Pro LCS

Live Communications Server Administration

Andrew Edney and
Rui Maximo

Apress®

Pro LCS: Live Communications Server Administration

Copyright © 2007 by Andrew Edney and Rui Maximo

ISBN-13 (pbk): 978-1-59059-836-8

ISBN-10 (pbk): 1-59059-836-9

Lead Editor: Jonathan Hassell
Technical Reviewer: John Lamb
Editorial Board: Steve Anglin, Ewan Buckingham, Gary Cornell, Jason Gilmore, Jonathan Gennick, Jonathan Hassell, James Huddleston, Chris Mills, Matthew Moodie, Jeff Pepper, Dominic Shakeshaft, Matt Wade
Project Manager: Beth Christmas
Copy Edit Manager: Nicole Flores
Copy Editor: Kim Wimpsett
Assistant Production Director: Kari Brooks-Copony
Production Editor: Ellie Fountain
Compositor: Susan Glinert
Proofreader: Patrick Vincent
Indexer: Rebecca Hornyak
Artist: Kinetic Publishing Services, LLC
Cover Designer: Kurt Krames
Manufacturing Director: Tom Debolski

Distributed to the book trade worldwide by Springer-Verlag New York, Inc., 233 Spring Street, 6th Floor, New York, NY 10013. Phone 1-800-SPRINGER, fax 201-348-4505, e-mail orders-ny@springer-sbm.com, or visit http://www.springeronline.com.

For information on translations, please contact Apress directly at 2855 Telegraph Avenue, Suite 600, Berkeley, CA 94705. Phone 510-549-5930, fax 510-549-5939, e-mail info@apress.com, or visit http://www.apress.com.

The source code for this book is available to readers at http://www.apress.com in the Source Code/Download section. You will need to answer questions pertaining to this book in order to successfully download the code.

For Katy
—Andrew Edney

To my wife, Anne, and my children, who keep me going when I can no longer.
—Rui Maximo

Contents at a Glance

PART 1 ▪▪▪ Introducing Live Communications Server

PART 2 ▪▪▪ Setting It Up

PART 3 ▪▪▪ Configuring Live Communications Server

PART 4 ▪▪▪ Getting the Most from LCS

Contents

PART 1 ▪▪▪ Introducing Live Communications Server

PART 2 ▪▪▪ Setting It Up

PART 3 ▪▪▪ **Configuring Live Communications Server**

PART 4 ■■■ Getting the Most from LCS

About the Authors

ANDREW EDNEY has been an IT professional for more than 12 years and has over the course of his career worked for a range of high-tech companies, such as Microsoft, Hewlett-Packard, and Fujitsu Services. He has a wide range of experience in virtually all aspects of Microsoft's computing solutions, having designed and architected large enterprise solutions for government and private-sector customers. Over the years, Andrew has made a number of guest appearances at major industry events, presenting on a wide range of information systems subjects, such as an appearance at the annual Microsoft Exchange Conference in Nice where he addressed the Microsoft technical community on mobility computing. Andrew is currently involved in numerous Microsoft beta programs, including next-generation Windows operating systems and next-generation Microsoft Office products, and he actively participates in all Windows Media Center beta programs. In addition, Andrew has written a number of books on topics such as Windows Media Center, PowerPoint 2007, networks, Windows Vista, and the Xbox 360. These include *Getting More from Your Microsoft Xbox 360* (Bernard Babani, 2006), *How to Set Up Your Home or Small Business Network* (Bernard Babani, 2006), *Using Microsoft Windows XP Media Center 2005* (Bernard Babani, 2006), *Windows Vista: An Ultimate Guide* (Bernard Babani, 2007), *PowerPoint 2007 in Easy Steps* (Computer Step, 2007), and *Windows Vista Media Center in Easy Steps* (Computer Step, 2007). You can reach him at andrew@firebirdconsulting.co.uk.

RUI MAXIMO has more than 14 years of experience shipping more than 10 commercial software products for IBM and Microsoft from educational software to operating systems, mobile devices, and server products. Rui has been a lead program manager working in the Unified Communications Group at Microsoft since 2003. He was a member of the engineering team that built Live Communications Server and worked on many different aspects of the project. He was responsible for the Active Directory schema extensions; the migration from Exchange 2000 IM; the definition of supported topologies; and the design of the Admin Tools MMC, WMI, LcsSync, and the MOM Pack. In addition to working on the management aspect of the product, Rui worked on VoIP for the upcoming release of Office Communications Server 2007 before leading the team that designed the Communicator Web Access product. He also contributed as a technical expert in developing the product's documentation, developing the Microsoft Professional Exam for Live Communications Server 2005, and presenting at major conferences. Rui has been living in the Pacific Northwest and working at Microsoft for the past 10 years as a software design engineer and program manager. You can reach him at ruim@ruimaximo.com. He looks forward to hearing from you!

About the Technical Reviewer

JOHN LAMB has more than 12 years of experience in software development and IT infrastructure design, including more than 8 years with Microsoft in the United States and United Kingdom holding senior roles in both product development and consulting. John recently left Microsoft to cofound Modality Systems in London, a company that specializes in the design and implementation of Live Communications Server and Office Communications Server real-time communications systems. The company's projects are notable for delivering advanced solutions to large enterprises, carriers, and hosting companies.

John is a Microsoft Certified Systems Engineer (MCSE) and was recently recognized by Microsoft, receiving the Unified Communications Group's Outstanding Contribution Award for his work with EMEA customers in 2006. In his spare time, John enjoys traveling with his wife, Nicole, and cooking authentic Mexican food for her.

Acknowledgments

First I want to thank my partner, Katy, for putting up with me writing yet another book! It takes quite a lot of patience and dedication to write a book and probably takes just as much to live with someone who is writing one, so thanks! I also want to thank Starbuck and Apollo for keeping me sane and for trying to help—well, eating or sitting on my work whilst I was trying to do it.

I also want to extend a big thank you to everyone at Apress who made this happen—Jonathan, Beth, Ellie, Kim, and everyone else who did fantastic work taking what we threw together and turning it into what you now have in your hands. These guys never get enough credit as far as I'm concerned.

Thanks also to Rosie for her assistance.

I also want to thank Rui for agreeing to work with me on this book; it's fun writing a book with someone else who has a similar passion to you.

And, finally, thanks to you, the reader, for buying the book; I hope you like it.

Andrew Edney

I want to thank my family for their love and understanding during the time I dedicated to writing this book. Writing a book late in the evening when everyone is sleeping isn't easy! For my mother, you taught me by example to always work hard.

I want to thank Jonathan for giving me the opportunity to write this book. Working with Beth, Ellie, and Kim has been a fantastic experience. The assistance they provided and always in a so friendly and courteous manner was a real pleasure. Thank you! It was a pleasure working with you.

I want to thank John Lamb for taking on the task of technical reviewer. I met John back in 2003 when we worked together on defining supported topologies for Live Communications Server 2003, and I continue to enjoy working with him.

To Joyce and Trish, UCG's technical writers, writing the technical documentation for Live Communications Server 2003 and Live Communications Server 2005 with you is what got me started at writing this book. I want to thank the UCG team for your expertise, help, and camaraderie.

Not to be forgotten, Andrew, thanks for being my coauthor. I couldn't imagine writing the entirety of this book. I would still be at it!

Thank you to our readers for your support. I look forward to hearing from you.

Rui Maximo

Introduction

Instant messaging has been around for a while now, and most people use it on a daily basis so are used to what it can do for them. Businesses are starting to wake up to the fact that IM is a great tool for work purposes, not just for chatting to your friends and family. However, this brings with it a whole new group of problems, issues, and concerns, not to mention complexity. Microsoft has had a couple of versions of Live Communications Server on the market now, with the latest version being Live Communications Server 2005 SP1. This book aims to give you a better understanding of what the Live Communications Server 2005 platform actually is; what it can do for you and your business; and how to deploy it, manage it, and troubleshoot it successfully.

Based on the SIP protocol as the control channel, Live Communications Server can easily extend its existing instant messaging capabilities into other media such as web conferencing, audio, and video. Live Communications Server introduces a paradigm shift that resonates with customers. Ultimately, people are trying to reach other people using the best and most convenient means of communication—whether it be by email, IM, telephone, or otherwise—without needing to recall personal information such as phone numbers. Live Communications Server centralizes these means of communications around the user's presence, intelligently exposing the most appropriate medium based on the user's current activities. In essence, Live Communications Server acts as your personal digital assistant.

So now that you know all that, wouldn't it be useful to have a single source of information and guidance for Live Communications Server 2005. Well, guess what? You have it right here in your hands. Yes, that's right, this very book will be your guide to everything that Live Communications 2005 has to offer, including how to install, configure, use, and troubleshoot it. It is packed with advice and guidance to help you get the most out of the product so that you can start benefiting from its use immediately.

PART 1

■■■

Introducing Live Communications Server

Welcome to Part 1 of *Pro LCS: Live Communications Server 2005 Administration*. In this part of the book, we will introduce you to Live Communications Server 2005 SP1, explain what it is, and explain what it does. We will also cover what instant messaging is and how to use presence to work smarter. We will then explore the underlying protocol that Live Communications Server uses, Session Initiation Protocol (SIP), including what it is and how Live Communications Server uses it. We will then cover the various server roles that are available with Live Communications Server, such as Enterprise Edition, Standard Edition, Access Proxy, and more. We will then look at the clients you can use with Live Communications Server and finally round off this part of the book by examining each of the topologies you can implement with Live Communications Server.

■ ■ ■

CHAPTER 1

What Is Live Communications Server?

Live Communications Server (LCS) is a Microsoft Office server product that enhances your organization's communications and productivity by providing real-time information about people's presence, availability, and preferred mode of communication.

Organizations must remain competitive by bringing out the best ideas from their employees. Such breakthroughs are best accomplished through teamwork and collaboration. Although collaboration can be accomplished asynchronously such as via email, most of our daily tasks require short bursts of synchronous communications such as asking a question, clarifying a statement, or making a request. Waiting for a response often breaks the momentum in being able to quickly resolve tasks right then and there. Luckily, we have the ability to walk down the hallway if the other person is within physical proximity. We can also use the telephone, but we've all experienced the frustration of not reaching an important individual by phone. This is where Live Communications Server comes into play to further increase the productivity of the information worker (IW).

Live Communications Server is a presence server and platform that allows individuals to publish their presence state to whom they choose, which allows their presence subscribers to quickly and conveniently determine their availability. So, the next time you decide to walk down the hallway to talk to a co-worker, first check their presence state to make sure they're not in a meeting. And before you end up listening to their voicemail greeting, check their presence so you can call at a better time.

Although the primary client for Live Communications Server is Microsoft Office Communicator, users' presence can be displayed in any application, including the applications that make up the Microsoft Office productivity suite. The presence icon, more informally referred to as the *jelly bean*, provides unobtrusive ways to view people's presence availability whether you're working in Outlook, Word, SharePoint, or Excel.

How Business Value Follows Productivity Improvements

It's no longer sufficient to have information at your fingertips. It's necessary to have experts and trusted individuals at your fingertips. Often, with all the information available, we do not know where to locate the information we need. Once obtained, we need to talk to trusted experts to help us interpret this information. In today's world, as information becomes ubiquitous, the time value of information quickly diminishes from the moment it is released. Therefore, it is important to remain up to date and be able to quickly take action given new information.

Live Communications Server not only helps you locate your experts more expediently, but it also makes it more convenient to communicate in real time with them regardless of location. Using Office Communicator 2005, you can determine when a person you're trying to reach will become available. Based on their presence state, you can initiate a telephone call knowing that you won't be greeted by their voicemail and end up playing "phone tag." If an individual who you need an urgent "yes" or "no" answer from is on a call, you can try a gentle interruption using instant messaging instead of calling and ending up with their voicemail, or you can wait until they are off the phone before you try to call. While in meetings, you can do quick follow-ups via instant messaging to answer questions without disrupting the ongoing discussion. In addition, Office Communicator 2005 is a convenient way to communicate with co-workers across the country or overseas without spending a dime on long-distance toll charges. Information workers on the road can continue to communicate with co-workers in the office in real time from home, their hotel room, or a customer's office.

With Office Communicator Mobile 2005 or Research in Motion's BlackBerry, you can put presence in your pocket wherever you go! Using Communicator Web Access, you can access presence and instant messaging from non-Windows desktops without installing any native client. We're only scratching the surface in terms of scenarios where communication can be faster as well as more cost efficient.

Being able to quickly peek into someone's presence availability is an incredible convenience. You can avoid placing a call if you know they are not available. However, seeing someone else's presence state is predicated on one important criterion: the accuracy of this presence information. Everyone is so busy these days that they don't need yet another application to manage. If people need to manually specify their presence state each time they are on the phone, in a meeting, out to lunch, or out of the office, they will quickly stop keeping this information up to date consistently, if at all. Live Communications Server 2005 goes a step further than just indicating whether a user is signed in. Communicator 2005 uses the user's calendar information available in Outlook to automatically update the user's presence state and display when the person will be available next. If Live Communications Server 2005 is integrated with your organization's phone system, the user's presence state can indicate whether the user is on the phone. All this improves the accuracy of the user's presence state and future availability.

With greater availability comes greater intrusion through interruptions as well as concerns regarding privacy. Similar concerns existed when email and the Internet became widely available. Companies were concerned that employees would spend their days browsing the Internet. Today, people are overwhelmed by email at the office and at home. Most of us spend a good ten minutes every day clearing out spam emails from our inboxes. Others have been trained "à la Pavlov" to immediately interrupt whatever they're doing to respond to the new email that just landed into their inboxes. These are not problems created by email, instant messaging, or telephones. Such technologies only exacerbated poor habits in controlling the interruptions. Removing email, instant messaging, and telephones is not the solution to the problem. Software and systems should empower users to control interruptions, define their privacy preferences, and make intelligent decisions about how and when to interrupt (or not interrupt!) others. Organizations understand the value of email, the Internet, and the telephone in improving their employees' productivity. Instead of removing instant messaging capabilities, organizations should implement solutions that are designed for business productivity rather than advertising-driven "free" systems that are designed for consumer consumption.

Using Live Communications Server 2005, communication is secure and restricted to internal employees with accounts in their Active Directory forest. The administrator controls this. However, the system can be connected externally as well. For example, your organization can choose to federate with other organizations or connect with consumer networks such as Yahoo!, AOL, and MSN. Live Communications Server 2005 employs the Access Proxy server role to do this safely and securely. This can enable organizations to allow employees to communicate with members of these public network using corporate identities without sacrificing security or compliance. The ability for employees to use their corporate identity instead of a consumer handle such as greathandles@aol.com can mean the difference between making a sale and losing future business. External parties can have higher confidence that they are dealing with an authorized company representative and not a social engineer impersonating a corporate employee (that is, a hacker). This feature is called PIC and is further described in Chapter 14.

Just as Live Communications Server 2005's integration with the Office suite of applications creates synergy to improve the information worker's productivity, the tight integration of Live Communications Server 2005 with Active Directory brings that synergy to the administrator's productivity by leveraging their existing expertise and the tools familiar to them such as the Active Directory Users and Computers MMC and Microsoft Operations Manager (MOM). This helps directly reduce total cost of ownership (TCO).

What Does This Book Cover?

Pro LCS: Live Communications Server 2005 Administration will help you harness the value proposition Live Communications Server offers to increase the adoption of technology within your organization while improving productivity. This book's chapters are self-contained. If a chapter relies on information already covered in another chapter, you will be invited to visit the other chapter for further information. There is a minimal amount of precedence to the chapters, which reflects the dependencies in the product.

Chapters 1–3 provide an overview of Live Communications Server 2005 SP1, the value of instant messaging, and the SIP protocol on which Live Communications Server is based. These chapters provide a background for those readers who are new to this technology.

Chapters 4–8 provide prerequisite information you need to know before you deploy your first Live Communications Server machine. Chapter 4 covers how you should use the different server roles depending on the scenarios you want to enable. Chapter 5 discusses the different clients available for Live Communications Server 2005 SP1 and what considerations to keep in mind when rolling them out to users. Chapter 6 covers the important topic of topologies. Nothing is more frustrating than starting down a path only to realize after expending a considerable amount of time, effort, and frustration in installing and configuring Live Communications Server 2005 SP1 that it wasn't intended to be deployed in that manner. Even worse, you might discover your deployment is not supported by Microsoft's Product Support Services. Please make sure to follow one of the supported topologies. It will help you avoid considerable frustration. Chapter 7 covers a required step before you can deploy the first server within your Active Directory infrastructure. In any medium to very large company with a tiered IT organization, various IT administrators are likely to hold different administrative privileges. You'll need to work with these key stakeholders to review and approve the schema extensions needed for Live Communications Server 2005 SP1 and other preparatory steps required. We've discovered that this process of preparing your Active Directory takes a considerable amount of time from the moment you begin evaluating the product until you deploy it within your organization.

We recommend you plan this effort early in the project to help reduce the deployment cycle. Because Live Communications Server 2005 SP1 leverages other existing technologies beside Active Directory such as DNS and PKI, Chapter 8 covers important considerations that have caused customers grief and resulted in high support calls for Microsoft.

Chapters 9 and 10 finally get into the step of deploying your Standard Edition Server and Enterprise pool. Instead of documenting the process step by step with screenshots of every wizard's page, we provide you with additional insight that complements the product's available documentation, which already gives step-by-step instructions. By their nature, wizards are intended to walk the user through the configuration process and need little additional instructions.

After deploying your Standard Edition Servers and Enterprise pools, you must configure them for the scenarios you want. Chapters 11–14 cover configuration. Specifically, Chapter 11 covers configuring users for Live Communications; otherwise, they won't be able to use the service. Chapter 12 discusses the Address Book Service. This service permits users to easily search and find other users within your organization similarly to how Outlook works. Chapter 13 talks about configuring your Live Communications Server infrastructure for federation to allow your users to communicate with users from other partner companies. Chapter 14 covers how to enable communications with external users subscribed to AOL's, Yahoo!'s, and MSN's instant messaging services.

Chapters 15–19 cover manageability topics such as backing up and restoring, profiling the server with logging, enabling archiving for compliance, using best practices to troubleshoot the system, and performing ongoing monitoring for high availability.

Chapter 20 introduces you to the Live Communications Server 2005 SP1 software development kit (SDK). Chapter 21 discusses how to configure Live Communications Server 2005 SP1 for Voice over IP (VoIP) so users can leverage Communicator 2005 to enhance their existing telephony experience by using their computer to do remote call control. Chapter 22 covers additional resources.

Finally, the appendix covers deploying Live Communications Server in a multiforest Active Directory environment, with flowchart aids to determine which Active Directory "prep steps" to run and a checklist for deploying a Standard Edition Server and an Enterprise pool.

Summary

Live Communications Server enhances your organization's communications and productivity by providing real-time information about people's presence, availability, and preferred mode of communication. In the upcoming chapters, we'll cover everything you need to know to install and deploy it in your organization.

CHAPTER 2

■ ■ ■

What Is Instant Messaging?

Unless you have been living under a rock for the past few years (and if you have, welcome!), you have probably heard of instant messaging. In fact, chances are you would not have bought this fantastic book if you did not already know what instant messaging actually is.

Just to make sure everyone reading this is sure exactly what instant messaging is, the next couple of pages will take a look at its history, its uses, and its future. If you know all this stuff already, feel free to skip this chapter; we won't be offended.

Instant messaging, or IM as it is most often referred to, is a way of communicating with one or more people in real time using a device such as a computer or mobile phone. This communication is mostly text-based messages, often referred as *chat*, or it could be a videoconference via an attached webcam. It could even be an exchange of audio, video, and pictures, amongst other things. The capabilities you have access to will depend on the type of device you are using and on the client software you have installed.

IM has become increasingly popular because it is quicker and easier to use than email, and you know that the person you want to communicate with is at the other end of the line. It is also considered to be less intrusive than a telephone call, and unlike email, IM is conversational and a lot less formal. It also provides collaboration functionality that you don't get with email or telephone conversations.

To use IM, after you have signed into your IM service, you start a conversation with someone either by picking them from your list of contacts, often referred to as your *buddy list*, or by entering their contact details in your IM program.

You then start the conversation by typing a message, such as "Hello . . .." This message will then appear on their device, and they in turn can reply to the initial message.

Figure 2-1 shows an example IM conversation using Microsoft Office Communicator.

This starts the dialogue, which will continue until someone in the conversation terminates the session. In the example, Andrew initiated the IM session with Rui, and within a few seconds, the conversation had begun. Andrew could see that Rui was available because his presence information indicated he was online and available. (For more about presence, see the "Presence" section later in this chapter.)

You can have more than two people in an IM conversation; inviting more people is easy.

To try to add something extra other than just text, a number of IM clients support the use of emoticons. *Emoticons* are graphical representations of various facial expressions, such as smiling, crying, kissing, and so on. These are really useful because they can add a depth that might not otherwise be in the text conversation and can certainly help to get a point across.

Figure 2-1. *An example IM conversation using Communicator*

Figure 2-2 shows some of the emoticons provided in Communicator.

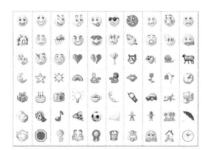

Figure 2-2. *Emoticons in Communicator*

Another benefit of IM is that you can save conversations to review them later. Also, Live Communications Server 2005 provides an archiving facility, which is discussed in Chapter 17.

More than 400 million instant messages are sent and received each day, and chances are you might have sent and received some of them yourself.

The History of Instant Messaging

IM has really been around now for more than ten years, although most people don't realize it. It became quite popular in chat rooms provided by online providers such as CompuServe and America Online (AOL), where users could talk to one another in real time. In this context, all the users in the chat room were part of a large IM conversation, but users could, if they wanted, have private, one-to-one conversations, which is really where IM was born.

In the early 1990s when the Internet started to be accessed by a wider audience, software developers started producing programs that could provide similar functionality to that provided by those online providers, and by 1996 ICQ was launched.

ICQ, which was short for *I seek you*, soon became popular as a way for people to easily communicate in real time with one another by installing a client application and connecting to the Internet. ICQ is still in use today. For more information about ICQ, including the latest version of the client software, go to `http://www.icq.com`.

AOL then launched a product called AIM, which stood for AOL Instant Messenger. This quickly became the leading IM tool of the time, which in no small part was because AOL had more than 20 million subscribers.

Other providers launched IM products, including Yahoo! with its IM product, called Yahoo! Messenger, and Microsoft with MSN Messenger. Microsoft has since released Windows Messenger, Windows Live Messenger (which was formally MSN Messenger), Communicator, and Communicator Web Access, to name but a few.

For anyone who is interested, the Internet Engineering Task Force (IETF) has even published a request for comments (RFC) on IM, which you can find at `http://www.ietf.org/rfc/rfc2779.txt`.

Now and the Future

It is not just computers that can be used to have IM conversations and send IM messages. Mobile phones now contain IM applications, personal digital assistants (PDAs) have IM applications (including versions of Microsoft IM tools), and you can even send instant messages through your television.

In fact, Windows Live Messenger now even enables users to communicate with Yahoo! Messenger users, which opens up the IM community to multiple providers and means you don't need multiple IM clients in order to speak to all of your contacts.

Nowadays, IM is not just used at home for pleasure; it has seen a huge take-up in businesses, with people being able to save considerable amounts of time communicating with colleagues and customers via IM. Enterprise instant messaging, as it has been dubbed, is increasing in popularity, and many companies such as Microsoft have released enterprise software to provide IM in these environments. Microsoft's original product was the Exchange Chat Server, which later evolved into Live Communications Server 2003 and is now Live Communications Server 2005 (the reason you bought this book).

For more information about the various clients that are supported by Live Communications Server 2005, take a look at Chapter 5.

The Downsides to Instant Messaging

IM does have some downsides. Only a few days ago a friend of ours said he felt sometimes he can talk to his kids only through IM! He was of course joking, but it just shows how many different people are using IM on a daily basis.

Some people consider the continual "popping up" of messages to be a source of great annoyance so they end up treating IM in the same way as a telephone and ignoring it when they are busy.

Probably the biggest concern to IM is security. This security concern revolves around viruses in attachments or even people intercepting and reading the IM communications. The concern about viruses is strong enough that a number of organizations actually ban the use of IM because often sending someone an attachment means that the organization's antivirus software could be circumvented. Fortunately, a number of antivirus products have been specifically designed to be used with IM.

In terms of the "eavesdropping" concern, again, organizations ban IM for this reason because a number of the IM solutions actually transmit the messages in clear text, which means that anyone could intercept and read them. Live Communications Server 2005 enables organizations to encrypt messages so that if they were to be intercepted, they would be unreadable.

Another growing annoyance is IM spam, or SPIM, as it is called. This is the same as SPAM emails in that unwanted IMs are sent to users without their approval, and because it is difficult to identify the source of IMs, these messages are difficult to stop. Live Communications Server 2005 provides a mechanism to fight SPIM with a component called the Intelligent Instant Message Filter.

The Intelligent Instant Message Filter includes enhanced uniform resource locator (URL) filtering, which means you can block URLs from being clicked if they are sent in IMs, you can even stop delivery of an IM if it contains a hyperlink, plus you can do much more. Also included is enhanced file transfer control and logging facilities.

You can find more information about the Live Communications Server 2005 Intelligent Instant Message Filter, including the ability to download it, at `http://www.microsoft.com/downloads/details.aspx?familyid=0ED13372-F3D2-40F0-BA5D-C880359A40F5&displaylang=en`.

Identity fraud is also a genuine concern, because an unscrupulous person could create an IM account claiming to be anyone and try to gain information from you that way. If you are not convinced of the identity of the person you are conversing with, do not give any personal details or business information away.

IM is not for everyone. However, if it is used properly, it can greatly increase business productivity and allow faster and easier levels of communication.

Presence

Having the ability to contact people using a multitude of different devices, be they mobile phones, PDAs, laptops, desktops, tablet PCs, or anything else, is great, but you often have to attempt to contact someone without even knowing whether they are actually available to communicate with you.

For example, when you send someone an email or you pick up the phone and call them, you often don't know whether they are there or whether they are available to respond or talk to you. Email is often used as a fire-and-forget mechanism because you have no idea when or if the person might respond. If the person you have called on the phone is not available and they have voicemail, you can leave a voicemail message and hope that they listen to it and that you get a timely response. This can cause delays, which can often account for a number of hours of unproductive time. This might not initially seem like a big deal, but if you imagine a few hours per person for a large organization, then it quickly becomes thousands, if not hundreds of thousands of dollars, worth of potential lost revenue.

With IM, there is a process that helps you by showing you whether one of your contacts is currently signed in, whether they are available or away, or whether they have displayed a user-defined message that can help you to determine whether they are contactable (for example "in a meeting – available").

This process is known as *presence* and can provide instant access to availability information of the person you want to communicate with, which in turn will save you valuable time in determining whether they are even contactable. Presence has even been referred to as the *killer app*. Those of us who have been in the game for a while have heard that all before; however, this time, it could actually be true!

Presence information is available in a number of programs, including the Microsoft Office suite, Communicator, and the SharePoint family of products. Presence information is also available on devices such as PDAs and smart phones. This presence information appears as an icon next to the person's name. For example, if you see a green icon beside a contact's name, you know that they are online and available.

Table 2-1 shows the Microsoft programs with presence awareness.

Table 2-1. *Presence-Aware Products from Microsoft*

Type	Application
IM	Windows Messenger MSN Messenger Communicator
Collaboration	Office SharePoint Portal Server Windows SharePoint Services
Communication	Outlook Live Communications Server
Productivity	Excel Word

You can see a good example of presence in Communicator. When you are signed in, you can see the status of all your contacts. This status includes whether they are also signed in and, if they are signed in, whether they are available. You, and indeed they, can set status flags to show whether you are busy, on the phone, out to lunch, and so on. Figure 2-3 shows an example of the status flags available in Communicator.

Figure 2-3. *Status flags in Communicator*

Let's say you want to start an IM session with your friend Rui. The first step to take is to check his presence information, as shown in Figure 2-4.

Figure 2-4. *Rui's presence information in Communicator*

So, you can easily see that Rui is online and that he is currently on the phone. You can then wait until he gets off the phone and changes his status flag, or you can easily ping him with an instant message asking him to call you when he is free. This will appear on his screen, and provided that he is near his screen, he will get instant visibility of your message (as shown in the example in Figure 2-5), which is certainly better than leaving him a voicemail message, which he might not pick up for some time.

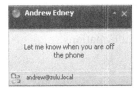

Figure 2-5. *Message pop-up*

Equally, if his status is shown as Online, you can easily start to communicate with him knowing that he should be available. This does of course rely heavily on users keeping their presence information up-to-date. The application can help a little here—for example, with Communicator, if you do not use your computer for five minutes, your status automatically changes to Away. This setting is configurable to 5, 10, 15, 30, and 60 minutes, or you can switch it off entirely.

When you use Live Communications Server 2005, presence information is enhanced further because Live Communications Server 2005 acts as the presence engine that provides presence information. For example, if you are using Communicator, Exchange 2003, and Outlook, your presence information can be tied into your calendar, so when you are in a meeting, your presence information is automatically updated to show that you are currently unavailable. You also have the ability to integrate with PBX and PSTN telephone services so that you can use Communicator to initiate phone calls, view pop-up alerts for incoming calls, have your presence changed to "on the phone" automatically for you, and much more.

As already mentioned, Live Communications Server 2005 provides integration into the Microsoft Office suite in order to provide presence information into applications such as Excel and SharePoint. For example, if you need to work on a report with Rui, you can see whether he is online, and if so, you can work on the report together.

Live Communications Server also provides a software development kit (SDK) that can help developers create enterprise line-of-business (LOB) applications that can leverage enhanced presence. You can find detailed information about this in Chapter 20 later in the book.

We'll show examples of presence, and how it can be configured to best help you and increase productivity, throughout this book.

As with IM, some problems come along with presence. First, presence really works effectively only when the information is kept up to date. It's no good if you sign in to your IM client, set your presence to online and available, and then go off to lunch. People will assume that because your presence information indicates that you are online and available, that you actually are online and available. They will start to communicate with you, and when you eventually return from lunch, you might have a number of messages and conversations waiting for you.

Another problem is the same one that affects IM, and that's compatibility. Other clients might not be able to see your presence information, depending on the client you are using. This means that to effectively use presence, anyone who wants to see where you are needs to be using the same client as you. That might be fine for an organization that can enforce the use of a single client, but that certainly becomes more difficult when you want to share information with people outside your organization. However, all is not lost because there is work being done to both standardize and translate presence states for different clients, making this problem a thing of the past.

Privacy is also considered an issue. Some people do not want others to know where they are and what they are doing during every minute of the day. This issue is addressed in part by setting permissions for users to be able to see or not see your presence information.

Summary

You probably already knew a lot about IM; in fact, you probably already use it either regularly or on occasion. What you might not have known, or you might have thought didn't affect you, were some of the downsides of using IM, such as the obvious security concerns, which are very real, and also the annoyance that some people experience when being constantly interrupted by instant messages. A real benefit to using IM is presence so that you can quickly and easily see whether the person you want to contact is available. This not only saves you time if they are not available, but it also reduces those annoying interruptions. We hope this chapter has given you a slightly larger picture of using IM and presence.

CHAPTER 3

■■■

Session Initiation Protocol

This chapter will introduce you to the Session Initiation Protocol (SIP) and will also give you an insight into the SIP message structure.

After reading through this chapter, you will have a better understanding of SIP, and having an awareness of SIP and its message structure will help you better understand and diagnose problems with client and server communications.

SIP was developed within the Multiparty Multimedia Session Control (MMUSIC) working group and is now maintained by the SIP working group for IETF; the result is RFC 3261. SIP is quite a detailed protocol, and because this chapter is only an overview, it will barely scratch the surface. Should you find yourself compelled to learn more about SIP, then please refer to RFC 3261 at http://www.ietf.org/rfc/rfc3261.txt. Be aware, though, that this RFC is more than 260 pages in length, so you might want to save it for one of those nights that you are having trouble sleeping or for that really long airplane journey!

SIP is an industry-standard application-layer signaling and call control protocol that Live Communications Server 2005 uses to communicate between client and server and between server and server. It is used to create, modify, and terminate SIP sessions, and it supports both unicast and multicast communication. It is used in conjunction with other supporting protocols, such as TCP, UDP, TLS, IP, and DNS, to describe the characteristics of the session to the potential session participants. It is used widely across the Internet for instant messaging, presence, conferencing, and Voice over IP (VoIP). If you are planning on using VoIP hardware (such as a handset), you will need to ensure it is SIP-compliant.

Within instant messaging conversations, SIP supports five main functions, as listed in Table 3-1.

Table 3-1. *SIP Functions in Instant Messaging*

Function	Description
User location	Determines the end system that will be used for the communication
User availability	Registers the availability of the user to communicate
User capabilities	Determines what media and media parameters can be used for the communication
Session setup	Establishes the session parameters that will be used between the calling party and the called party
Session management	Modifies session parameters, invoking other services and terminating the session

Like HTTP, SIP is based on a request-and-response design—a request must always be paired with a response, although BENOTIFY may be the exception (covered later in this chapter). A number of different requests and responses exist, which we will cover shortly.

An extension to SIP is SIP Instant Messaging and Presence Leveraging Extensions (SIMPLE), which provides SIP-compliant support for instant messaging and presence functionality. SIMPLE includes a number of specifications, including SIP, HTTP, and XML. Live Communications Server 2005 utilizes SIMPLE to leverage presence information and receive notifications of when certain events occur, such as when a user logs in or sets their availability to Away.

When you extend the Active Directory schema in preparation of installing Live Communications Server 2005, you add a large number of SIP attributes. To review these and find out more about extending the Active Directory schema, go to Chapter 7.

As we mentioned, SIP is a client-server protocol, and as such it has both a client and a server agent element:

User Agent Client (UAC): The client sends the SIP request to the server and can be either software based (such as Communicator or Windows Messenger) or hardware based (such as a SIP telephone).

User Agent Server (UAS): The server receives and responds to the request from the client and can again be software based (such as Live Communications Server 2005) or a hardware appliance.

The following steps take place for a typical IM conversation, as shown in Figure 3-1:

1. When a user invites another user into a session, an INVITE message is sent.

2. The calling user might receive an interim response, such as Trying, before the user being called accepts the invitation.

3. When the calling user accepts the incoming call, an OK message is sent back to the calling user client.

4. The calling user client responds with an ACK.

5. Live communication then takes place. This can include instant messages, video, or voice.

6. When one of the users ends the session, a BYE message is generated and sent to another client.

7. That client then sends an OK confirmation, and the session ends.

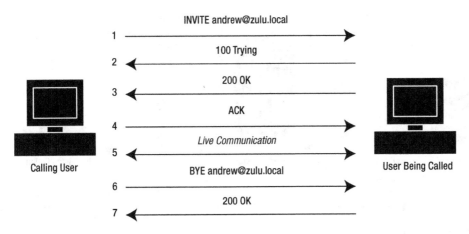

Figure 3-1. *UAC SIP call*

Each user agent has its own SIP address. In the case of a client, their SIP URI is often their email address. A word of warning: It is imperative that you define what you will use prior to beginning deployment.

A SIP server can have one of three roles:

SIP proxy. The proxy will act as an intermediary between a user agent client and a user agent server. The proxy can forward the request or modify it before sending it on.

SIP redirect. The redirect server accepts the INVITE request from the calling user agent, obtains the correct SIP address of the called user agent, and replies to the calling user agent with that address.

SIP registrar. The registrar server accepts the registration request and maps a client's address to a user's sign-in name (or SIP URI). In Live Communications Server 2005, the registrar is referred to as a *home server.*

Often times, the registrar server is also the proxy and the redirect server. Live Communications Server 2005 with Service Pack 1 (SP1) provides the functionality of all three of the different SIP server roles where necessary.

The call flow when using the proxy server is essentially the same as the user agent client call flow but with the proxy server acting as the midpoint, functioning as both a user agent server and a user agent client. When it acts as the user agent server, the proxy receives and forwards the SIP requests to the destination user agent client. When it acts as a user agent client, it receives the SIP responses and forwards them to the destination user agent client as shown in Figure 3-2.

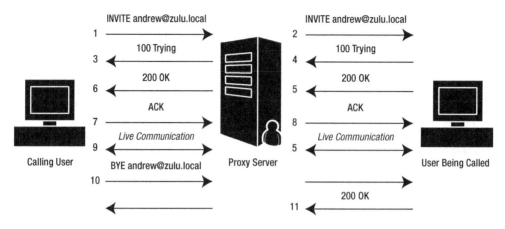

Figure 3-2. *Proxy server SIP call*

The registrar server accepts REGISTER requests from the UAC, which indicate the addresses where the user agent client can be contacted, as shown in Figure 3-3.

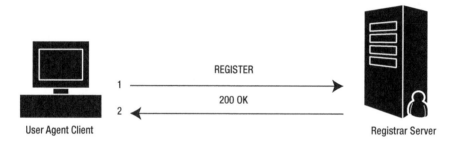

Figure 3-3. *Registrar server SIP call*

The following steps take place when a call to another user is redirected to a different location, as shown in Figure 3-4:

1. When a user invites another user into a session, an INVITE message is sent.

2. The redirect server responds with the 302 Moved response, which indicates that the user being called has temporarily moved.

3. The calling user client responds with an ACK.

4. The calling user client then sends another INVITE request, this time directly to the newly acquired address for the user being called.

5. When the calling user accepts the incoming call, an OK message is sent back to the calling user client.

6. The calling user client responds with an ACK.

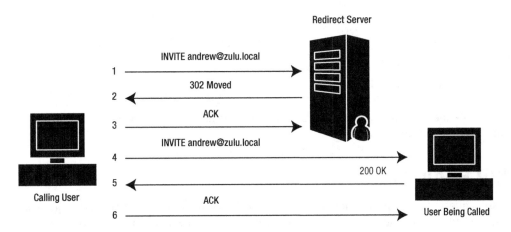

Figure 3-4. *Redirect server SIP call*

SIP Message Structures

Because SIP is a text-based protocol, it is easy to read. This has some security implications, because anyone who can capture the SIP packets could gain access to information. However, because it is easy to read, it also makes troubleshooting problems a little bit easier.

A SIP message can be a request to a server from a client or a response to the client from the server, or it can be a message proxied from one server to another.

Each message contains a start line followed by at least one header and then a message body. Table 3-2 describes the SIP message parts.

Table 3-2. *SIP Message Structures*

SIP Message Part	Description
Start line	This part includes the method type and the SIP address, or general URL of the destination receiving the request. It also includes the SIP version, a numeric status code, and a reason phrase.
Headers	This part contains the header type and any associated variables. Headers can span multiple lines, and some headers can appear several times in a message.
Message body	This part contains information that is provided by the Session Description Protocol (SDP) such as the description of the media capabilities for the SIP session (for example, in a multimedia session, it might include the codec types that are used for audio and video).

Figure 3-5 shows an example structure of a SIP message.

```
Message = start-line
*message header
CRLF
[message-body]
```

Figure 3-5. *Structure of a SIP message*

SIP defines the values for both the start line and the headers, with the SDP defining the values for the message body.

SIP Request

A SIP request consists of a method token called a *verb*, which is used to identify the request; a request URI, which is the address of the destined device; and the SIP version. Table 3-3 describes each of the SIP methods.

Table 3-3. *SIP Requests*

SIP Methods	Description
INVITE	This method establishes sessions between different user agents. The message body can also include information about the initiating caller along with other information such as the media type and any security information.
ACK	This is the acknowledgment that is sent to confirm establishment of the session.
BYE	This terminates the current established session.
CANCEL	This ends a pending request, such as an outstanding INVITE. An example could include an instant messaging session where a user invites another user to start a collaboration session; however, before it has been accepted, it is cancelled, but the instant messaging session continues.
OPTIONS	This checks the capabilities of the server or device before issuing an INVITE. It is also used to discover the current availability.
REGISTER	This is used by the client to log in and register its address with the SIP registrar server.
SUBSCRIBE	This allows the user to subscribe to events such as contact details and the presence status of other users and other notifications. Each SUBSCRIBE will trigger at least one NOTIFY.
NOTIFY	This informs the user when an event they have subscribed to occurs. It is also used by Windows Messenger or Microsoft Office Communicator to request contacts and groups, allow and block lists from the server, and get the presence information of any contacts. Live Communications Server 2005 uses it to deliver data obtained by the SUBSCRIBE method back to whichever client is used.
MESSAGE	This transports an instant message from one user to another user. The actual message itself is carried in the message body as a MIME attachment.
INFO	This transfers information during a session; for example, in an instant messaging session, a message appears on the screen to show that another user is typing a message.

Table 3-3. *SIP Requests*

SIP Methods	Description
SERVICE	This searches for contacts in a SIP domain. It is also used by Windows Messenger to add contacts and groups on the server.
NEGOTIATE	This negotiates different parameters, such as the first SIP server message exchange after TLS negotiation has been completed but before any user level SIP data is exchanged. It is also used by Live Communications 2005 Server to provide compression between clients and servers.
REFER	This enables the sender of the request to instruct the receiver to contact a third party using the contact details provided in the request, such as forwarding the call to a cellular phone or other device.

In the example SIP request shown in Figure 3-6, Andrew is sending Rui an INVITE to start a messaging session with him. As you can also see from the message body, several SDP parameters are displayed, as shown in Table 3-4.

```
INVITE sip:192.168.205.1:1390;transport=tcp;ms-received-cid=800 SIP/2.0
contact: <sip:andrew@zulu.local:1037;maddr=192.168.1.73;transport=tcp;ms-
received-cid=600>
via: SIP/2.0/TCP 192.168.1.73:11715;ms-received-port=1037;ms-received-
cid=600
max-forwards: 70
from: "Andrew Edney"
<sip:andrew@zulu.local>;tag=39959c4112;epid=85cbf0bfa8
to: <sip:rui@zulu.local>;epid=d94ae100f2
call-id: f0f8b6c1dac44f8cb33d93d34a578584
cseq: 1 INVITE
user-agent: LCC/1.3
Ms-Conversation-ID: 0120E37C-0332-410F-B601-84122BA29E7D
ms-text-format: text/plain; charset=UTF-
8;msgr=WAAtAE0ATQBTAC0ASQBNAC0ARgBvAHIAbQBhAHQAOgAgAgAEYAT
gA9AE0AUwAIADIAMABTAGgGAZQBsAGwAJQAyADAARABsAGcAOwAgAEUA
RgA9ADsAIABDAE8APQAwADsAIABDAFMAPQAwADsAIABBQAEYAPQAwAAA0
ACgANAAoA;ms-body=SGkgUnVpIC0gYXJlIHIvdSBmcmVlIHRvIHRhbGs/
supported: ms-delayed-accept
supported: ms-renders-gif
Roster-Manager: sip:andrew@zulu.local
EndPoints: "Andrew Edney" <sip:andrew@zulu.local>, <sip:rui@zulu.local>
supported: com.microsoft.rtc-multiparty
content-type: application/sdp
content-length: 117

v=0
o=- 0 0 IN IP4 192.168.1.73
s=session
c=IN IP4 192.168.1.73
t=0 0
m=message 5060 sip sip:andrew@zulu.local
```

Figure 3-6. *A SIP request*

Table 3-4. *SDP Parameters*

SDP Parameter	Description
v	Version number
o	Origin
s	Subject
c	Connection
t	Time
m	Media

SIP Response

A SIP response is generated in response to a request and contains a three-digit number that indicates the outcome of that request. It also contains a reason phrase that is a description of the outcome of the request, which helps you understand what happened if you read through the SIP response.

The SIP response begins with a status line, the SIP status codes are from 100 to 699, and the first digit is the response class, as shown in Table 3-5.

Table 3-5. *SIP Responses*

Class Name	Description
1xx: Provisional	The request is received and is being processed.
2xx: Success	The action was received, understood, and accepted.
3xx: Redirection	Further action is needed to complete the request.
4xx: Client Error	The request contains bad syntax or cannot be fulfilled at this server.
5xx: Server Error	The server failed to fulfill a valid request.
6xx: Global Failure	The request cannot be fulfilled at any server.

In the example SIP response shown in Figure 3-7, Rui has accepted the INVITE to start a messaging session with Andrew.

```
SIP/2.0 200 OK
contact: <sip:rui@zulu.local:1390;maddr=192.168.205.1;transport=tcp;ms-
received-cid=800>
via: SIP/2.0/TCP 192.168.1.73:11715;ms-received-port=1037;ms-received-
cid=600
from: "Andrew Edney"
<sip:andrew@zulu.local>;tag=39959c4112;epid=85cbf0bfa8
to: <sip:rui@zulu.local>;epid=d94ae100f2;tag=df47dd91cf
call-id: f0f8b6c1dac44f8cb33d93d34a578584
cseq: 1 INVITE
record-route: <sip:ae-1.zulu.local;transport=tcp;lr;ms-route-
sig=aa5X71lXTw1teRVLlluGbCVD6AtKaQ>;tag=EE19C0CFAA770A833130863
85D80D483
user-agent: LCC/1.3
supported: com.microsoft.rtc-multiparty
supported: ms-text-format
supported: ms-renders-gif
content-type: application/sdp
content-length: 116

v=0
o=- 0 0 IN IP4 192.168.205.1
s=session
c=IN IP4 192.168.205.1
t=0 0
m=message 5060 sip sip:rui@zulu.local
```

Figure 3-7. *A SIP response*

SIP Headers

A SIP message also contains message headers, which include information that can help the message to be handled correctly. The headers depend on whether the message is a request or a response.

These headers include the following:

General headers: These headers contain basic information and are used in both requests and responses.

Request headers: These headers provide additional information to the server about the request or the client.

Response headers: These headers apply only to status messages and are used to provide additional information that cannot be or is not included in the status line.

The SIP proxy server inspects those message headers to determine message processing and routing.

Table 3-6 shows some of the headers that Live Communications Server 2005 with SP1 uses.

Table 3-6. *SIP Headers*

Header	Description
To	This is the identity of the intended recipient of the request. The identity always has the prefix "Sip:" followed by user@domain, which is the SIP URL.
From	This is the identity of the user sending the message.
Call-ID	This is a unique identifier for the SIP invitation.
Contact	This is the user's actual address rather than the address of the server hosting the user. Once the client has received the Contact address, further communication can be handled directly without needing to go through the server.
Record-Route	A server that proxies a message can add its own URI to the Record-Route header to indicate that it wants to remain in the path for all SIP traffic in the current conversation. A Live Communications Server 2005 proxy server uses the Record-Route header for all traffic that originates from a corporate branch office to ensure that all traffic will route through it before passing through the branch office firewall.
Route	This is a list of SIP-URIs of all entities that are in the path of the request. At each point along the path, the Live Communications Server will remove the Route header that identifies it and will forward the message to the next URI in the list.
Via	This lists all of the Live Communications Server instances that have handled the request.

In a Live Communications Server SIP network, requests are routed to endpoints that represent SIP-enabled Windows user accounts. If there is no user account for a URL stored in Active Directory, routing is based on the static routing tables of federation rules.

SIP Protocol Optimizations

Live Communications Server 2005 with SP1 includes a number of SIP protocol optimizations. The optimizations are included to enhance server performance and are listed in Table 3-7.

Table 3-7. *SIP Protocol Optimizations*

SIP Optimization	Description
Batch presence subscriptions	SUBSCRIBE requests and NOTIFY responses for all users in a contact list are sent in single batches rather than for each individual contact as was the case with Live Communications Server 2003. This significantly reduces network traffic.
BENOTIFY (Best Effort NOTIFY)	BENOTIFY is a proprietary SIP method introduced in Live Communications Server 2005 and is used to reduce SIP signaling traffic because it does not require a response like a standard NOTIFY requires. Applications that do not require a response can greatly enhance their performance by enabling BENOTIFY. This feature is important for deployments with large amounts of users on each server.

Table 3-7. *SIP Protocol Optimizations*

SIP Optimization	Description
Whitespace keep-alives	This provides accurate presence information. Clients and servers need to detect the state of the connection between them on a continual basis. With Live Communications Server 2003, this was accomplished by repeated client re-registration. In Live Communications Server 2005, the client sends carriage return line feeds (CRLFs) to the server. If the server does not receive a CRLF or another communication back from the client, it closes the connection and reports that the user is not available.

Summary

Now you should have some insight into SIP, its origins, and how it actually works. You learned about the different SIP functions used for instant messaging, and you learned about the different roles that a SIP server can have and how Live Communications Server 2005 uses those functions and roles to operate. You also learned about the SIP message structures and saw examples of SIP requests, responses, and headers and how Live Communications Server 2005 SP1 includes a number of SIP protocol optimizations to provide enhanced server performance. All of this information combined should give you a better understanding of what SIP is and where to look in the event of a problem where you need to examine SIP packets.

CHAPTER 4

■■■

Server Roles

You can deploy Live Communications Server 2005 SP1 in one of several server roles. These server roles perform specific tasks that enable different scenarios. The configuration of these server roles in relation to each other defines a topology. Chapter 6 describes the set of topologies supported by Live Communications Server 2005 SP1. This chapter focuses on understanding the different server roles that are available and when to use them.

Home Server/Pool

The basic scenario is to initially deploy Live Communications Server 2005 SP1 internally within your organization with no connectivity to the Internet. In this scenario, the building block is the home server or pool. A *home server* refers to a Standard Edition Server role with users enabled for Live Communications (that is, SIP) assigned to it. A *home pool* refers to an Enterprise Edition pool with users enabled for Live Communications assigned to it. Subsequent scenarios rely on the home server/pool. The home server is equivalent to the SIP registrar and SIP proxy as defined in RFC 3261 and is discussed in Chapter 3.

Standard Edition Server

The Standard Edition Server is both a SIP registrar and a SIP proxy in a single physical server. Users enabled for Live Communications are homed on a Standard Edition Server. When installing a Standard Edition role, the Microsoft SQL Server Desktop Engine (MSDE) database is automatically installed. This database stores data of all users enabled for Live Communications homed on this server.

The data that is stored for each user includes the following:

- Contact information

- Permissions

- Endpoints

- Subscription information

- Live Communications Server user settings published in Active Directory.

Contact information includes the list of contacts and groups created by the user and how these contacts are organized within these groups (see Figure 4-1).

Figure 4-1. *Contact list*

Permissions refer to whether users are allowed or blocked from viewing your presence state. The administrator can configure these permissions on behalf of the user by clicking the View/Edit button in the user's Live Communications property page, as shown in Figure 4-2.

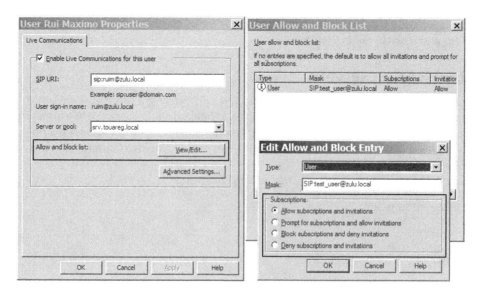

Figure 4-2. *Administrator control for managing permissions of user's contacts*

Permissions can be edited at three different levels. The administrator can modify the Allow and Block entries at the individual contact level, can modify all contacts in the Active Directory domain, or can modify all contacts including federated and PIC contacts. The user has the ability to directly block or allow contacts from viewing their information including presence and from initiating IM conversations with them (as shown in Figure 4-3).

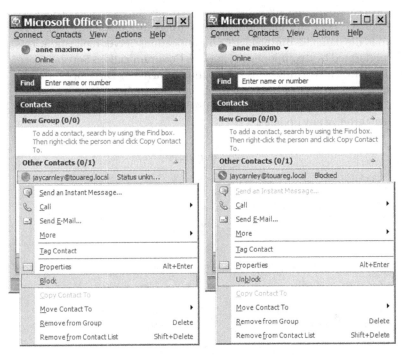

Figure 4-3. *Blocking contact from viewing presence information and initiating IM conversations*

Endpoints refer to each of the clients from where the same user is signed in to Live Communications Server. This is not uncommon for users to be signed in from multiple devices. Users may be simultaneously signed in to Live Communications Server from Office Communicator from their desktop computer, from their laptop, from their smart phone running Office Communicator Mobile, or from Communicator Web Access running on a web browser. The server tracks each of these endpoints to determine the most accurate presence state of the user. When an incoming invitation is sent to the user, Live Communications Server forks the invitation by sending the invitation to all of the user's endpoints. The user responds from one of her devices. The server stops forking incoming messages from that contact and routes all subsequent messages for this session to that device where the user accepted the original invite. Once the session is terminated, any new messages from the same contact or any other contact are again forked to all endpoints to which the user is signed in.

Subscription information contains the list of contacts to which you are a subscriber. Don't confuse this with the list of users subscribed to your presence information; this subscription information tracks all the users from which you want to get presence updates. Examples of presence updates include getting notifications when your contact signs in to Live Communications Server, getting notifications when your contact changes their presence state such as being in a call, and so on.

Figure 4-4 shows the Live Communications Server user settings stored in Active Directory. User information and global Live Communications Server settings stored in Active Directory are synchronized down to the database during Live Communications Server replication. This replication process is performed by a component of the Live Communications Server service called the *user replicator* (UR). The UR only reads information from Active Directory and never writes back to it. The logic of this process, UR, is to contact the closest Active Directory global catalog (GC). If this GC is unavailable, the Standard Edition Server cannot start up; if it's already running, it will fail to synchronize any updates.

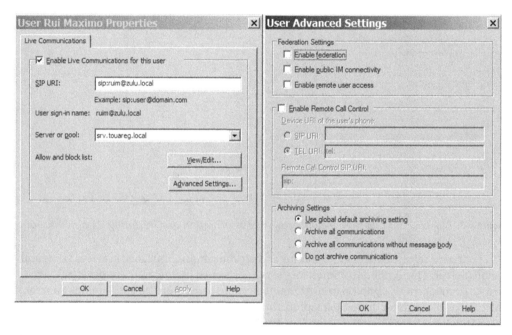

Figure 4-4. *User settings in Active Directory*

As a single-server solution, this becomes a single point of failure. Because a Standard Edition Server maintains user information, it is important to periodically back up the database so in the event of a server failure, this data can be restored. See Chapter 15 for further information.

A Standard Edition Server can handle up to 15,000 users simultaneously logged on. Because of its scale characteristics and ease of deployment as a stand-alone server, the Standard Edition Server targets small- to medium-sized businesses or branch offices within large organizations.

Table 4-1 lists the system requirements for Live Communications Server 2005 Standard Edition. To get the most up-to-date information, refer to http://www.microsoft.com/office/livecomm/prodinfo/standreq.mspx.

Table 4-1. *Hardware and Software Requirements for Standard Edition Servers*

Component	Requirement
Computer and processor	PC with 2.0GHz or faster processor; two or more processors recommended.
Memory	256MB of RAM (2GB or greater recommended).
Hard disk	Dual Ultra2 small computer system interface (SCSI) hard drives with 36GB of available hard disk space recommended.
Operating system	Windows Server 2003 Standard Edition, Windows Server 2003 R2 Standard Edition, Windows Server 2003 Enterprise Edition, Windows Server 2003 R2 Enterprise Edition, Windows Server 2003 Datacenter Edition (supports 32-bit versions of Windows Server 2003), or Windows Server 2003 R2 Datacenter Edition.
Other	Active Directory directory service for Windows Server 2003 or Windows 2000 with Service Pack 3 required. *Database requirements*: Installation of the User Services Component of Live Communications Server 2005 Standard Edition results in the installation of a dedicated SQL Server 2000 Desktop Engine (MSDE) Service Pack 3a database. The Archiving Service requires a separate server running SQL Server 2000 Standard Edition, SQL Server 2000 Enterprise Edition with Service Pack 3a, SQL Server 2005 SP1 Standard Edition, or SQL Server 2005 SP1 Enterprise Edition. *Client requirements*: Microsoft Windows Messenger 5.1 works for basic presence, instant messaging (IM), and federation scenarios; however, Microsoft Office Communicator 2005 is the recommended client for Live Communications Server 2005 with Service Pack 1 (SP1).

Enterprise Pool

The Enterprise Edition improves the scalability and availability of a Standard Edition Server by using a two-tier architecture. An Enterprise Edition deployment is referred to as an *Enterprise pool* because such a deployment involves multiple physical servers. An Enterprise pool decouples the database to a back-end server running SQL Server and the SIP proxy service to front-end servers. The front-end servers no longer maintain persistent data since this is stored in the SQL back-end server. This is an advantage because in the eventuality of a system failure, you can quickly bring up a new front-end server to replace it. A Live Communications Server 2005 Enterprise pool requires a minimum of two front-end servers.

An Enterprise Edition pool deployment requires a hardware load balancer (HLB) to load balance client connections to the front-end servers. The HLB's virtual IP (VIP) is published in Active Directory and DNS when performing the deployment step Create Pool in setup. Clients will connect to this VIP to sign in to the Enterprise pool. The HLB is configured to load balance incoming client requests among the front-end servers.

Each front-end server can scale up to 25,000 users simultaneously. An Enterprise pool can scale up to five front-end servers with a maximum of 125,000 users simultaneously signed in. Its scale characteristics makes the Enterprise pool the better option for large companies wanting to centralize their servers.

For high availability on the back-end since the back-end server is a SQL Server, it can be clustered by taking advantage of Microsoft Clustering Service (MSCS). MSCS is a feature of Enterprise Edition and Datacenter Edition of Windows Server 2003 and Windows Server 2003 R2. Microsoft officially supports *only* active-passive SQL clustering. Active-passive SQL clustering means one SQL node is active while the other SQL node is passive. The front-end servers in the pool are connected to the active node. The passive node takes over when the active node fails. The passive node must be an exact replica of the active node in system configuration. If you're wondering whether Live Communications Server 2005 SP1 supports active-active SQL clustering or 64-bit SQL, you can stop wondering. Microsoft does not officially support these configurations for your Enterprise pool back end. The back-end server cannot be colocated on the same physical server with a front-end server. Since only the back-end server stores persistent information about each user homed on the pool, the front-end servers maintain transient information only for the duration of a user's session, such as its logged-on state and any IM conversations.

All servers belonging to an Enterprise pool must be running on a Windows Server 2003 or Windows Server 2003 R2 computer joined to an Active Directory domain. Deploying half of the front-end servers in domain A, the other half in domain B, and the back-end servers in domain C is not supported by Microsoft. Also, all servers in an Enterprise pool should be within geographic proximity with 1GB connectivity between front-end servers and back-end server(s).

Table 4-2 lists the system requirements for Live Communications Server 2005, Enterprise Edition. To get the most up-to-date information, refer to `http://www.microsoft.com/office/livecomm/prodinfo/enterprisereq.mspx`.

Table 4-2. *Hardware and Software Requirements for Front-End Servers*

Component	Requirement
Computer and processor	PC with 2.0GHz or faster processor; two or more processors recommended.
Memory	256MB of RAM (2GB or greater recommended).
Hard disk	Single Ultra2 small computer system interface (SCSI) hard drive with 36GB of available hard disk space.
Operating system	Windows Server 2003 Standard Edition, Windows Server 2003 R2 Standard Edition, Windows Server 2003 Enterprise Edition, Windows Server 2003 R2 Enterprise Edition, Windows Server 2003 Datacenter Edition (supports 32-bit versions of Windows Server 2003), or Windows Server 2003 R2 Datacenter Edition.
Other	Active Directory directory service for Windows Server 2003 or Windows 2000 with Service Pack 3 required.
	Database requirements: The installation of Live Communications Server 2005 Enterprise Edition requires a separate server running SQL Server 2000 Standard Edition, SQL Server 2000 Enterprise Edition with Service Pack 3a, SQL Server 2005 SP1 Standard Edition, or SQL Server 2005 SP1 Enterprise Edition.
	The Archiving Service requires SQL Server 2000 Standard Edition, SQL Server 2000 Enterprise Edition, SQL Server 2005 SP1 Standard Edition, or SQL Server 2005 SP1 Enterprise Edition.
	Client requirements: Microsoft Windows Messenger 5.1 works for basic presence, instant messaging, and federation scenarios; however, Microsoft Office Communicator 2005 is the recommended client for Live Communications Server 2005 with Service Pack 1 (SP1).

Director

When deploying a single home server/pool, your topology remains simple. However, as the number of home servers/pools grows within your organization, complexity creeps in. Deploying multiple home servers/pools might be necessary to handle the large number of users, to handle geographically dispersed users within your organization, or both. In such situations, it is recommended to deploy a Director or array of Directors. Before explaining why, a bit of background information is necessary.

When users sign in to Live Communications Server, the client (that is, Office Communicator or Windows Messenger) performs a DNS SRV query. Once the client determines the IP address of this server, it connects to it and attempts to sign in. If this server is the user's home server or pool, then the server/pool signs in the user. This will always be the case if your organization has only a single home server or pool. Mission accomplished! However, if you've deployed multiple Live Communications Servers within your organization, then the DNS SRV query might or might not return the user's home server. If the DNS query returns the FQDN of a Live Communications Server that is not the user's home server, then this server must redirect the client to the user's correct home server. This makes the initial sign-in traffic nondeterministic since clients signing in are not guaranteed to reach the user's home server in the first hop. This nondeterministic configuration has several impacts. First, each home server and pool must account for the performance load created from redirecting client requests attempting to sign in users not homed on that server/pool. In the worse-case scenario, every home server and pool needs to handle the load of redirecting sign-in traffic for all users in your organization that are enabled for Live Communications. Second, if the DNS query returned directs the client to a server that is unavailable, the sign-in experience will be substantially impacted because the client must wait for the network timeout to expire before attempting to connect to another server. If the user is using Windows Messenger, this client will not reattempt the sign-in process. The user will need to reinitiate the sign-in process again. Therefore, it is recommended that you deploy a Director role when your organization hosts multiple home servers and pools. The Director role forces the sign-in traffic into a deterministic path. Instead of publishing the FQDN of the home servers/pools in DNS, the DNS SRV publishes the FQDN of the Director or bank of Directors. When Communicator attempts to sign in the user, its DNS SRV query returns the FQDN of the Director. The Director knows how to locate the user's home server and redirects the client to that server. The Director's role is to redirect internal clients to the correct home server or pool where the user is homed on (see Figure 4-5). This configuration allows home servers and pools to handle SIP traffic only for its users.

Besides helping route traffic for internal deployments, a Director is also useful for external topologies. Again, the best usage of a Director is when your organization has a deployment of Live Communications Server with multiple servers and pools.

When configuring federation, public IM connectivity, or remote access, deploying a Director as the Access Proxy's next hop is strongly recommended. By using a Director or bank of Directors, the only socket (that is, IP address and port number) that needs to be opened on the internal firewall separating servers in the network perimeter and servers in the internal network is access to the Director on port 5061. By restricting the Access Proxy to reach only the Director, you can limit damages to your internal network if the Access Proxy was ever compromised. None of the internal home servers and Enterprise pools is directly accessible to the Access Proxy.

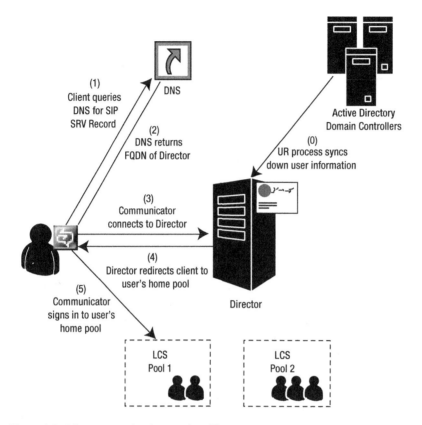

Figure 4-5. *Director routing internal traffic*

The Director provides the following benefits:

- Authenticates remote users before proxying the client connection to the user's home server. The Director insulates the internal servers from denial of service (DoS) attacks from unauthorized users.

- Proxies remote user connections to the correct Standard Edition Server or Enterprise pool. This is necessary since the connection cannot be redirected.

- Verifies the intended recipient of a message is a valid user before proxying to an internal server. This protects internal servers from processing invalid messages from a PIC or federated partner.

The Director is responsible for authenticating the user and routing the client connection to the correct home server or pool. The home server or pool responds to the client request by routing the messages through the Director. From a security perspective, the Director serves as an additional security barrier. For outgoing connections to the Access Proxy, the home servers and pools route traffic destined for external users (that is, federated contacts, PIC contacts, and remote users) to the Director. The Director then proxies the connection to the Access Proxy.

Figure 4-6 illustrates this.

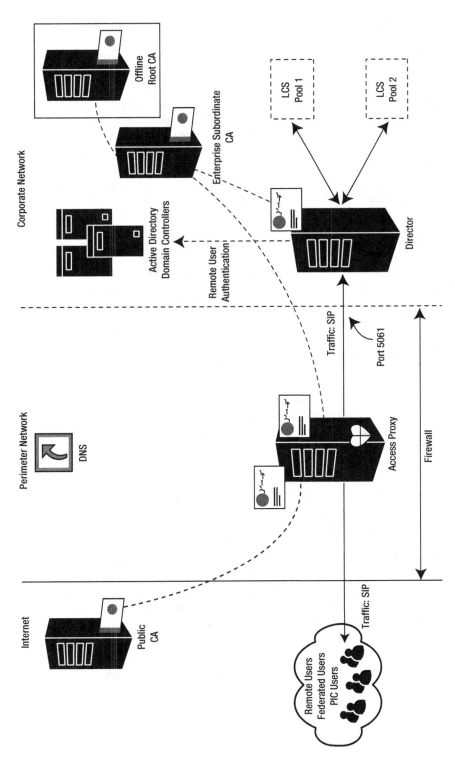

Figure 4-6. *Director routing external traffic*

Archiving Service

If your organization has a policy that requires that every communication must be logged for compliance purposes, then you need to deploy the Archiving Service. This server role enables archiving of all messages at the server level. Since all IM conversations travel through the user's home server or pool, it is possible to enforce archiving at the server level without requiring any cooperation from the client. This architecture offers the most control to the administrator.

The Archiving Service must be installed on a Windows Server 2003 or Windows Server 2003 R2 computer with SQL Server 2000 SP3a (or higher) or SQL Server 2005 SP1 (or higher) installed. The Archiving Service cannot be colocated on the same physical server as the Access Proxy or home server or pool. An Archiving Service can archive IM traffic from up to four Standard Edition Servers or front-end servers. For additional information, please refer to Chapter 17.

Access Proxy

The Access Proxy is a server role that is deployed in the network perimeter. The Access Proxy must be deployed if you want to enable federation, PIC, or remote user access. Since most organizations do not have Active Directory access from their network perimeter for security reasons, the Access Proxy is deployed on a computer running Windows Server 2003 or Windows Server 2003 R2 in a WORKGROUP environment. The system requirements for an Access Proxy are the same as for a Standard Edition Server.

The Access Proxy cannot be colocated on the same physical server with any other service such as Microsoft Internet Security and Acceleration Server (ISA). For IT administrators who are cost sensitive (that is, most of us), the question might have crossed your mind, why does Live Communications Server not provide the functionality of the Access Proxy as an ISA filter? The primary reason is because the tasks that an Access Proxy performs are much more complex than can be supported by ISA.

The Access Proxy must be configured with two NICs. One network card is connected to the Internet, and the second network card is connected to the corporate network. If the Access Proxy is protected by firewalls on both sides of the network perimeter, the internal firewall must be configured to open port 5061 so the Access Proxy can connect to the Director in the corporate network, and vice versa. If configuring federation or PIC, port 5061 must be opened on the external firewall to allow connectivity from the Internet to the Access Proxy. If remote user access is configured, then you have the option to configure whichever port number you prefer because you control the client connecting since these are internal users. The recommendation is to open port 5061 or 443. Best practice is to open port 443 because this allows your users to connect back to your Access Proxy from another organization's network since this port number is usually open. This is particularly important for professionals such as consultants who work on-site at a customer's site.

To provide high availability, a bank of Access Proxy servers can be deployed. An HLB must be configured on both sides of the Access Proxy server, as shown in Figure 4-7.

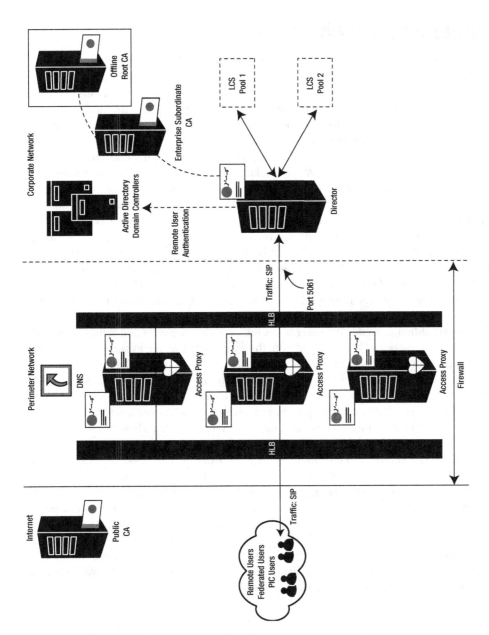

Figure 4-7. *Access Proxy servers*

Communicator Web Access

Communicator Web Access for Live Communications Server 2005 SP1 is a web service that allows users to sign in to Live Communications Server without needing to install Microsoft Office Communicator. This server role makes it possible to connect to Live Communications Server with simply a web browser. This browser-based client for Live Communications Server 2005 SP1 makes it possible for users using non-Windows systems and locked-down Windows systems to have a similar experience as those users using Office Communicator.

If you're trying to find where this server role is located in the Setup menu, you won't find it there. Communicator Web Access (CWA) is available only as a web download from Microsoft, which makes it difficult for customers to discover. You can find it at `http://www.microsoft.com/downloads/details.aspx?familyid=A7499AC3-09A6-4491-BDD1-1E41F4719E90&displaylang=en`. CWA provides its own setup and management console (MMC), which is why CWA servers cannot be managed from the same MMC as Live Communications Servers. This server role must be installed on a computer joined to your Active Directory forest because it needs Active Directory connectivity to authenticate and authorize user access. When a user connects to CWA, the web service authenticates the user. CWA supports forms-based authentication or integrated Windows authentication (IWA). Integrated Windows authentication refers to the native authentication protocols Kerberos and NTLM supported by Active Directory. Once the user is properly authenticated, CWA determines the user's home server and signs in the user. At this point, CWA proxies all traffic to and from the user's home server, as shown in Figure 4-8.

Communicator Web Access can be installed on a separate computer that may be running other web services, or it can be installed on the same computer running a Standard Edition Server or front-end server. If installing Communicator Web Access on a home server/pool, beware that the overall performance of your home server/pool will be reduced. If you expect to have 1,000 users or more connecting to Communicator Web Access, it's best to install CWA on its own computer. For valuable tips on how to optimize the performance of your Communicator Web Access server, refer to the following TechNet article: `http://www.microsoft.com/technet/prodtechnol/office/livecomm/library/cwa/capacityplanning/cwacpl_3.mspx`.

Notice how CWA performs a similar role as the Director except it always proxies client connections instead of redirecting them for internal users. Microsoft supports colocating Communicator Web Access on the same physical server with a Standard Edition Server. This makes CWA a prime candidate to be deployed on the same physical server as a Director, which is what most customers we've encountered do to avoid the cost and management of yet another server. If you've deployed Office Communicator to all your users, the usage of CWA is likely to be light enough that a Director could easily handle it.

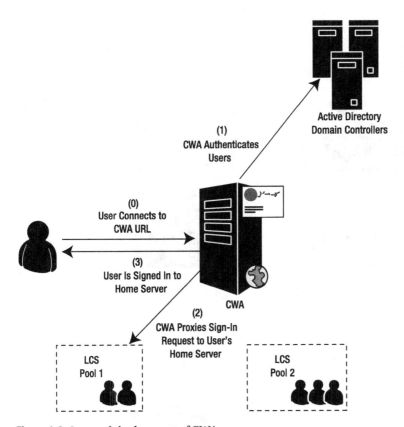

Figure 4-8. *Internal deployment of CWA*

Communicator Web Access can also be accessible from outside your organization's fire-wall. To properly secure your CWA server, it is strongly recommended that you use a reverse proxy such as ISA behind the firewalls in your network perimeter. When configuring CWA for external access, you should use port 443. Figure 4-9 illustrates this topology.

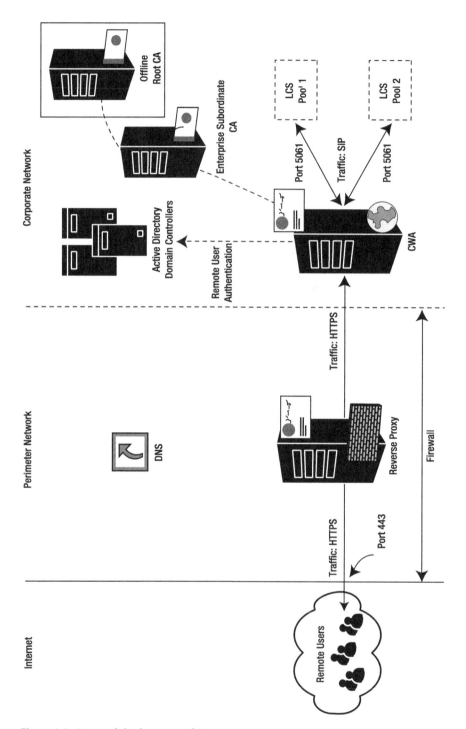

Figure 4-9. *External deployment of CWA*

Table 4-3 lists the system requirements for Communicator Web Access, including the various browsers that are supported. To get the most up-to-date information, refer to http://www.microsoft.com/office/communicator/webaccess/prodinfo/sysreq.mspx.

Table 4-3. *Hardware and Software Requirements for CWA*

Component	Requirement
Computer and processor	Dual Intel Xeon 3.06GHz, 1MB cache, 533MHz FSB (front-side bus)
Memory	2B DDR (double data rate), 266MHz RAM
Hard disk	18GB of available hard disk space
Network adapter	100Mb or higher network adapter
Operating system	Microsoft Windows Server 2003 Service Pack 1 (SP1)
Supported browsers	Internet Explorer 6.0 (SP1 recommended), Firefox 1.0, Safari 1.2.4, Netscape 7.2
Other	Live Communications Server 2005 SP1, .NET Framework 2.0, ASP.NET 2.0, Public Key Certificates for transport layer security (TLS), and HTTPS

Proxy

The Proxy server role functions as the proxy server as defined in RTC 3261: a *proxy server* receives SIP requests and forwards them on behalf of the requestor. This server role is often referred to as the *forwarding proxy* in Microsoft's Live Communications Server 2005 documentation. This server role is recommended for use in branch office scenarios to compression SIP traffic over low-bandwidth WAN connections. This proxy functionality is also present in the home server/pool (Standard/Enterprise Edition) and Access Proxy roles. Similar to other server roles, value-added functionality can be built on top of Live Communications Server's Proxy such as complex routing applications using Microsoft SIP Processing Language (MSPL) and managed code. As such, this server role is seldom used directly by customers.

Summary

Live Communications Server 2005 SP1 provides seven different server roles with specific usages to build an Enterprise instant messaging system:

- Standard Edition

- Enterprise Edition

- Director

- Access Proxy

- Archiving Service

- Communicator Web Access

- Proxy

The Enterprise Edition scales the capacity of the Standard Edition Server to a larger magnitude by splitting the different logical functionality into separate physical servers. The Director is a logical server role and really is a Standard Edition Server or an Enterprise Edition pool. What differentiates the Director from a Standard Edition Server or Enterprise pool is the lack of users homed on it. It serves to proxy and/or redirect user connections to the user's home server or home pool. The Access Proxy is deployed in the network perimeter to enable connectivity outside the organization's private network. The Access Proxy allows remote users to sign in to their organization's Live Communications Server infrastructure and allows employees to communicate with federated partners as well as subscribers to any of the three public IM providers (AOL, MSN, Yahoo!). The Archiving Service serves the role of performing server-side archiving of all IM communications of employees within the organization's network as well as outside. Communicator Web Access provides a Communicator client experience from a web browser for users without Office Communicator installed on their local computers. Finally, the Proxy server role is a basic proxy server as defined in RFC 3261 that can be used by vendors to provide special value-added services on top of SIP.

CHAPTER 5

■■■

Live Communications Server Clients

Live Communications Server 2005 SP1 is a client-server architecture product geared for enterprises. Microsoft offers several clients to connect to Live Communications Server: Windows Messenger 5.1, Office Communicator 2005, Communicator Web Access, and Office Communicator Mobile. In this chapter, we'll discuss each of these clients in detail.

In the case of Communicator 2005, Windows Messenger 5.1, and Communicator Mobile, these clients must be locally installed on the user's computer or device. Organizations can use various ways to get the client installed on users' computers. First, organizations can create entire desktop images containing all the approved software packaged into a single download that are then pushed to computers via third-party desktop management tools. Second, a network share on a server can serve as a software distribution point where users can download the latest software approved by the organization's IT. In addition, enterprises often use software distribution solutions such as Microsoft Systems Management Server (SMS), IBM Tivoli, and CA Unicenter to distribute software. Alternatively, companies can use a logon script to automatically download the latest software the next time the user logs on to their corporate computer. Finally, Windows Server 2000 and Windows Server 2003 offer tools such as Group Policy and IntelliMirror to deploy and manage the installation of software.

Whichever method you choose to install Communicator and Windows Messenger 5.1, managing the desktop software still remains a nontrivial cost to IT. Communicator Web Access avoids this deployment and management cost entirely.

Communicator

Communicator is the preferred client for Live Communications Server 2005 SP1. Communicator sports a new user interface compared to Windows Messenger. Communicator's user interface is well suited for enterprise usage because it allows users to view presence information and interact over instant messaging with other users in the organization without requiring employees to add each other to their contact lists first. If you were required to wait until the other person accepted your invitation before you could contact them over IM, the use of IM would become impractical for an organization setting. Also, imagine managing a contact list that is the size of the employee base of your company! For large organizations, the sign-in time performance would be horribly slow as the client downloaded the user's contact list and subscribed to each contact's presence information. Communicator makes searching for contacts and immediately displaying their presence state so the user can determine which means of communication is best suited to reach this contact a primary feature of the client. This way, the contact list can remain manageable with only the contacts the user communicates with the most.

Users using Communicator have the ability to search their organization's Active Directory directory services directly as long as they are not connected to the internal network remotely. To search Active Directory, select Contacts ➤ Add a Contact, as shown in Figure 5-1.

Figure 5-1. *Selecting Add a Contact in Communicator*

The Add a Contact Wizard will appear. To search Active Directory for a contact, select the option Search for a Contact (see Figure 5-2).

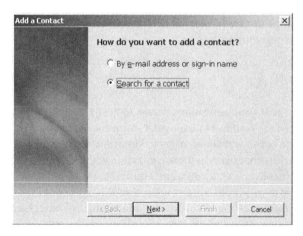

Figure 5-2. *Specifying a search*

Users have the option of searching based on the parameters shown in Figure 5-3.

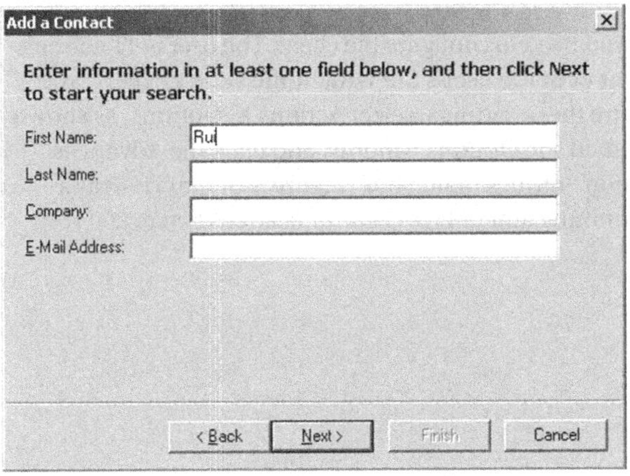

Figure 5-3. *Specifying parameters*

Search results are immediately returned to the user. The user can then select which entries to add as contacts, as shown in Figure 5-4.

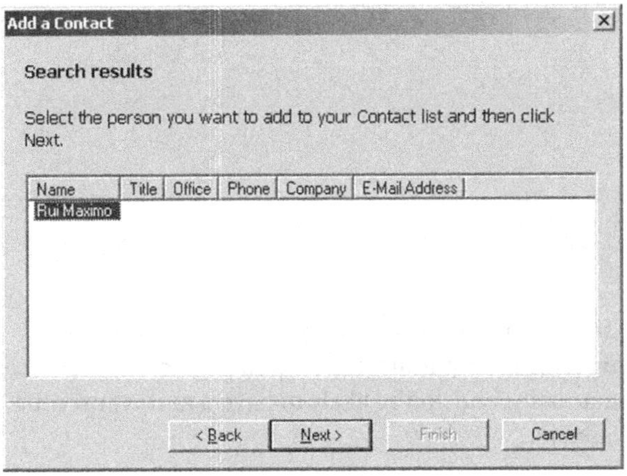

Figure 5-4. *Active Directory search results*

A subtle feature of Communicator is the lack of a multitude of consumer features that can easily distract workers from their immediate task, which is to contact a particular user regarding a work-related effort or project.

If you want to prevent users from walking through the steps of installing Communicator 2005 to avoid any user errors, you can install Communicator in silent mode by using the /q switch in a script or batch file as such:

```
Communicator.msi /q
```

Once installed, you can start Communicator 2005 by calling the following command:

```
%Program Files%\ Microsoft Office Communicator\communicator.exe
```

After installing Communicator 2005, you need to configure the client. The user or IT adminis-trator configures the Communicator client with the user's SIP URI, home server FQDN, and connection type (TCP or TLS). To configure these settings, select Actions ➤ Options, as shown in Figure 5-5. Navigate to the Accounts tab in the Options window, and click the Advanced button. Notice in the Advanced Connection Settings dialog box (Figure 5-6) that UDP as a transport protocol is not supported by Communicator or Live Communications Server 2005 SP1.

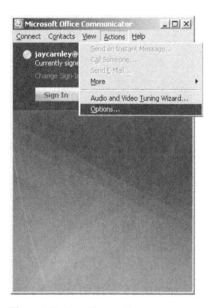

Figure 5-5. *Locating options*

The best kind of configuration an IT administrator must perform on a user's computer is no configuration, if at all possible. Try convincing an IT administrator to configure hundreds to tens of thousands of desktop computers manually, and you're likely to have a mutiny on your hands. Luckily, a couple of options are available:

Automatic Configuration: Set up a Standard Edition Server as a Director, or a bank of Stan-dard Edition Servers as a bank of Directors, that clients can locate via a DNS SRV record for SIP. When users sign in, Communicator performs a query for the DNS SRV record and connects to the Director. The Director, or bank of Directors, then redirects the client to the user's home server or pool.

Manual Configuration: Package the installation payload for Communicator with a script that queries Active Directory for the user's SIP URI and home server or pool and configures Communicator with these settings.

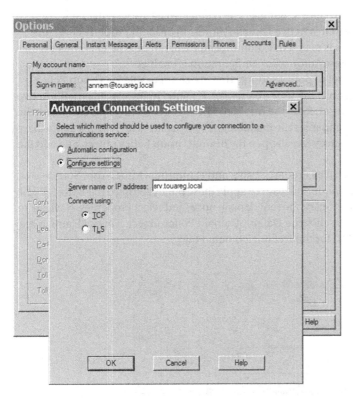

Figure 5-6. *Configuring an account*

The Automatic Configuration option has the advantage of being a server-side solution. No clients need to be configured. If you consider that your organization's workforce starts around 8 a.m., the Director is likely to experience a spike in activity as users file into work. Even though the Director's load will be nominal during the rest of the day, you must account for the performance impact during peak hours. Another consideration to keep in mind is if your organization's workforce is geographically dispersed in different regions or countries. Suppose the Director is deployed in Redmond, Washington. Users in the Beijing, China, office will have to connect to the Director before they get redirected to their home server, which is humming in the server closet a few doors down the hallway. If the WAN connection is reliable, this arrangement might work. However, if the WAN connection is unreliable, it would be unfortunate that users in the remote office cannot sign in even though their Standard Edition Server is operational and ready to service them. If this issue will be a problem for your organization's environment, you should consider the Manual Configuration option. You can find more details in the "Automatic Configuration" section.

The Manual Configuration option has the advantages that no Director server needs to be deployed and no DNS SRV record needs to be created. It avoids the problem of traversing a WAN link to connect to a Director when users sign in. It has the disadvantage that you need to configure each Communicator client installed on every computer in your organization. However, since Communicator must be installed on every user's computer, why not package a configuration script with this payload so that it will configure Communicator before running it? The script queries Active Directory for a user's settings and configures the appropriate registry keys needed by Communicator. This requires that users be connected to the internal network at least once to query the organization's Active Directory forest in order to properly configure Communicator. If remote access is enabled, Communicator will not be able to connect to the organization's Access Proxy unless Automatic Configuration is enabled.

Communicator provides a set of policy settings that are configurable via Group Policy. These settings will be applied only if the user's computer is joined to the organization's Active Directory forest and is not logging on from the Internet. These policy settings are defined in the file, `Communicator.adm`, that accompanies the installation file, `Communicator.msi`. To apply these policy settings to the Active Directory forest, open the desired Group Policy object, and add the `Communicator.adm` policy file.

For example, launch the Active Directory Users and Computers MMC from Start ➤ Administrative Tools. Select the node you want to apply these policy settings. In Figure 5-7, the root domain node is selected. Right-click the root domain node, and select Properties. Navigate to the Group Policy tab, and double-click the Default Domain Policy object. This will launch the Group Policy Object Editor MMC for the Default Domain Policy.

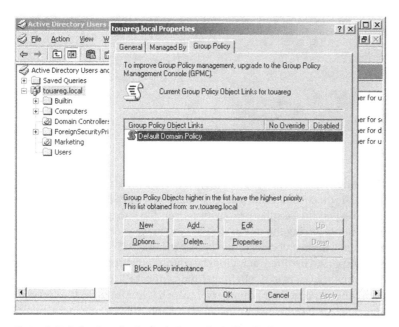

Figure 5-7. *Selecting the Default Domain Policy link*

Right-click the Administrative Templates node, and select Add/Remove Templates, as shown in Figure 5-8. In the Add/Remove Templates dialog box, click the Add button to add the Communicator.adm file.

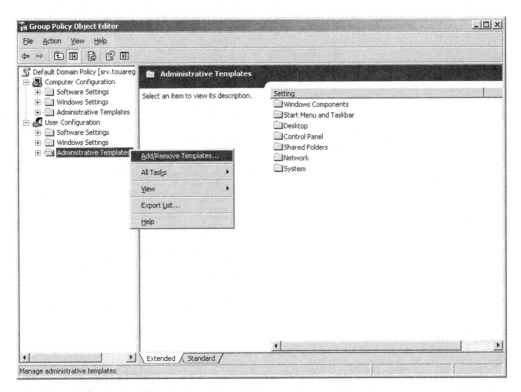

Figure 5-8. *Adding the Communicator administrative template*

You can now configure the Communicator-specific policy settings under the Microsoft Office Communicator Feature Policies node, as shown in Figure 5-9. We won't explain each policy setting because the description provided in the Extended view already provides a comprehensive explanation of each setting.

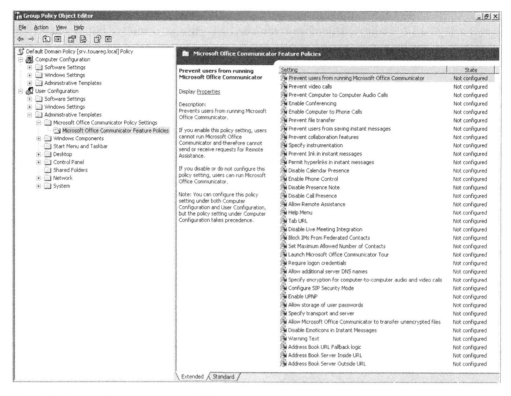

Figure 5-9. *Setting Communicator policies*

To enable the Microsoft Office 2003 integration of presence information, you must set the following registry keys. Although Office integration is enabled by default, it's a good idea to set them in case users disable this setting by mistake.

```
[HKEY_CURRENT_USER\Software\Policies\Microsoft\Office\11.0\Outlook\IM]
"Enabled"=dword:00000001
"EnablePresence"=dword:00000001
```

By default, Office applications display presence information only for contacts in a user's contact list. To configure Office to display presence information for any user in your organization, set the following registry key:

```
[HKEY_CURRENT_USER\Software\Policies\Microsoft\Office\11.0\Common\
    PersonaMenu] "QueryServiceForStatus"=dword:00000002
```

To remove the dependency of the Outlook 2003 and Communicator 2005 start order, set this registry key:

```
[HKEY_CURRENT_USER\Software\policies\Microsoft\Office\11.0\Common\PersonaMenu]
    "EnableDynamicPresence"=dword:00000001
```

To avoid manually touching every desktop to configure these registry settings, you can configure these via Group Policy. The easiest option is to add the Office11.adm policy as an administrative template in the same way you added the `Communicator.adm` policy. This ADM file defines these registry keys as policies for presence integration in Office. It is available in the Office 2003 Policy Template Files and Deployment Planning Tools. This download contains updated Office group policy template files (ADMs) for Office 2003 Service Pack 2. It is available at `http://download.microsoft.com/download/9/5/f/95f7e000-d7ab-4b86-8a5d-804b124c7a69/ORKSP2AT.EXE`. Once you've added `Office11.adm` as an administrative template, you can find these settings under the node Administrative Templates ➤ Microsoft Office 2003 ➤ Instant Messaging Integration (see Figure 5-10).

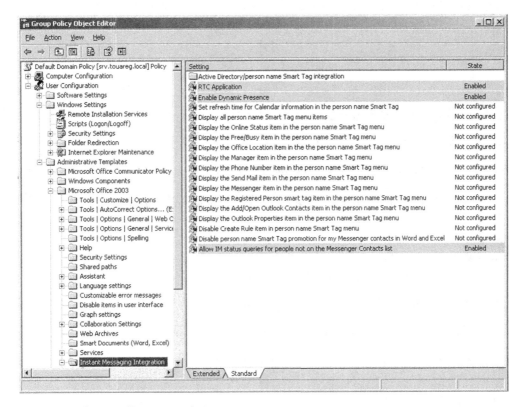

Figure 5-10. *Setting Office 2003 policies*

The policy settings corresponding to the presence integration registry keys are as follows:

- RTC Application

- Enable Dynamic Presence

- Allow IM Status Queries for People Not on the Messenger Contacts List

Configure the RTC Application policy, as shown in Figure 5-11.

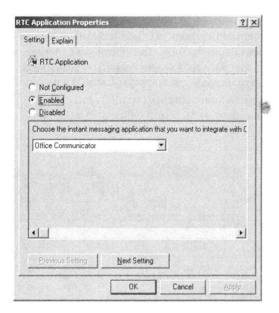

Figure 5-11. *Office 2003: RTC Application policy*

Configure the Enable Dynamic Presence policy, as shown in Figure 5-12.

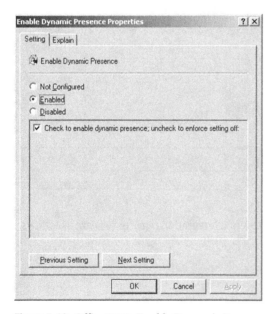

Figure 5-12. *Office 2003: Enable Dynamic Presence policy*

Configure the Allow IM Status Queries for People Not on the Messenger Contacts List policy, as shown in Figure 5-13.

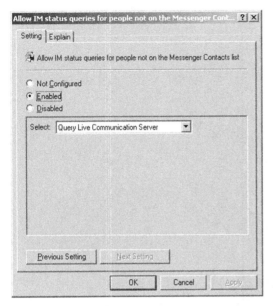

Figure 5-13. *Office 2003: Allow IM Status Queries for People Not on the Messenger Contacts List policy*

When trying to troubleshoot why a particular user is experiencing problems, it's sometimes necessary to enable the client-side tracing of Communicator. The generated log file can then be reviewed by Microsoft's Product Support Services to hone in on the problem. To turn on tracing, set the following registry key:

```
[HKEY_CURRENT_USER\Software\Microsoft\Tracing\Communicator]
   "EnableFileTracing"=dword:00000001
```

Instead of explaining to users how to set this registry key, you can use the free tool available from LcsSolutions.com called the Communicator 2005 Trace Utility. This utility makes it easy and error free to configure this setting. You can download this utility at http://lcssolutions.com/Downloads/tabid/58/Default.aspx. To enable tracing, simply start the utility, and click the button Communicator Tracing Is Off to turn it on. After restarting Communicator and reproducing the problem, the user can send you the trace log by clicking the button Browse Tracing Directory. This will open the directory C:\Documents and Settings\%username%\Tracing, where the user can easily locate the log file (see Figure 5-14).

Figure 5-14. *Using the free Communicator 2005 Trace Utility*

Automatic Configuration

To publish the Director or bank of Directors so Communicator clients can discover it, you must create a DNS SRV record in the organization's primary DNS server, as shown in Figure 5-15 and Figure 5-16. The SRV record that should be created can be one of the following forms. Communicator queries for the SRV record in the following order of priority:

1. **_sipfederationtls.**_tcp.<domain>, which is used by Communicator clients for external access only over port 5061

2. **_sipinternaltls.**_tcp.<domain>, which is used only by Communicator clients for internal TLS access over port 5061

3. **_sipinternal.**_tcp.<domain>, which is used only by Communicator clients for internal TCP access over port 5060

4. **_sip._tls.**_tcp.<domain>, which is used by Windows Messenger 5.1 and Communicator for internal and external TLS access over port 5061

5. **_sip.**_tcp.<domain>, which is used by Windows Messenger 5.1 and Communicator for internal TCP access over port 5060

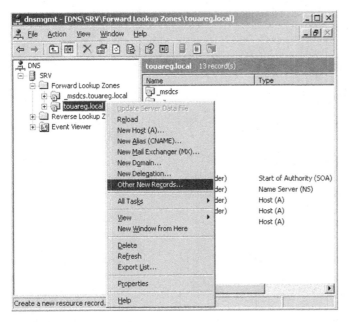

Figure 5-15. *DNS snap-in*

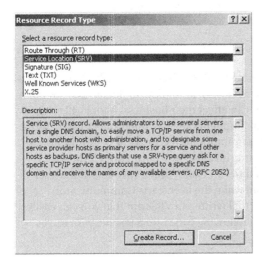

Figure 5-16. *Creating a DNS SRV record*

When creating the SRV record, the prefix (marked in bold earlier) before the "._tcp.<domain>" suffix is entered in the Service field, as shown in Figure 5-17. The Protocol field should always be set to _*tcp* and not _*udp* because Live Communications Server supports TCP only as a transport protocol. For internal access (_sipinternaltls, _sipinternal, _sip._tls, or _sip._tcp), the FQDN of the Director (or in the case of a bank of Directors, the FQDN of the hardware load balancer) is entered in the field called, Host Offering This Service. For external access (_sipfederationtls or _sip._tls), the

FQDN of the Access Proxy (or in the case of a bank of access proxies, the FQDN of hardware load balancer) is entered in this field.

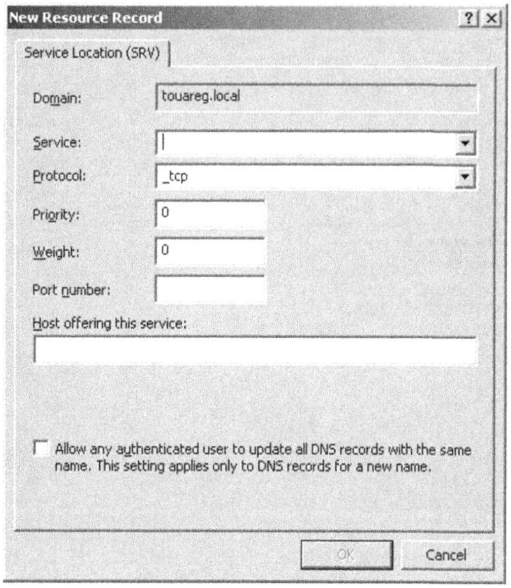

Figure 5-17. *Configuring a DNS SRV record*

Manual Configuration

Since manually configuring each user's Communicator settings is not practical, an IT administrator's best friends are tools that automate the work for them so they can focus their valuable time on investigating how the latest technologies can affect their business. A tool will retrieve the username and domain name from the user's environment variables, query Active Directory for the user's SIP URI and home server FQDN, and set the appropriate registry keys for Communicator. To avoid potential problems after Communicator is installed and configured if the user is moved to another home server, the tool will need to run again, preferably before the user reports a problem. A good choice is to run the tool when the user starts Communicator.

The following is a working example of such a tool written in VBScript that you can easily customize for your needs. Just copy and paste the following code into a text file with a .vbs extension, and run it:

```
On Error Resume Next
set WshShell = WScript.CreateObject("WScript.Shell")
'

' Obtain currently logged on user's DN
' stored in the value: ADSysInfo.UserName
'

Set ADSysInfo = CreateObject("ADSystemInfo")

'
```

```
' Query user's SIP URI and home server DN
' using the following WMI class:
'
' class MSFT_SIPESUserSetting
' {
'     string DisplayName;
'     boolean Enabled;
'     string HomeServerDN;
'     [key] string InstanceID;
'     string PrimaryURI;
'     string TargetServerDNIfMoving;
'     string UserDN;
' };
'
Set oUsers = GetObject("winmgmts:\\").ExecQuery("SELECT * FROM
  MSFT_SIPESUserSetting WHERE UserDN = '" & ADSysInfo.UserName & "'")
' Since the user DN is unique, we're expecting a single result.
for each User in oUsers
    Wscript.echo User.DisplayName
    sipURI = User.PrimaryURI
    Wscript.echo sipURI
    poolDN = User.HomeServerDN
next

' Exit if user is not enabled for Live Communications.
if IsEmpty(sipURI) then
    Wscript.echo "ERROR: user is not enabled for Live Communications"
    Wscript.Quit
end if

' Exit if user is orphaned.
if IsNull(poolDN) then
    Wscript.echo "ERROR: user is not assigned to a home server"
    Wscript.Quit
end if

'
' Convert home server DN into FQDN
' using the following WMI class:
'
' class MSFT_SIPPoolSetting
' {
'     string BackEndDBPath;
'     [key] string InstanceID;
'     uint32 MajorVersion;
'     uint32 MinorVersion;
'     string PoolDisplayName;
```

```
'      string PoolDN;
'      string PoolFQDN;
'      string [] PoolMemberList;
'      string PoolType;
' };
'
Set oServers = GetObject("winmgmts:\\").ExecQuery("SELECT * FROM
   MSFT_SIPPoolSetting WHERE PoolDN = '" & poolDN & "'")
' Since the pool DN is unique, we're only expecting a single FQDN.
for each HS in oServers
    Wscript.echo HS.poolFQDN
    poolFQDN = HS.PoolFQDN
next

' Exit if user's home server FQDN cannot be determined.
if IsEmpty(poolFQDN) then
    Wscript.echo "ERROR: failed to determine user's home server FQDN"
    Wscript.Quit
end if

'
' Retrieve user's domain
'
set WshShell = WScript.CreateObject("WScript.Shell")
domain = WshShell.ExpandEnvironmentStrings("%USERDOMAIN%")

'
' Parse the SIP URI into the format:
' 'sip:user@company.com' -> 'user@company.com %domain%\user'
' where %domain% is the user's domain name
'
Set myRegExp = New RegExp
myRegExp.IgnoreCase = True
myRegExp.Global = True
myRegExp.Pattern = "sip:([^~]+)@([^~]+)"
replaceString = "$1@$2 " & domain & "\$1"
userURI = myRegExp.Replace(sipURI, replaceString)
Wscript.echo userURI

'
' Configure Communicator registry keys
'
WshShell.RegWrite
   "HKCU\Software\Microsoft\Communicator\UserMicrosoft RTC Instant Messaging",
   userURI, "REG_SZ"
```

```
WshShell.RegWrite
    "HKCU\Software\Microsoft\Communicator\ServerAddress",
    poolFQDN, "REG_SZ"
WshShell.RegWrite
    "HKCU\Software\Microsoft\Communicator\ConfigurationMode",
    1, "REG_DWORD"
' Set type to 2 for TCP or set type to 4 for TLS
const TransportType = 2
WshShell.RegWrite
    "HKCU\Software\Microsoft\Communicator\Transport",
    TransportType, "REG_DWORD"

'

' Start Communicator.exe
'

WshShell.Run "Communicator.exe", 1
```

This tool can then be packaged with the installer for Communicator, Communicator.msi, into a single payload if users have sufficient permissions to install software locally on their computers. A simple and free option is to use the IExpress.exe tool. This is a powerful tool if you haven't used it before. IExpress can package the files, Communicator.msi, and the tool into a single executable that can be run silently (as a logon script, for example) without requiring any user interaction. Creating an installation package with IExpress is very simple and takes only a couple of minutes to complete. IExpress is available on Windows 2000, Windows XP, and Windows Server 2003. From Start ➤ Run, type **IExpress** to start the IExpress wizard. To use the Self Extraction Directive (SED) file available on the companion CD, select the second option, and select the file InstallCommunicator.SED file. This SED file automatically installs Communicator in silent mode so users do not need to go through the Communicator installation wizard and runs the tool (called configure.vbs) once the installation is complete to configure Communicator for the user.

Windows Messenger 5.1

Several versions of Windows Messenger (WM) exist; however, only version 5.1 works with Live Communications Server 2005 SP1. WM is considered a legacy client, and Microsoft recommends using Communicator as the preferred client. If your users are not running Microsoft Office 2003 SR2 or later, Windows Messenger 5.1 must still be installed on users' desktops to light up Microsoft Office 2003 with presence integration. Communicator and Windows Messenger can coexist on the same computer. Windows Messenger 5.1 should not be confused with the version of Windows Messenger that gets installed when you set up Windows XP. You should uninstall this version, Windows Messenger 4.8 or 5.0, because it doesn't work with Live Communications Server 2005 SP1.

To install Windows Messenger in silent mode to avoid users from installing it manually, run the installation with the /q switch:

```
Messenger.msi /q
```

If you do not have any Exchange IM 2000 servers running and want to avoid users from running two clients, Communicator and Windows Messenger (which could be confusing to users and likely result in support calls), you can disable Windows Messenger from running by disabling Autorun from Windows Messenger's Options.

WM is a triple-stack client. This means a user using WM can log into Live Communications Server, MSN, and Exchange IM 2000 (the predecessor to Live Communications Server 2003). Since few customers are using it (none that we know of at this point because the ones we are aware of have already migrated to Live Communications Server and Communicator), we won't cover this client in further detail. If you do have a user base running WM and you need to migrate your users' contact list to Live Communications Server, you have two options. The Live Communications Server 2005 SP1 Resource Kit contains a set of scripts to perform a server-side migration of users and their contact lists. The other option is to use a freely available tool found at `http://www.download.com` to allow users to migrate their contact lists to Communicator by themselves. Users must already have Communicator installed and running before migrating their contacts.

Communicator Web Access

Communicator Web Access extends the reach of Communicator beyond the Windows desktop for any organization with a heterogeneous computing environment. Communicator Web Access is a browser-based client that offers a user experience similar to Communicator. Users with network connectivity to their Live Communications Server and access to a web browser can sign in without needing to use a computer running Windows 2000 or XP with Communicator installed. The best part is that Communicator Web Access is a free download from Microsoft. Communicator Web Access is Live Communications Server 2005 SP1's solution for organizations with non-Windows desktops, locked-down Windows desktops where users are not authorized to install any software, or users who want to sign in to Live Communications Server from a kiosk computer. Users can simply navigate to the URL published for Communicator Web Access to sign in. No client-side configuration is necessary.

You can download Communicator Web Access from `http://www.microsoft.com/downloads/details.aspx?FamilyId=A7499AC3-09A6-4491-BDD1-1E41F4719E90&displaylang=en`. Before installing Communicator Web Access, you must have Internet Information Services (IIS), ASP.NET, and the .NET Framework installed on the computer. Installing Communicator Web Access is a three-step process. First you install the files, then you activate the server role, and finally you create a virtual server. Each of these steps is straightforward to complete via the provided wizards. If you plan to make Communicator Web Access accessible externally, then you must create two virtual servers, one for internal access and another for external access. Although you can configure the virtual server used for internal access to use HTTP or HTTPS, you must configure the virtual server for external access for HTTPS. You'll need to request a web server certificate and configure the virtual server with it.

After installing Communicator Web Access, you should install the Hotfix KB 915066, `CWA-KB915066.msp`, found at `http://www.microsoft.com/downloads/details.aspx?FamilyID=5ffbd0da-124c-4ffc-a810-4a9e9e50d80d&DisplayLang=en`.

Communicator Mobile

Similarly, Communicator Mobile extends the reach of Communicator beyond the desktop. Using Communicator Mobile, users with Windows Mobile–powered devices can quickly locate co-workers and communicate with them via IM or voice calls while on the road or away from their offices. Users using Communicator Mobile can easily escalate into a voice call from a contact's presence indicator.

You can download Communicator Mobile from `http://www.microsoft.com/downloads/details.aspx?familyid=BC89EC5E-5F3B-47D2-955B-B0C1DEAC94D8&displaylang=en`. It is supported on the following devices:

- Windows Mobile 2003 SE for Pocket PCs

- Windows Mobile 5.0 for Pocket PCs

- Windows Mobile 2003 SE for smart phones

- Windows Mobile 5.0 for smart phones

In addition to installing Communicator Mobile on your Windows Mobile device, users will need to install the public root authority certificate in order to trust the server certificate used by your Access Proxy. If you requested a server certificate for the external edge of your Access Proxy from VeriSign, then the VeriSign certificate authority must be installed on your Windows Mobile devices.

If your users are experiencing any of the issues listed next, then it's recommended to install the following update available at `http://support.microsoft.com/kb/919950`:

- You are not notified that a "File Transfer" or a "Remote Assistance" request from Communicator 2005 to Communicator Mobile could not be delivered.

- The home screen layout on a Motorola Q device changes when Communicator Mobile is installed.

- A "Call Computer" request in Communicator 2005 is not established when the recipient is a Communicator Mobile user.

- Nothing occurs when you single-tap the My Status screen in Communicator Mobile on a Pocket PC.

- ActiveSync may try to install the incorrect version of Communicator Mobile on a device.

- Updated phone forward settings may not be displayed on a Windows Mobile–based smart phone that uses Communicator Mobile.

- The bottom of the text in the second row of a contact note is truncated in Communicator Mobile.

Blackberry Instant Messaging for Microsoft Live Communications Server 2005

Research in Motion (RIM) developed a Communicator Mobile–like client for the BlackBerry called the BlackBerry Enterprise Instant Messaging device software. Now BlackBerry users who are connected to their emails can equally be signed in to Live Communications Server 2005 at all times. To gain advantage to this feature, organizations need to install the BlackBerry Enterprise Server (BES) v4.1+. With BES, administrators are able to push the client software to users over the air.

Summary

Different types of clients are available for Live Communications Server 2005 SP1, including Office Communicator 2005 for desktops, Communicator Web Access for browsers, and Communicator Mobile for smart phones. Connectivity to Live Communications Server 2005 SP1 is even possible on RIM's BlackBerry with the client pushed over the air by the BlackBerry Enterprise Server. These different clients extend your connectivity with co-workers, partners, friends, and family. Each endpoint (that is, client) publishes your presence information, which gets aggregated at the server. A user can use one or all of these clients to remain connected.

CHAPTER 6

■■■

Topologies

You can deploy Live Communications Server in a variety of configurations. Since it's nearly impossible for the development team to cover all the possible configurations, the product team has defined a set of topologies supported by Product Support Services. Since Live Communications Server uses Active Directory, it must be deployed within a forest environment. Multiple Standard Edition Servers and Enterprise pools deployed within a single Active Directory forest can communicate with each other. Standard Edition Servers and Enterprise pools deployed in different Active Directory forests can communicate with each other only over a federation connection. The "Single-Forest Topologies" section covers unique types of topologies supported within a single Active Directory forest.

If an organization has multiple Active Directory forests, such as a large company with a separate forest for each business unit, using federation to enable the communication of Standard Edition Servers and Enterprise pools between forests is not a viable option. Users from one forest would not be able to search users in another forest. Users would not be able to immediately initiate an IM conversation until the other party accepted an invitation to add them to their contact list. Users would become confused with this user experience, which is different for users within their forest versus users in another forest, and this could likely result in support calls. This is to be expected because federation is intended for communication across organization boundaries. Federation is more restrictive because the intended design is to protect the privacy of users between different companies. A different approach is required when deploying Live Communications Server in a multiforest environment; the "Multiforest Topologies" section details this.

In addition to topology configurations that are dependent on your Active Directory infrastructure, other topologies are independent of your Active Directory topology; the "Network Topologies" section covers them.

Understanding which type of topology best fits your organization's existing infrastructure and needs will help you in your architectural decisions. Once you decide on a Live Communications Server topology, evaluate how your deployment is likely to affect your IP network. A tool to help you evaluate your capacity requirements is the Live Communications Server 2005 SP1 Capacity Planning Toolkit available at http://www.microsoft.com/downloads/details.aspx?familyid=F249A48A-FC42-4D30-B60B-CB91BF8F2191&displaylang=en.

Single-Forest Topologies

A single-forest topology offers three main types of configuration:

- Single-domain forest

- Multidomain forest

- Multitree forest

The most widely deployed configuration of Active Directory in a single forest is of three types. The simplest configuration is a single-domain forest, as illustrated in Figure 6-1.

Figure 6-1. *Single-domain forest*

The most common configuration is a single forest with multiple child domains. The more common practice is to keep the root domain empty (no users and no servers) and multiple child domains. Rarely did the depth of child domains go beyond three levels deep. Although not required, some organizations separated servers and user accounts in different child domains as a best practice. This practice created some headaches because it required understanding what Prep Domain and Prep DomainAdd steps were necessary to administer users from a different domain onto servers located in another domain. (Chapter 9 covers this intricacy.) Figure 6-2 shows an Active Directory forest of this type.

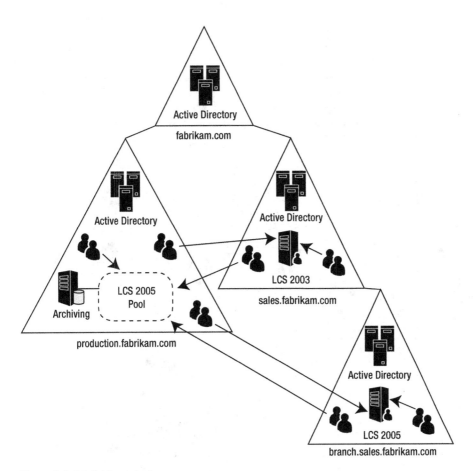

Figure 6-2. *Multidomain forest*

The third and less common configuration of an Active Directory single forest is a multiple tree configuration within a single forest. Each tree has a distinct DNS namespace that is disjoint from other trees within the same forest. If this terminology is foreign to you, you don't have to worry about it because your organization probably hasn't deployed it. As odd as it might sound, a single forest can have multiple root domains. Each root domain has a distinct DNS namespace. For some historical perspective, Live Communications Server 2005 required installing a hotfix (KB 889327) to support this type of Active Directory topology. We know. We once made the mistake of not being aware of customers with such Active Directory topologies. Luckily, if you're deploying Live Communications Server 2005 SP1, you don't need to worry about installing this hotfix. Figure 6-3 illustrates a multitree Active Directory single forest.

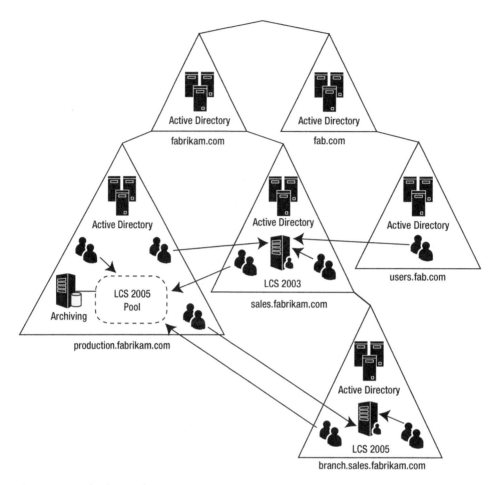

Figure 6-3. *Multiple-tree forest*

In the last two single-forest topologies, one issue to keep in mind when planning your deployment of an Enterprise pool is that all servers (that is, SQL back-end server and front-end servers) in a pool must be joined to the same domain. For cross-domain permissions required, please refer to Chapter 7.

Multiforest Topologies

An organization might have multiple Active Directory forests for a variety of reasons. Business units within the company might choose to have complete autonomy of their security and Active Directory schema independent of what other business units might choose to do. An organization might inherit another Active Directory forest from another company in a merger. Such organizations planning a deployment of Live Communications Server are likely to want to provide presence and instant messaging services to all employees across the different Active Directory forests. Deploying Standard Edition Servers and Enterprise pools in each forest will not work because users from one forest will not be able to search and initiate a conversation with a user from another forest as easily as if the user were in the same forest. To provide a consistent and seamless user experience, the recommended approach is to deploy Live Communications Server in a single Active Directory forest that services users from all the other forests. Two models are available: the resource forest topology and the central forest topology. These two models centralize the deployment of Live Communications Server in slightly different ways.

Resource Forest Topology

A resource forest topology consists of dedicating an Active Directory forest for hosting Live Communications Server and potentially other services such as Exchange Server, SharePoint, and so on, for the benefit of users with primary user (NT principal) accounts in other forests. This forest is referred to as the *resource forest*. Live Communications Server 2005 SP1 is deployed in the resource forest in the same way that it is deployed in a single-forest environment. The difference is in how users are enabled for Live Communications. Since the users you want to enable have accounts in other forests, referred to as *user forests*, it is not possible to enable those accounts directly for Live Communications. Figure 6-4 illustrates this problem.

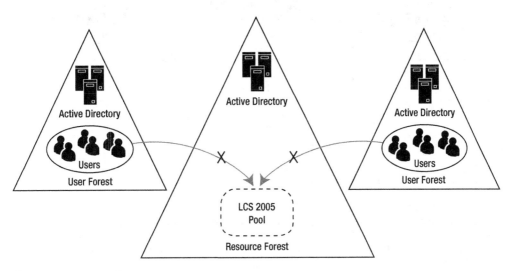

Figure 6-4. *Resource forest*

The way to solve this problem is to use user accounts in the resource forest as proxies for the user accounts, referred to as *NT principal accounts*, used by users in the user forests (this solution was first introduced by Exchange Server). The NT principal accounts have corresponding disabled user accounts in the resource forest. The purpose for disabling the user accounts in the resource forest is for security reasons. A hacker with knowledge of the user's password could log on with the user account in the resource forest without the user's knowledge or the IT administrator noticing. Disabling the user account protects against this type of security vulnerability. The disabled user account is then mapped to the NT principal account in the user forest. This operation permits users to sign in to Live Communications Server without being prompted for credentials again. For single sign-on to work, you must establish a one-way trust between the resource forest and the user forests. The resource forest must trust the user forests. If a two-way trust already exists, then you're covered. This trust can be a forest-level trust if both Active Directory forests are native Windows Server 2003 forests or can be a domain-level trust.

After the disabled account is mapped to the NT principal account, you can then enable it for Live Communications. Once these steps are completed, the user can sign in to their home server or pool as if the server or pool were deployed within their Active Directory forest. Figure 6-5 shows this configuration.

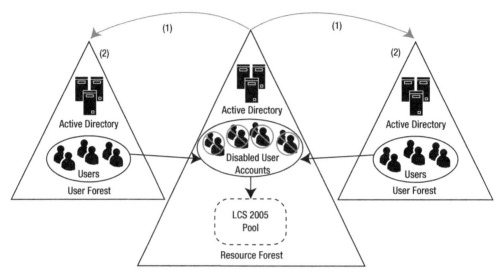

Figure 6-5. *Resource forest configuration*

The advantages of this topology are as follows:

- No Active Directory schema extensions are necessary in the user forests. The Active Directory schema extensions are limited to the resource forest.

- The resource forest can be used to host Exchange and Live Communications Server. The same disabled user accounts can be used for both services.

- All users regardless of which Active Directory forest their account is in can use their existing credentials to sign in to Live Communications Server, search other users with accounts in other forests, and initiate IM conversations as if those users had accounts in the same Active Directory forest.

The drawbacks to this topology are as follows:

- For every user account created in a user forest, a corresponding disabled user account must be created and mapped to the NT principal account before the user can be enabled for Live Communications. This requires some coordination between IT administrators, assuming that different individuals manage each forest.

- Mapping the NT principal account to the disabled account is left as a manual process for each organization to determine how best to implement.

- If a hacker manages to reenable a disabled account, they can log in with this account and go unnoticed for a while.

For more details about how to implement Live Communications Server in a resource forest topology, please refer to the appendix.

Central Forest Topology

The central forest topology is similar to the resource forest topology with the exception that instead of using disabled user accounts, contact objects are used. When working with Microsoft IT (MSIT) on planning the rollout of Live Communications Server 2005 in 2004, the feedback received from MSIT was to use contact objects because they are more lightweight Active Directory objects than user objects. Fewer attributes are associated with a contact object, and a hacker cannot log in using a contact object, which addresses the drawbacks of using disabled user accounts. To distinguish a resource forest using disabled user accounts versus contact accounts, this configuration was referred to as the *central forest* topology. Instead of referring to a resource forest using contact objects, which is a bit of a mouthful, central forest topology was an easier way to refer to it. The difference in the two topologies is the choice of accounts used to represent the user in the forest where Live Communications Server is deployed. Figure 6-6 illustrates this topology.

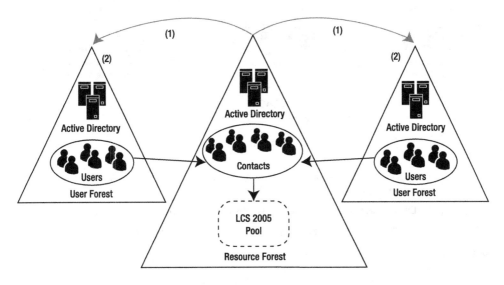

(1) The minimum trust requirement between forests is a one-way trust. The resource forest must trust the user forests.

(2) The Live Communications Server schema does not need to be extended in this forest.

Figure 6-6. *Central forest*

To address the lack of automation in creating a contact object for every new user account created in one of the user forests and mapping the contact object to this user account, you can use the Identity Integration Feature Pack (IIFP) to synchronize user accounts as contact objects and automatically perform the mapping. IIFP is a freely available solution available from Microsoft. IIFP is a trimmed-down version of Microsoft Identity Integration Server (MIIS). MIIS is a server product for synchronizing data between directory services such as Novell eDirectory, IBM Directory Server, iPlanet Directory, and so on. IIFP restricts synchronizing data to only between Active Directory directory services. The logic to synchronize the information needed by Live Communications Server is defined in a Management Agent, which IIFP or MIIS then automates. Luckily, the Live Communications Server Resource Kit provides such a Management Agent with full source code so it can be fully customized. This Management Agent is located in the LcsSync subdirectory. A white paper is available in the same subdirectory that explains in detail the logic of the LcsSync Management Agent. Figure 6-7 shows the final topology for a central forest.

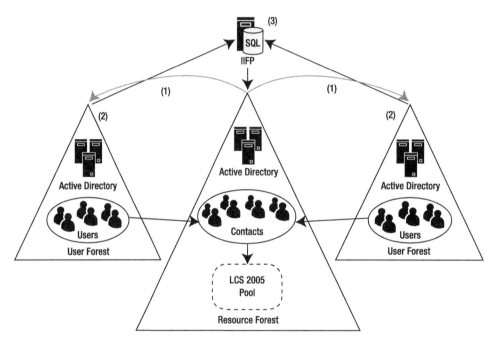

(1) The minimum trust requirement between forests is a one-way trust. The resource forest must trust the user forests.

(2) The Live Communications Server schema does not need to be extended in this forest.

(3) IIFP (Identity Integration Feature Pack) synchronizes users as contacts in the central forest.

Figure 6-7. *Central forest configuration*

The central forest provides all the same benefits as the resource forest and addresses all its drawbacks. By using IIFP or MIIS, the complexity of the deployment substantially increases because the learning curve for MIIS is rather steep.

Network Topologies

In addition to deploying Live Communications Server as a member server to your Active Directory, the Access Proxy server role is targeted to be deployed in your network perimeter to enable remote access without a VPN and federate with other partners. Live Communications Server can also be integrated with your PBX telephony system. You should keep any special considerations in mind when deploying Live Communications Server across WAN links.

Active Directory Dependent Topologies

Since Live Communications Server depends on Active Directory, it needs to contact the closest domain controller available. If it fails to contact a domain controller during startup, it will fail to run. Given this dependency, it's important to make sure a domain controller is available within the network site where your Live Communications Server is deployed to avoid problems when your site's WAN link goes down, as shown in Figure 6-8.

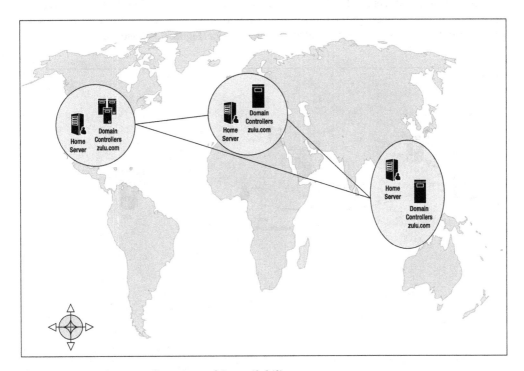

Figure 6-8. *Domain controller geographic availability*

Network Perimeter Topologies

Chapter 5 covered the different server roles. The only server role that is deployable in the network perimeter is Live Communications Server's Access Proxy. This server role enables remote access, federation with other companies, and PIC access with subscribers to AOL, Yahoo!, and MSN instant messaging. If you plan to enable any or all of these scenarios, you will need to deploy an Access Proxy.

Multiple Access Proxy servers can be deployed as a bank of servers abstracted as a single FQDN by a hardware load balancer. An Access Proxy must be a dual-NIC computer with two edges—one network connection to the internal network and the other network connection to the Internet. When deploying a bank of Access Proxy servers, the internal edge must be abstracted by a VIP (provided by a hardware load balancer), and the external edge must also be abstracted by another VIP.

Since the external edge of the Access Proxy is exposed to the Internet, it needs to be published so that remote users and enhanced federated partners can locate it. You can do this by creating a DNS SRV record of the type _sipfederationtls._tcp.<domain> on the public domain (see Chapter 6). This exposes a single entry point to your organization's SIP traffic. This implies that for large organizations with multiple points of presence in different geographic locations, remote users cannot dynamically locate the Access Proxy closest to them. They will have to connect to a single location (such as a data center) even if it's located across the world. The Access Proxy or bank of Access Proxy servers will proxy the connection to the user's home server on the internal network. This home server might likely be located in their hometown. This network traffic route certainly isn't efficient when there could be a perfectly valid Access Proxy within closer proximity to the user's location that would be a better choice. Figure 6-9 illustrates this problem.

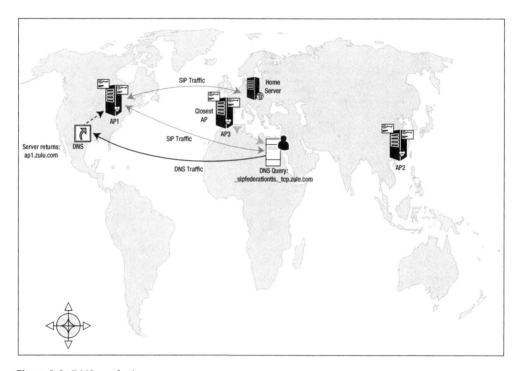

Figure 6-9. *DNS resolution*

Ideally, the user can connect to the closest Access Proxy deployed by the organization, as shown in Figure 6-10.

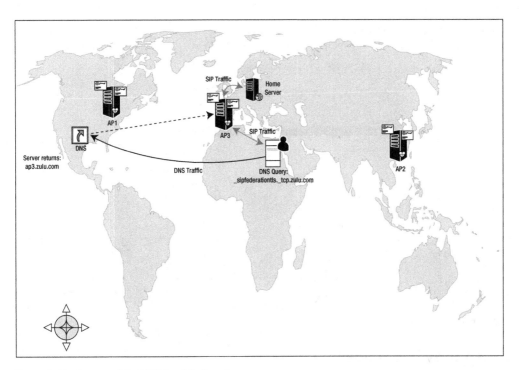

Figure 6-10. *Geographic DNS load balancing*

A solution to this problem is to use a DNS server that does geographic-specific resolution (also referred to *geographic load balancing*) such as PowerDNS, geoDNS for BIND, or 3DNS. Since the client needs to first resolve the query for _sipfederationtls._tcp.<domain> by contacting the company's authoritative DNS server, the FQDN of the closest Access Proxy is returned to the client based on geographic or topology information by client IP address. Once the closest Access Proxy is returned, all SIP traffic is optimized by routing to the closest Access Proxy.

Another option is to hard-code the FQDN of the closest Access Proxy to the user's home server. This second solution amounts to an approximation and might just be adequate. Alternatively, an organization could use different SIP domain namespaces for each geographic region. Users in North America could have a SIP URI with a domain name suffix of user@us.touareg.com. Users in EMEA could have a SIP URI with a domain name suffix of user@emea.touareg.com. Each of these SIP domain namespaces would need to be published in DNS as SRV records as well as in the Domains table, as shown in Figure 6-11.

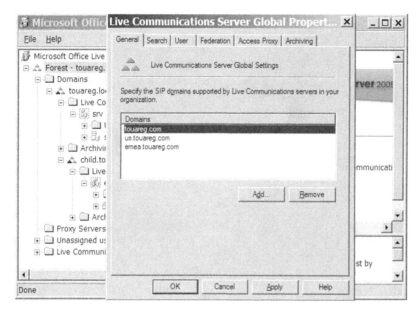

Figure 6-11. *SIP domains*

Telephony Topologies

When enabling remote call control (RCC) scenarios such as users getting call notification toasts from Communicator and initiating calls from Communicator but taking the calls from their PBX phones, a Computer-Supported Telephony Applications (CSTA) gateway is required. A CSTA gateway bridges the gap between the SIP network and the proprietary PBX network. Communicator sends CSTA commands over SIP to the PBX server. These CSTA commands control the user's phone. Depending on whether your CSTA gateway supports Mutual Transport Layer Security (MTLS), your telephony topology will need to be adjusted to prevent users from snooping and spoofing your CSTA traffic to the gateway.

If your CSTA gateway supports MTLS, configure every Live Communications Server deployed within your organization to directly communicate with your CSTA gateway via a static route (see Figure 6-12).

If your CSTA gateway does not support MTLS, you'll want to isolate this traffic onto its own private subnet that is not reachable from anyone within your network except via a specific Live Communications Server running as a Director role. This server is configured with two network cards, with the first network interface connected to the CSTA gateway and the second network interface accessible from the rest of your internal network. Your Standard Edition Servers and Enterprise pools send CSTA commands to the Director on its second interface. This way, the TCP traffic from the Director to the CSTA gateway is protected by isolating it in its own subnet that is not directly accessible from anywhere else on the internal network except via the Director. Figure 6-13 illustrates this topology. (Chapter 21 covers telephony integration in more detail.)

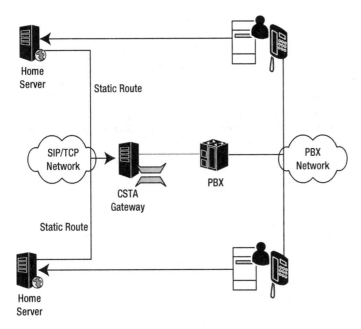

Figure 6-12. *CSTA configuration*

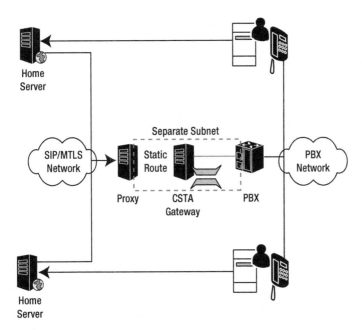

Figure 6-13. *Recommended CSTA configuration*

Summary

Before deploying Live Communications Server, it is important to consider how your Active Directory and your network topology impact your deployment strategy because of the constraints of your environment. Your deployment strategy will be different depending on whether you have a single forest or multiple forests that your Live Communications Server deployment will need to service. Domain controller placement across WAN links can also impact the availability of your Live Communications Servers. To get support from Microsoft's Product Support Services, your deployment should fall under one of the supported topologies.

PART 2

■ ■ ■

Setting It Up

Now that you know all about Live Communications Server, it's time to learn how to actually deploy it. In this part, we will examine the role that Active Directory plays and show how to prepare for the required changes that are needed in Active Directory to install and run Live Communications Server. We will then cover the Domain Name System (DNS) and its function within the environment. Last but by no means least, we will teach you how to install both Standard Edition and Enterprise Edition of Live Communications Server 2005.

CHAPTER 7

■ ■ ■

Preparing Active Directory

If your organization is already using Active Directory as the primary directory services, then we don't need to explain the value of Active Directory. It is worthwhile, however, to understand how Live Communications Server 2005 SP1 extracts value from Active Directory. The integration of Live Communications Server 2005 SP1 and Active Directory makes managing Live Communications Server machines simpler and more convenient. For example, global information that needs to be shared by all Live Communications Servers can be stored in Active Directory instead of replicating it across servers. In addition, server information can be published in Active Directory for easy discoverability. This makes it possible to remotely manage Live Communications Server machines from any computer joined to the Active Directory forest with Live Communications Server's Admin Tools installed. By using Active Directory, users can sign in to Live Communications Server using their Windows credentials (that is, username and password). This single sign-in avoids requiring users to manage separate credentials. Live Communications Server leverages Active Directory to determine whether a user is authorized to access certain information such as by searching for other users in the organization.

Live Communications Server stores *global settings*, information that is needed by every server in the forest, in the System container of the root domain of the forest. Active Directory replicates information stored in the System container only among the domain controllers (DCs) and global catalogs (GCs) in the root domain. DCs and GCs in child domains will not have the Live Communications Server global settings replicated to them. Every Live Communications Server deployed in the forest will need to connect to a root domain GC to obtain this information. Since the best practice is to deploy Live Communications Servers in a child domain of the forest, the Live Communications Servers will fail to activate if they are restricted from accessing the root domain DCs/GCs by firewalls—or if already activated, they will fail to start. Figure 7-1 shows this root domain GC dependency.

Live Communications Server leverages Active Directory to publish service information. This means Standard Edition Servers and Enterprise pools are discoverable by querying Active Directory. A visible example of this feature is the automatic population of servers deployed in your Active Directory forest when opening the Live Communications Server MMC. If you're wondering when a Standard Edition Server or Enterprise Edition front-end server publishes this information to Active Directory, the answer is during activation. This is why activation, when deploying a Standard Edition Server or front-end server, requires RTCDomainServer-Admins privileges or being a member of the Domain Admins group. The administrator needs sufficient rights to write to Active Directory during activation.

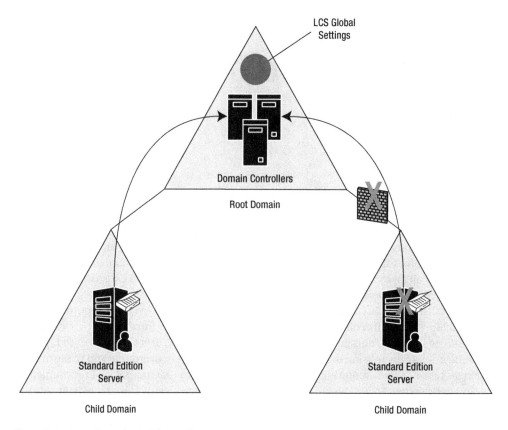

Figure 7-1. *Root domain GC dependency*

During activation, the Setup program creates a service principal name (SPN) and registers this SPN with the service account used to run the service. By default, this service account is a user account called LCService. The SPN is registered in the servicePrincipalName attribute of this object and is of the form *sip/<fqdn>* (see Figure 7-2). For a detailed understanding of how SPNs and SCPs work, see TechNet: http://technet2.microsoft.com/WindowsServer/en/library/8127f5ed-4e05-4822-bfa9-402ceede47441033.mspx?mfr=true.

Activation publishes server information in three locations in Active Directory. Following Microsoft's best practices for Active Directory, Live Communications Server creates a service connection point (SCP) on the computer object belonging to the physical server where Live Communications Server is installed. By creating an SCP on the computer object, third-party asset management applications can query the types of services running on each machine. This SCP, called RTC Services, appears below the Microsoft node under the computer object. In the example shown in Figure 7-3, we've used the MMC snap-in, adsiedit.msc, to view the SCP on the computer object called SRV. Of the most important SCP attributes (keywords, serviceDNSName, serviceDNSNameType, serviceClassName, and serviceBindingInformation), Live Communications Server 2005 SP1 populates only the keywords attribute with GUID values to represent the service.

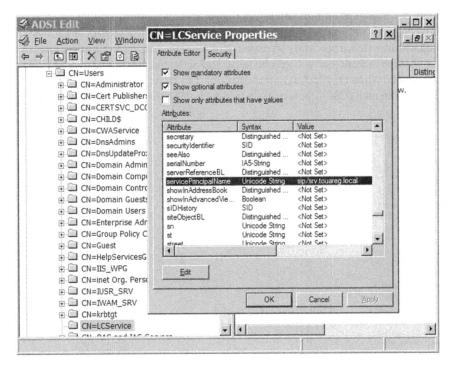

Figure 7-2. *Service principal name*

Figure 7-3. *LCS 2005 SP1 Active Directory global settings*

adsiedit.msc is available as a web download from Microsoft as part of the Windows Support Tools. You'll need to register the DLL, adsiedit.dll, first by running the regsvr32 adsiedit.dll command from a Command Prompt window. For more information about this handy tool, refer to http://technet2.microsoft.com/WindowsServer/en/library/ebca3324-5427-471a-bc19-9aa1decd3d401033.mspx?mfr=true.

When a Standard Edition Server is activated (see Chapter 9) or when an Enterprise pool is created (see Chapter 10), Live Communications Server creates a new entry under the msRTCSIP-Pools container in Active Directory. Each entry represents a logical pool and is of class type msRTCSIP-Pool. The msRTCSIP-Pool class defines the FQDN of the pool as well as the association between the front-end servers and the back-end server to a pool.

You can think of a Standard Edition Server as a pool with a single front-end server colocated on the same physical computer as the back-end server. Every time a new Standard Edition Server is installed and activated, a new entry is created. This is not the case for front-end servers in an Enterprise pool. When a front-end server is installed and activated, it is linked to an existing entry previously created when creating an Enterprise pool. The common name (CN) of each object created under the msRTCSIP-Pools container is defined by the name of the pool (see Figure 7-4).

Figure 7-4. *LCS pool representation in Active Directory*

The third location where the server information is published in Active Directory is in the Trusted Server list. The FQDN of each front-end server for every Enterprise pool and the FQDN of every Standard Edition Server are published in this Trusted Server list. In addition to using server certificates to verify the authenticity of a server that claims to own a specific FQDN, the Trusted Server list is used to determine whether the server can be trusted. Without an entry containing its FQDN, a server will not be trusted by other Standard Edition Servers or Enterprise Edition front-end servers and therefore will not be able to establish any communication with these other servers. If you find that users homed on a particular pool are not able to communicate with users homed on other pools, this could be the reason. Check that the pool's FQDN is listed in the Trusted Server list in Active Directory.

It may seem odd that every server's FQDN is defined again in the Trusted Server list when it is already available on the computer object. After all, you could determine the set of computers running Live Communications Server by querying all computer objects with the RTC Services SCP.

The primary reason why Live Communications Server does not use this approach is speed. For large organizations with tens of thousands of users, the number of computers tends to be at least as large as, if not larger than, the number of users. Querying all the computers in the organization to determine which are running Live Communications Server would be time-consuming. Such a query would substantially impact the administrator's experience when loading the Live Communications Server's Admin Tools. Searching a smaller list makes it possible for the MMC to load faster.

The way the Trusted Server list is represented in Active Directory is rather obscure. Each Trusted Server entry is represented as a GUID under the Global Settings container. The GUID is generated during the activation step. To determine which GUID object matches a particular Standard Edition Server or Enterprise Edition front-end server, you need to look at the properties of the object. The attribute msRTCSIP-TrustedServerFQDN contains the FQDN of the server that you'll then be able to recognize. You can find the Global Settings container in the System container under Microsoft/RTC Service. In our example of the Standard Edition Server named SRV, its Trusted Server entry is represented by the GUID highlighted in Figure 7-5.

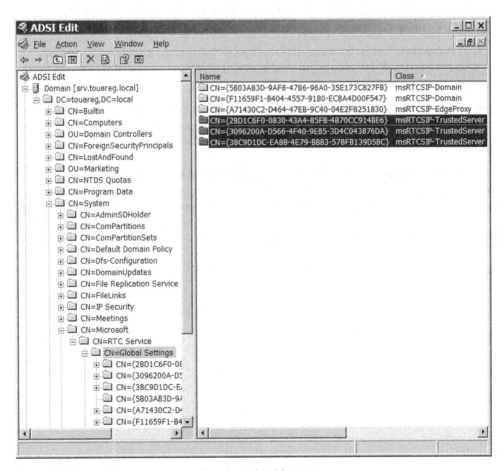

Figure 7-5. *Trusted Server representation in Active Directory*

Not all GUIDs under the Global Settings container represent GUIDs of trusted servers. As the name indicates, the Global Settings container contains settings that are global to Live Communications Server.

In addition to storing global settings in Active Directory and publishing Live Communications Server information, the user class that represents a user account in Active Directory is extended with attributes specific to Live Communications Server. Such attributes define settings that are configurable by an administrator member of the RTCDomainUserAdmins or RTCDomainServerAdmins group. Chapter 16 covers user settings in greater detail.

Before Live Communications Server can add this information to the Active Directory services, the Active Directory schema must be extended. This is the first step in preparing the Active Directory forest. Live Communications Server 2005 SP1 has four steps to prep an organization's Active Directory forest (see Figure 7-6):

1. *Prep Schema*: This step extends the Active Directory schema with new classes and attributes specific to Live Communications Server 2005 SP1.

2. *Prep Forest*: This step creates the global settings in the System container in the root domain of the forest, which is used by all Live Communications Servers.

3. *Prep Domain*: This step creates domain-level global security groups in the domain where it is run. These groups are used to manage Live Communications Servers deployed in the domain.

4. *Prep DomainAdd (referred to as DomainAdd to Forest Root in the Setup program)*: This step adds permissions to the domain global security groups (created in step 3) to access and modify specific global settings in the forest's root domain.

These steps are the same in both the Standard Edition and Enterprise Edition SKUs. It doesn't matter whether you complete them with the Standard Edition or Enterprise Edition SKU. Setup will automatically detect whether any required steps were not run and will prevent the administrator from activating a Standard Edition Server or Enterprise Edition front-end server until these steps are completed successfully.

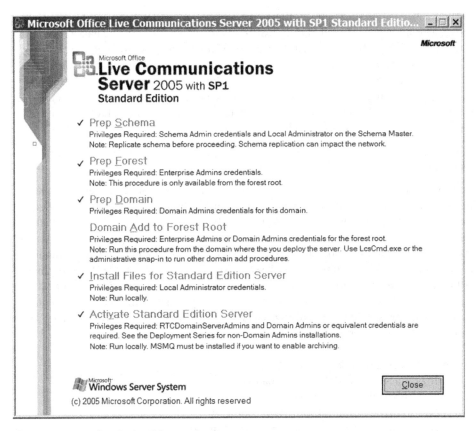

Figure 7-6. *Prepping Active Directory*

Prep Schema

To fully leverage Active Directory, Live Communications Server extends the schema with requirements specific to its needs similarly to how Exchange Server extends the schema. Live Communications Server 2005 SP1 extends the schema with seven new classes and twenty-two new attributes. An administrator member of the Schema Admins group must run this step once on a domain controller acting as the schema master in the root domain of the forest (see Figure 7-7).

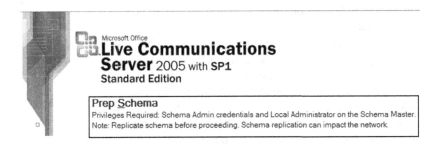

Figure 7-7. *Prep Schema step*

All schema extensions start with a unique namespace that is specific to Live Communications Server. This namespace is called msRTCSIP-"*name*", where *name* is the name of a class or attribute. RTC, which refers to *real-time communications*, was the original name of the product group at Microsoft responsible for building Live Communications Server. SIP stands for Session Initiation Protocol (RFC 3261), which Live Communications Servers is based on. Chapter 3 covers SIP in more detail. By using a common namespace for all schema extensions, schema administrators can clearly identify which extensions are specific to Live Communications Server and know not to reuse them for a different purpose.

Global Settings

Live Communications Server 2005 SP1 creates new containers and objects under the System container in the root domain of the forest with global settings. These settings are tucked under an SCP called RTC Service. This SCP is of class type msRTCSIP-Service with no attributes associated with it. Subordinate to this SCP are two nodes. One node, called Global Settings, is a single instance of the class of type msRTCSIP-GlobalContainer. The class msRTCSIP-GlobalContainer contains twenty-five attributes and two subordinate classes. This class contains all the global settings visible when viewing the properties of the Forest node in Live Communications Server 2005 SP1's Admin Tools. The other node is a class container of type msRTCSIP-Pools called Pools that contains all the pool objects deployed in the Active Directory forest. This Pool class contains five attributes and one subordinate class:

RTC Service (class type: msRTCSIP-Service)
  Global Settings (class type: msRTCSIP-GlobalContainer)
    msRTCSIP-Archive (class type: auxiliary)
      msRTCSIP-ArchiveDefault (attribute type: Boolean)
      msRTCSIP-ArchiveDefaultFlags (attribute type: Integer)
      msRTCSIP-ArchiveFederationDefault (attribute type: Boolean)
      msRTCSIP-ArchiveFederationDefaultFlags (attribute type: Integer)
    msRTCSIP-Federation (class type: auxiliary)
      msRTCSIP-EnableFederation (attribute type: Boolean)
      msRTCSIP-DefaultRouteToEdgeProxy (attribute type: Unicode String)
      msRTCSIP-DefaultRouteToEdgeProxyPort (attribute type: Integer)
    msRTCSIP-Search (class type: auxiliary)
      msRTCSIP-SearchMaxRequests (attribute type: Integer)
      msRTCSIP-SearchMaxResults (attribute type: Integer)
      msRTCSIP-MaxNumOutstandingSearchPerServer (attribute type: Integer)
    msRTCSIP-Registrar (class type: auxiliary)
      msRTCSIP-DefPresenceSubscriptionTimeout (attribute type: Integer)
      msRTCSIP-DefRegistrationTimeout (attribute type: Integer)
      msRTCSIP-DefRoamingDataSubscriptionTimeout (attribute type: Integer)
      msRTCSIP-MaxNumSubscriptionsPerUser (attribute type: Integer)
      msRTCSIP-MaxPresenceSubscriptionTimeout (attribute type: Integer)
      msRTCSIP-MaxRegistrationTimeout (attribute type: Integer)
      msRTCSIP-MaxRoamingDataSubscriptionTimeout (attribute type: Integer)
      msRTCSIP-MinPresenceSubscriptionTimeout (attribute type: Integer)
      msRTCSIP-MinRegistrationTimeout (attribute type: Integer)
      msRTCSIP-MinRoamingDataSubscriptionTimeout (type: Integer)

msRTCSIP-NumDevicesPerUser (attribute type: Integer)
msRTCSIP-UserDomainList (attribute type: multivalued DN)
msRTCSIP-EnableBestEffortNotify (attribute type: Boolean)
msRTCSIP-GlobalSettingsData (attribute type: multivalued Unicode String)[1]

{GUID} (class type: msRTCSIP-Domain)[2]
msRTCSIP-DomainName (attribute type: Unicode String)
msRTCSIP-DomainData (attribute type: multivalued Unicode String)[3]

{GUID} (class type: msRTCSIP-TrustedServer)[4]
msRTCSIP-TrustedServerFQDN (attribute type: Unicode String)
msRTCSIP-TrustedServerVersion (attribute type: Integer)
msRTCSIP-TrustedServerData (attribute type: Unicode String)[5]

Pools (class type: msRTCSIP-Pools)
CN (class type: msRTCSIP-Pool)[6]
msRTCSIP-PoolDisplayName (attribute type: Unicode String)
msRTCSIP-PoolType (attribute type: Integer)
msRTCSIP-PoolVersion (attribute type: Integer)
msRTCSIP-BackEndServer (attribute type: Unicode String)
msRTCSIP-PoolData (attribute type: Unicode String)

Microsoft (class type: container)[7]
LC Services (class type: msRTCSIP-PoolService)
msRTCSIP-FrontEndServers (attribute type: multivalued DN)[8]

Computer Settings

For every Standard Edition Server or Enterprise Edition front-end server installed and activated, an SCP is defined. This SCP specifies the type of service running on the computer, its version, and the address of the pool to which it belongs:

---

1. This attribute is reserved by Live Communications Server 2005 SP1 for future use.
2. A new instance of the class msRTCSIP-Domain is created (with a new GUID) for every SIP domain name the administrator defines.
3. This attribute is reserved by Live Communications Server 2005 SP1 for future use.
4. A new instance of the class msRTCSIP-TrustedServer is created (with a new GUID) for every Standard Edition Server and Enterprise Edition front-end server upon activation.
5. This attribute is reserved by Live Communications Server 2005 SP1 for future use.
6. A new instance of the class msRTCSIP-Pool is created for every pool. An instance of the class msRTCSIP-Pool called a *pool object* is created when a Standard Edition Server is activated or an Enterprise pool is created. The CCN of a pool object is initially set to the same value of the attribute msRTCSIP-PoolDisplayName.
7. This attribute is reserved by Live Communications Server 2005 SP1 for future use.
8. The LC Services class subordinate to the msRTCSIP-Pool class is an SCP. This SCP lists the front-end servers associated with the pool. If the pool is a Standard Edition Server, it will contain a single entry. If the pool is an Enterprise pool, then it will contain one entry for each front-end server associated with the pool.

Computers (class type: container)
  CN (class type: computer)[9]
    Microsoft (class type: serviceConnectionPoint)
      RTC Services (class type: msRTCSIP-Server)
        msRTCSIP-EnterpriseServices (attribute type: Boolean)
        msRTCSIP-PoolAddress (attribute type: DN)
        msRTCSIP-ServerData (attribute type: multivalued Unicode String)[10]

User Settings

Users can be enabled for Live Communications, federation, remote access, archiving, remote call control, and other features. These user configurations must be persisted in Active Directory, so any Live Communications Server deployed within the forest can query this information. These settings are stored on the user class, which is extended to accommodate them. Active Directory provides different user-type classes such as the user class, contact class, and inetOrgPerson class. Live Communications Server 2005 SP1 extends each of these classes with the same set of per-user settings.

Users (class type: container)
  CN (class type: user/contact/inetOrgPerson)[11]
    msRTCSIP-UserEnabled (attribute type: Boolean)
    msRTCSIP-PrimaryUserAddress (attribute type: Unicode String)
    msRTCSIP-PrimaryHomeServer (attribute type: DN)
    msRTCSIP-TargetHomeServer (attribute type: DN)
    msRTCSIP-ArchivingEnabled (attribute type: Integer)
    msRTCSIP-FederationEnabled (attribute type: Boolean)
    msRTCSIP-InternetAccessEnabled (attribute type: Boolean)
    msRTCSIP-Line (attribute type: Unicode String)
    msRTCSIP-LineServer (attribute type: Unicode String)
    msRTCSIP-OptionFlags (attribute type: Integer)
    msRTCSIP-OriginatorSid (attribute type: SID)
    msRTCSIP-UserExtension (attribute type: multivalued Unicode String)[12]

Prep Forest

Once you've extended the forest's Active Directory schema by defining the new classes and attributes, you must perform the step Prep Forest next. No objects have been created in Active Directory after completing the Prep Schema step. The step Prep Forest must be run from the forest's root domain and needs to be run only once (see Figure 7-8). Until Prep Schema is completed successfully, the Setup program disables this step.

---

9. This is the CN of the computer object.
10. This attribute is reserved by Live Communications Server 2005 SP1 for future use.
11. This is the CN of the user/contact/inetOrgPerson object.
12. This attribute is reserved by Live Communications Server 2005 SP1 for future use.

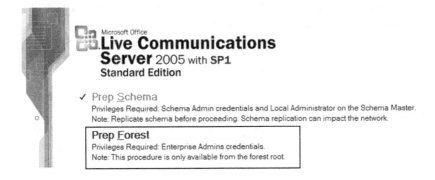

Figure 7-8. *Prep Forest step*

Running the Prep Forest step creates an instance of the msRTCSIP-GlobalContainer class called an *object* and populates its attributes with default values. This object contains the global settings used by Live Communications Server. Prep Forest creates the Pools container of class type msRTCSIP-Pools. At this point, this container is empty because no pool objects have been created yet. An instance of the class, msRTCSIP-Domain, with a unique GUID as the name for the object is defined. This object defines the default SIP domain name for which this Active Directory forest will be authoritative. The default SIP domain name is set to the forest's root domain FQDN.

Archive Settings

Live Communications Server defines global-level archive settings to make it more convenient for administrators to configure all users without each account individually. User-level archive settings are also available, but keep in mind that the user-level archive settings take precedence over global-level archive settings:

msRTCSIP-ArchiveDefault: This attribute specifies whether IM conversations between internal users should be archived. This does not include IM conversations between internal users and federated users. If set to TRUE, all internal conversations are logged. By default, this setting is set to FALSE.

msRTCSIP-ArchiveDefaultFlags: This attribute defines whether the content of the IM conversation should be archived. If the value is set to 0, then the entire conversation body is archived. If set to 1, then the message content is not archived, but the occurrence of the conversation is still logged. This setting is enforced only if the attribute msRTCSIP-ArchiveDefault is set to TRUE.

msRTCSIP-ArchiveFederationDefault: This attribute specifies whether IM conversations between internal users and federated users should be archived. For legal reasons, organizations need to differentiate archiving between internal users only and between internal and external users because external users must be notified that their conversations are being recorded. If set to TRUE, all federated conversations are logged. By default, this setting is set to FALSE.

msRTCSIP-ArchiveFederationDefaultFlags: This attribute defines whether the content of the IM conversation between internal users and federated users should be archived. If the value is set to 0, then the entire conversation body is archived. If set to 1, then the message content is not archived, but the occurrence of the conversation is still logged. This setting is enforced only if the attribute msRTCSIP-ArchiveFederationDefault is set to TRUE.

These attributes are directly exposed in the Live Communications Server's Admin Tools. To access them, launch the Live Communications Server 2005 link from the Administrative Tools folder. Right-click the Forest node, and select Properties. Navigate to the Archiving tab. Figure 7-9 shows the mapping from the Active Directory attribute to the MMC setting. Chapter 17 covers more about how to configure archiving.

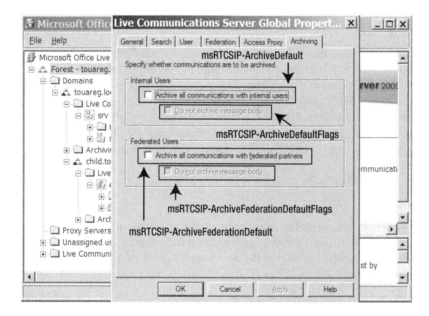

Figure 7-9. *Global archiving settings*

Federation Settings

The following global settings are related to Federation. These attributes are organized under the msRTCSIP-Federation auxiliary class of the Global Settings object:

msRTCSIP-EnableFederation: This attribute determines whether federation is enabled or disabled at the forest level. Federation cannot be turned on unless this setting is set to TRUE. By default, this attribute is set to FALSE.

msRTCSIP-DefaultRouteToEdgeProxy: This attribute defines the FQDN of the server where all outgoing traffic destined to a federated partner should be routed to. This is either the FQDN of a Director or the FQDN of the Access Proxy for small deployments. By default, this attribute is undefined.

msRTCSIP-DefaultRouteToEdgeProxyPort: This attribute defines the port number that should be used to connect to the FQDN as specified in the attribute msRTCSIP-DefaultRouteToEdgeProxy. By default, this attribute is undefined. However, once the administrator specifies an FQDN, the port number as specified in the SIP RFC should be 5061.

These attributes are directly exposed in Live Communications Server's Admin Tools. To access them, click the Live Communications Server 2005 link from the `Administrative Tools` folder. Right-click the Forest node, and select Properties. Navigate to the Federation tab. Figure 7-10 shows the mapping from the Active Directory attribute to the MMC setting. We'll cover these federation global settings in Chapter 13.

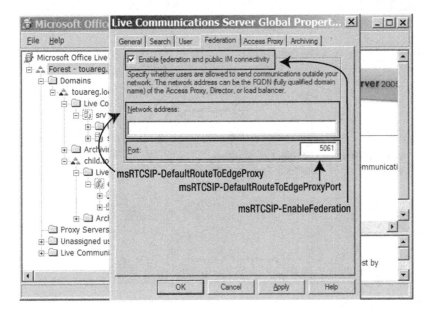

Figure 7-10. *Global federation settings*

Search Settings

The following three attributes are members of the auxiliary class msRTCSIP-Search under the Global Settings container. This auxiliary class defines Active Directory search limits that servers deployed in the forest can perform against DC/GCs.

msRTCSIP-SearchMaxResults: This attribute defines a server-side limit on the maximum number of objects that can be returned to any client search request (such as Office Communicator, Communicator Mobile, or Windows Messenger). The default value is a maximum of 20 objects returned in any single search query.

msRTCSIP-SearchMaxRequests: This attribute defines the maximum number of objects to return from a server-side search query against Active Directory. By default, this maximum value is set to 200. If your Live Communications Server instances are slamming your domain controllers, reducing this number might help.

msRTCSIP-MaxNumOutstandingSearchPerServer. This attribute defines the maximum number of requests that a server is permitted to perform against Active Directory. This limit helps prevent your Live Communications Server machines from slamming your domain controllers with AD queries. The default value is a maximum of 80 queries that any Live Communications Server can perform.

These attributes are directly exposed in Live Communications Server's Admin Tools. To access them, click the Live Communications Server 2005 link from the `Administrative Tools` folder. Right-click the Forest node, and select Properties. Navigate to the Search tab. Figure 7-11 shows the mapping from the Active Directory attribute to the MMC setting.

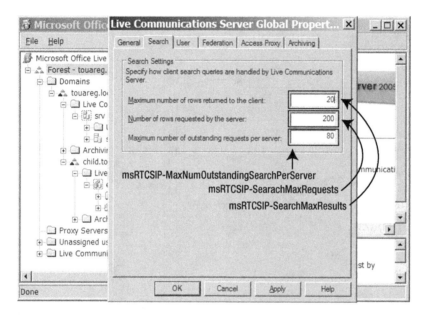

Figure 7-11. *Global search settings*

Registrar Settings

SIP (RFC 3261) specifies that client and server transactions are driven based on timeouts rather than retransmit counts. The first nine attributes shown next define timeout settings. Since administrators rarely need to configure these timeout values, they are not exposed in the Live Communications Server 2005 MMC.

msRTCSIP-MinPresenceSubscriptionTimeout. This attribute defines the minimum timeout value that clients (such as Communicator) can specify when subscribing to presence information. If a client requests a timeout less than this minimum, the server rejects the request. By default, the minimum subscription timeout is set to 1200.

msRTCSIP-DefPresenceSubscriptionTimeout: This attribute defines the default timeout value for clients to subscribe to other users' presence information. If the client does not specify a timeout, the server sets the timeout to this value. By default, this value is set to 28800.

msRTCSIP-MaxPresenceSubscriptionTimeout: This attribute defines the maximum timeout value that a client can request for presence subscription. If a client requests a timeout value greater than this maximum, the server resets it to this value. By default, the maximum subscription timeout is set to 43200.

msRTCSIP-MinRegistrationTimeout: This attribute defines the minimum timeout value before a client must re-register with the server. If a client requests a registration timeout less than this minimum, the server rejects the request (see RFC 3261, section 21.4.17 423). By default, the minimum registration timeout is set to 300.

msRTCSIP-DefRegistrationTimeout: This attribute defines the default timeout value before clients must re-register with the server. If the client does not specify a timeout, the server sets the timeout to this value. By default, this value is set to 600.

msRTCSIP-MaxRegistrationTimeout: This attribute defines the maximum timeout value that a client can request for registration. If a client requests a timeout value greater than this maximum, the server resets it to this value. By default, the maximum registration timeout is set to 900.

msRTCSIP-MinRoamingDataSubscriptionTimeout: This attribute defines the minimum timeout value clients can specify when subscribing to the user's roaming data (that is, a user's contact list and permissions list). If a client requests a registration timeout less than this minimum, the server rejects the request. By default, the minimum subscription timeout is set to 900.

msRTCSIP-DefRoamingDataSubscriptionTimeout: This attribute defines the default timeout value clients can specify to the server for subscribing to roaming data. If the client does not specify a timeout, the server sets the timeout to this value. By default, this value is set to 43200.

msRTCSIP-MaxRoamingDataSubscriptionTimeout: This attribute defines the maximum timeout value that a client can request for roaming data subscription. If a client requests a timeout value greater than this maximum, the server resets it to this value. By default, the maximum roaming data subscription timeout is set to 86340.

msRTCSIP-MaxNumSubscriptionsPerUser: This attribute defines the maximum number of people who can simultaneously subscribe to a user's presence. This setting is exposed in the Live Communications Server 2005 MMC in the User tab of the forest's properties. The default value is 200. (See Figure 7-12.)

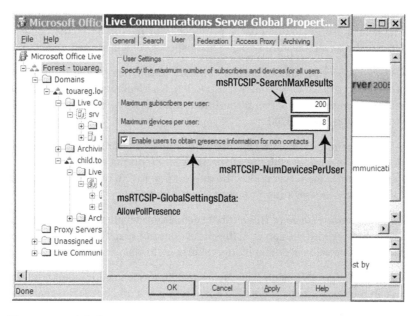

Figure 7-12. *Global user settings*

msRTCSIP-NumDevicesPerUser. This attribute specifies the maximum number of devices from which a user can be simultaneously signed in to Live Communications Server. These devices, also referred to as *points of presence* (POP), can be any client used to sign in users such as Communicator, Windows Messenger, Communicator Mobile, and Communicator Web Access. Users can be simultaneously connected from their desktop computer, laptop, browser, and phone. To limit the number of points of presence users can be signed in from, reduce this value. This setting is exposed in the Live Communications Server 2005 MMC in the User tab of the forest's properties (see Figure 7-12). By default, the maximum number of devices per user is eight devices.

msRTCSIP-UserDomainList. This attribute provides the ability for administrators to specify which Active Directory domains will host users enabled for Live Communications. The default value is an empty list, which implies that all domains in the forest can host users for Live Communications Server. Most administrators do not need to restrict which domains should not be allowed to host users configured for Live Communications Server. Therefore, this setting is not exposed in the Live Communications Server 2005 MMC.

msRTCSIP-EnableBestEffortNotify. This attribute enables a performance optimization introduced in Live Communications Server 2005 previously not available in Live Communications Server 2003. This is a nonstandard extension to the SIP RFC to improve the performance of Standard Edition Servers and Enterprise Edition front-end servers. A NOTIFY request requires a 200 OK response. By using a BENOTIFY request, no response is required, reducing the need for a return message. By default, this performance optimization is turned on and set to TRUE. Since there will seldom be the need to turn off this optimization (unless organizations have Live Communications Server 2003 deployed for which they need servers running Live Communications Server 2005 SP1 to interoperate with), this setting is not exposed in the Live Communications Server 2005 MMC.

msRTCSIP-GlobalSettingsData. This attribute is a Microsoft reserved field. Live Communications Server 2005 SP1 creates a reserved attribute for every new class it defines. These reserved attributes store name/value pairs. This allows multiple settings to be stored in a single Active Directory attribute instead of creating an attribute for a single setting. In the case of this reserved attribute, the following name/value pair was defined: AllowPollPresence = TRUE. This setting is exposed in the Live Communications Server 2005 MMC in the User tab of the forest's properties (see Figure 7-12). By default, the value of the setting, AllowPollPresence, is set to TRUE. This setting allows Office applications to query and display presence information of users who are not in the current user's contact list within the application such as SharePoint, Word, Outlook, and so on.

After creating the global objects, Prep Forest defines two new property sets. With a *property set*, you can group a number of attributes into a set. You can apply security permissions to the property set instead of each individual attribute through a single access control entry (ACE). These property sets are called RTCPropertySet and RTCUserSearchPropertySet and are of class type controlAccessRight. They are defined under the Extended-Rights object in the Configuration container, as shown in Figure 7-13.

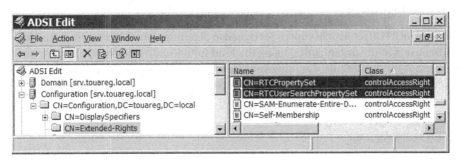

Figure 7-13. *Live Communications Server property sets*

The property set RTCPropertySet contains all the user attributes extended by Live Communications Server. To configure users for Live Communications Server, administrators must have read/write privileges to this property set. Domain-level security groups, which are created in the next step called Prep Domain, are given access to this property set. The RTCDomainServerAdmins security group is given read permission to this property set so administrators of this group can view user configuration details but cannot configure users. The RTCDomainUserAdmins security group is given read and write permissions to the property set so administrators of this group are able to configure users for Live Communications Server. The RTCHSDomainServices security group is given read and write permissions to this property set.

The RTCPropertySet property set is composed of the following attributes:

- msRTCSIP-PrimaryUserAddress

- msRTCSIP-PrimaryHomeServer

- msRTCSIP-TargetHomeServer

- msRTCSIP-OptionFlags

- msRTCSIP-UserEnabled

- msRTCSIP-ArchivingEnabled

- msRTCSIP-FederationEnabled

- msRTCSIP-InternetAccessEnabled

- msRTCSIP-OriginatorSid

- msRTCSIP-Line

- msRTCSIP-LineServer

- msRTCSIP-UserExtension

The property set RTCUserSearchPropertySet is used to determine whether a user is authorized to search other users in the organization using the Find functionality available in Communicator (see Figure 7-14). By default, domain users are allowed to search each other without restriction, and only the RTCDomainUsersAdmins group has full permissions on this property set.

Figure 7-14. *Finding users in Active Directory*

RTCUserSearchPropertySet is composed of a single attribute:

- msRTCSIP-PrimaryUserAddress

Prep Domain

Once Prep Forest is successfully completed, the step Prep Domain becomes available in the Setup program (see Figure 7-15). Unlike Prep Schema and Prep Forest, Prep Domain remains available to run again in another child domain where Prep Domain hasn't been run yet.

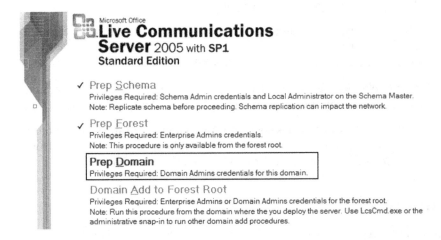

Figure 7-15. *Prep Domain step*

The rule of thumb for knowing when to run Prep Domain is simple. This step must be run in every Active Directory domain where a Live Communications Server will be deployed. It needs to be run only once per domain. If no servers running Live Communications Server will be deployed in the domain, then running this step is not necessary. Domain administrator privileges are required to run Prep Domain.

Prep Domain creates the following security group in the domain where it is run from and adds permissions for these groups to manage domain users:

RTCDomainUserAdmins: Members of this domain global security group are permitted to administer its domain users for Live Communications Server. Administrators from this group can enable users for Live Communications; configure them for other settings such as federation, remote access, archiving, remote call control; and move users between Enterprise pools and Standard Edition Servers. Prep Domain grants this group read/write permissions to RTCPropertySet.

RTCDomainServerAdmins: Members of this domain global security group are permitted to administer and manage Standard Edition Servers, Enterprise pools, and Archiving Services deployed within the domain. By granting this group read permissions to RTCPropertySet, members of this group can view Live Communications Server user settings and move users between Enterprise pools and Standard Edition Servers.

RTCHSDomainServices: Members of this domain global security group are service accounts used to run the Live Communications Server 2005 SP1 services on Standard Edition Servers and Enterprise Edition front-end servers. This group allows servers to read/write Live Communications Server global settings in the forest's root domain as well as user objects in Active Directory. This group has full access to RTCPropertySet. The name of this group might seem a bit cryptic. The HS in the name of the group refers to *home server*, which can be a Standard Edition Server or an Enterprise pool.

RTCArchivingDomainServices: Members of this domain global security group are service accounts used to run the Live Communications Server 2005 SP1's Archiving Service. This group provides permission to access the Archiving Service's database.

RTCProxyDomainServices: Members of this domain global security group are service accounts used to run the Live Communications Server 2005 SP1's Proxy server.

RTCABSDomainServices: Members of this domain global security group are service accounts used to run the Live Communications Server 2005 SP1's Address Book Service. This group provides permission to access the Enterprise pool's back-end server database.

Prep DomainAdd

Once you've completed Prep Domain successfully, you can run the Prep DomainAdd step, which is referred to Domain Add to Forest Root in the Setup program (see Figure 7-16). If your organization runs a single domain forest, you can skip this step. To run this step, log in to a computer joined to the child domain as an administrator member of the forest's root domain Domain Admins group or member of the Enterprise Admins group. There are two scenarios where Prep DomainAdd should be run.

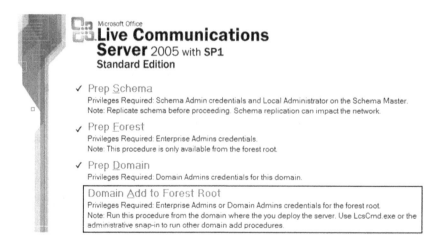

Figure 7-16. *Prep DomainAdd step*

The first scenario is necessary for any Active Directory forest with child domains in which you plan to deploy Live Communications Server machines. Prep DomainAdd to Root Domain must be run from the forest's root domain, specifying the child domain hosting Live Communications Servers. You should do this step after completing the Prep Domain step, which is run from the domain where Live Communications Servers will be hosted. Completing this step gives the domain's security groups (created during Prep Domain) access to the Live Communications Server global settings and pool objects created in the forest's root domain. The RTCDomainUserAdmins security group is given limited read access to pool settings and access only to global settings that affect user settings such as the global archiving settings and user search settings. The RTCDomainServerAdmins security group is given full access to manage all global settings in addition to being able to administer Live Communications Servers; however, this group is not permitted to manage Live Communications Server users. Without running this step, Enterprise pools cannot be created from the child domain, and Standard Edition Servers and Enterprise Edition front-end servers installed in the child domain cannot be activated and run. By running Prep DomainAdd, the RTCHSDomainServices group gains access to the Live Communications Global Settings.

A secondary use of Prep DomainAdd is to enable cross-domain administration scenarios. This is best explained via examples. There are three basic examples to consider.

For example, child domain A has domain user accounts enabled for Live Communications homed on an Enterprise pool hosted on child domain B. Administrators of the Enterprise pool in domain B must be able to manage these domain A users. How are these administrators granted permission to manage these users? To enable this scenario, Prep DomainAdd must be run from domain A specifying domain B. You must do this from the command-line tool, using LcsCmd.exe with the following parameters:

```
LcsCmd.exe /domain:DomainA_FQDN /action:DomainAdd /refdomain:DomainB_FQDN
```

Another scenario is a slight variation of the previous one. Child domain A has users homed on the Enterprise pool hosted in child domain B. However, this time only administrators in both domain A and domain B can manage these users for Live Communications Server. How do you achieve this? In this case, you must perform three steps:

1. Prep Domain is run from domain A. You can easily do this from Setup. The corresponding LcsCmd.exe command is as follows:

   ```
   LcsCmd.exe /domain:DomainA_FQDN /action:DomainPrep
   ```

2. Prep DomainAdd is run from domain A with the users-only option specifying domain B. Performing this action is done using the command-line tool:

   ```
   LcsCmd.exe /domain:DomainA_FQDN /action:DomainAdd
                  /refdomain:DomainB_FQDN /usersonly:TRUE
   ```

3. Prep DomainAdd to Root Domain is run from domain A specifying the root domain. This step is easily done from Setup. The corresponding LcsCmd.exe command is as follows:

   ```
   LcsCmd.exe /domain:DomainA_FQDN /action:DomainAdd
                  /refdomain:RootDomain_FQDN
   ```

All three steps can be batched up into a single command using `LcsCmd.exe`. The following XML file batches these three commands. You'll need to modify the FQDN placeholder text.

```xml
<?xml version="1.0" encoding="UTF-8" ?>
<LcsCmd>
    <Domain>
        <Action Name ="DomainPrep" domain ="DomainA_FQDN" />
    </Domain>
    <Domain>
        <Action Name ="DomainAdd"
            domain ="DomainA_FQDN"
            refdomain ="DomainB_FQDN"
            useronly ="TRUE" />
    </Domain>
    <Domain>
        <Action Name ="DomainAdd"
            domain ="DomainA_FQDN"
            refdomain ="RootDomain_FQDN" />
    </Domain>
</LcsCmd>
```

In an Active Directory forest with some child domains hosting and other child domains not hosting Live Communications Server, it's recommended that you do the previously mentioned step 2 for every domain not hosting Live Communications Server against every domain hosting Live Communications Server. Doing so will enable the Live Communications Servers to search users across the entire forest.

Summary

Live Communications Server 2005 SP1 relies on Active Directory to publish and replicate global settings, server settings, and user settings. In addition to publishing information for all Live Communications Servers to be able to find, Active Directory authenticates and authorizes users using Kerberos and NTLM to provide a secure single sign-in experience. Active Directory's integration with PKI enables server-to-server communication to be secure. Live Communications Server 2005 SP1 takes full advantage of the benefits that Active Directory provides. Carefully plan your Active Directory GC resources for servicing Live Communications Server 2005 SP1. To aid administrators in figuring out which Active Directory "prep steps" to perform and when, the appendix provides a flowchart that summarizes the steps to run depending on the scenario you want to enable. This flowchart is the same tool used by Microsoft's field and product support personnel to assist customers.

■■■

CHAPTER 8

Considering DNS and PKI Issues

Where appropriate, Live Communications Server leverages existing technology such as Active Directory (which we covered in Chapter 7), SQL Server, Microsoft Operations Manager (see Chapter 19), DNS, and PKI. This chapter covers these last two related concepts: SIP DNS namespaces and PKI certificates. It is important to understand these concepts and how they relate before requesting certificates for your Live Communications Servers.

SIP Namespaces

Live Communications Server uses the concept of SIP namespaces, or domains, to route SIP requests internally and externally by using DNS. This is similar to how emails are routed.

When installing Live Communications Server 2005 SP1, the default SIP domain the server becomes authoritative for is the Active Directory's forest (that is, root domain) name. For example, if your forest's FQDN is `zulu.local`, then your Live Communications Server will be authoritative for the SIP domain `@zulu.local`. In the case of a multitree Active Directory forest, Live Communications Server 2005 SP1 picks up only the first tree's FQDN as its SIP domain. The other tree's FQDN will need to be defined manually. In reality, however, this default namespace is probably not the namespace you will want to expose externally. In most cases, you will want to make the user's SIP URI identical to the user's email address for simplicity. This is not a requirement, but it keeps the user's corporate identity consistent. If your corporate email namespace does not match your Active Directory root domain FQDN, you'll need to change the default SIP namespace to match your SMTP namespace. Luckily, you can modify the list of SIP domains.

You can easily modify the set of authoritative SIP domains through the Administrative Tools MMC. Right-click the Forest node, and select Properties to open the global settings. The General tab will appear by default. Use the Add and Remove buttons to modify the list of authoritative SIP domains, as shown in Figure 8-1.

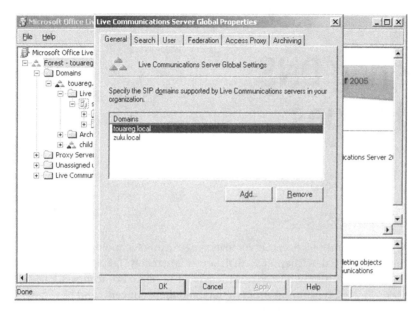

Figure 8-1. *Configuring SIP domains for Live Communications Server*

Users in your organization must be enabled for Live Communications with a SIP URI that has a domain suffix supported by the Live Communications Servers in your organization.

After the initial configuration, there is little need to add or remove SIP domains; however, sometimes this need does arise. For example, if a company changes its public identity, then the old SIP domain needs to be discontinued, and the new SIP domain needs to be added. If a company with an existing deployment of Live Communications Server is merged with your organization and you want to support only a single SIP domain namespace, then the acquired company's SIP domain name needs to be added to your Domains list until the migration is completed. For these and other reasons, simply adding the new SIP domain to the Domains list and removing the old SIP domain isn't sufficient. In addition to this step, you'll need to migrate all users whose SIP URI uses the old SIP domain to the new SIP domain. Each user's contacts will also need to be updated from the old SIP domain to the new SIP domain to remain valid.

Migrating users from one SIP namespace to another is a four-step process:

1. Add the new SIP domain to the Domains list.

2. Update every user's SIP URI to the new SIP domain suffix.

3. Update every user's contact to the new SIP domain suffix.

4. Update all Access Proxy public certificates to include the new SIP domain.

Performing step 1 is easy; however, steps 2 and 3 become more challenging because there are no tools to perform these steps. Luckily, Live Communications Server 2005 SP1 provides WMI APIs to automate these steps.

One approach is to query all users in Active Directory that are enabled for Live Communications, check whether any user matches the source SIP domain to change, and change the domain portion of the SIP URI (leaving the username portion intact) to the target SIP domain desired. Since users could have been added as contacts with SIP URIs that you need to change to match the new SIP domain name, this utility would need to "peek" into each user enabled for Live Communications, check whether any contact's SIP URI matches the same source SIP domain, and update the domain portion of the contact's SIP URI. Wouldn't that be a handy tool to have in your toolbox? Luckily, instead of leaving this problem as an exercise for you (which we often disliked reading in our college textbooks), the book's website includes a tool we have written to perform steps 2 and 3. The tool is a command-line utility called sipchange.exe. Figure 8-2 shows an example of its output.

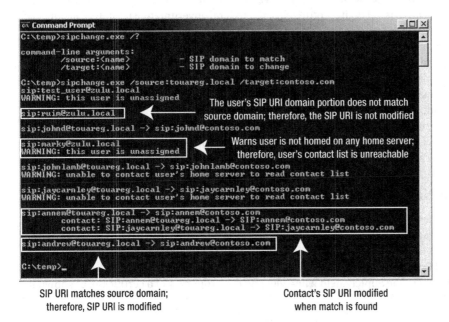

SIP URI matches source domain;   Contact's SIP URI modified
therefore, SIP URI is modified   when match is found

Figure 8-2. *Migrating user's SIP URI to a different SIP domain with* sipchange.exe

Step 4 involves requesting a new server certificate from your preferred public CA provider. For more details, see the "Subject Alternate Name" section later in this chapter.

Certificates

Since Live Communications Server 2005 SP1 leverages certificates to enforce the strong authentication of servers, it's important for administrators to understand how Live Communications Servers use certificates. Certificates are digital equivalents to a driver's license or a passport. Their purpose is to authoritatively identify an entity, in this case a server. Similar to a driver's license and passport, which identifies your height, weight, hair and eye color, address, and so on, the digital certificate provides specific properties that identify the server.

Every certificate is tied to a public key. Any information encrypted with this public key can be decrypted only by the holder of the corresponding private key. This is a public and private key pair and is unique. If you can determine that I hold the private key, then you know that you're communicating with the owner of the public key and therefore the owner of the certificate.

To determine whether I hold the private key, you generate a random piece of information that only you know (that is, the secret), encrypt it with the public key, and send it to me. If I'm able to send back the plain text (that is, the secret) by decrypting the message you sent, then you will know that I hold the private key to the certificate.

Knowing that I hold the private key proves only that much: that I hold the private key to the certificate. The certificate could claim that I'm Bill Gates just in the same way that a fake driver's license could identify me as Bill Gates. How do you determine whether the information contained in the certificate can be trusted? Since you cannot trust me to tell the truth, you will need to rely on a more reliable source to validate that the information contained in the certificate is legal. In the case of a driver's license or passport, this source of authority is the government of the United States. In the case of digital certificates, the federal government isn't in the business of issuing certificates to private businesses and citizens (yet). So, you must rely on trusted public certificate authorities (CAs), such as VeriSign, eTrust, and so on, to issue certificates that other organizations are likely to trust. Certificates for Access Proxy servers must be requested and issued from public CAs. Certificates for internal Live Communications Servers that interact with other servers only within your organizations can be issued certificates from a private CA trusted only within your organization to reduce cost.

Understanding how Live Communications Servers use the different properties of a certificate will go a long way in avoiding pitfalls in configuring your servers. Wikipedia.org provides a good overview at http://en.wikipedia.org/wiki/X.509.

Common Name or Subject Name

The common name (CN), also known as the *subject name* (SN), of a certificate in the case of a Live Communications Server identifies the server's FQDN as defined in Active Directory. In the case of a front-end server member of an Enterprise pool, the CN must match the pool's FQDN. For a Standard Edition Server, the CN should match the computer's FQDN. You can find the CN of a certificate in the Subject field when viewing the properties of a certificate, as shown in Figure 8-3.

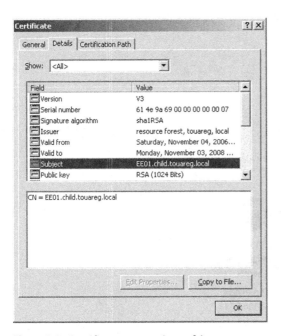

Figure 8-3. *Certificate properties: subject*

Although an organization's internal DNS service is considered to be trustworthy, it is possible for a rogue server to do DNS cache poisoning and take over another server's FQDN. To prevent such possible attacks, the CN is used to authoritatively tie a Live Communications Server to its FQDN. Live Communications Servers locate other Live Communications Servers via their FQDNs. After resolving the FQDN to an IP address, they validate that the server they've reached is not a rogue server by verifying that the CN of the server's certificate lists the right FQDN. This allows any connecting server to authenticate the Live Communications Server. Figure 8-4 illustrates this authentication process.

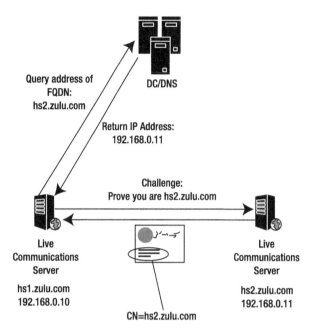

Figure 8-4. *Authenticating Live Communications Servers*

To verify that the server is an authorized Live Communications Server within your organization, the connecting server checks that the server's FQDN is listed in the Trusted Server list in Active Directory, as illustrated in Figure 8-5.

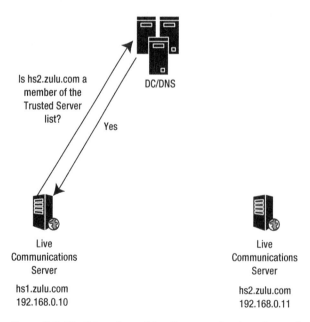

Figure 8-5. *Verifying that a Live Communications Server is a trusted server*

Subject Alternate Name

The subject alternate name (SAN) is used to expose multiple SIP domains. An organization (such as a multinational corporation) may have multiple SIP domains that it wants to publish to the public (that is, the Internet). Each SIP domain may represent a different business unit's brand of the organization. For example, the company Zulu Inc. has three brands, Zuave, Zesty, and Zulu. It would be confusing for customers, partners, and vendors unaware of this brand's parent structure to reach Zuave employees with a SIP URI of user@zulu.com. It would be more intuitive for those employees to have a SIP URI of user@zuave.com. Such an organization can expose multiple SIP domains to the Internet, as discussed in the "SIP Namespaces" section (see step 4).

The certificate of an Access Proxy may certify multiple SIP domains by placing additional SIP domains in the SAN field. If a SAN field is present, the SAN should contain the CN of the certificate (that is, the FQDN of the Access Proxy) as the first entry in the SAN to bind the original name into the SAN followed by the complete list of SIP domains for which your organization is authoritative. The use of the SAN allows a single Access Proxy to be authoritative for multiple SIP domains. Without this approach, you could expose only one SIP domain per Access Proxy. This would require deploying multiple Access Proxy servers to expose multiple SIP domains as in the case of Zulu Inc. Figure 8-6 illustrates an example of a certificate with a populated SAN.

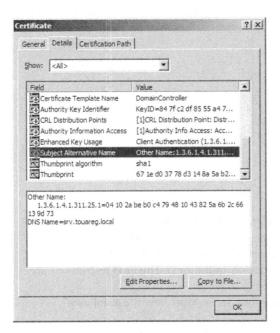

Figure 8-6. *Certificate properties: subject alternative name*

Using a SAN can also be beneficial for your internal deployment of Live Communications Server, particularly when you do not want to deploy a Director. If the DNS SRV record for Zulu Inc., _sipinternaltls._tcp.zulu.com, points to the A record, sip.zulu.com, and if every home server's certificate contains sip.zulu.com in the SAN field, then clients configured for automatic configuration will successfully authenticate these home servers. Because the A record, sip.zulu.com, matches the server's certificate SAN field, users will be able to sign in.

CRL Distribution Points

The certificate distribution point (CDP) is a field used to publish the distribution point(s) from where you can download certificate revocation lists (CRLs). The CRL is used to verify that the certificate hasn't been revoked since the time it was issued. You can download CRLs via a variety of methods indicated in the CDP. The most common CDPs are HTTP and LDAP URLs. Access Proxy servers should be configured to download CRLs. Figure 8-7 illustrates an example of a CDP.

Figure 8-7. *Certificate properties: CRL distribution points*

Enhanced Key Usage

The enhanced key usage (EKU) is a field that identifies the intended purpose of the certificate. If no EKU field is present in the certificate, the certificate is valid for all uses; however, the intended purpose of the certificate can be limited based on the EKU listed in the CA's part of the certificate path (not having an EKU provides no limitations). The EKU restrictions are inherited from the issuing parent CAs.

The two EKUs that every Live Communications Server must have are as follows:

- Server Authentication
- Client Authentication

Figure 8-8 illustrates these two EKUs.

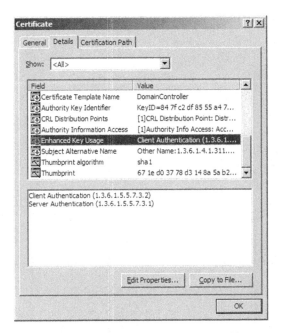

Figure 8-8. *Certificate properties: enhanced key usage*

Server Authentication

This EKU must be present in order to grant the certificate the right to act as a server. This EKU is required for the host to be treated as a server when using MTLS.

Client Authentication

This EKU must be present in order to initiate outbound MTLS connections with the following server types:

- Live Communications Server 2003

- Live Communications Server 2005

- Public IM Connectivity (PIC) to AOL

Live Communications Server 2005 SP1 has removed the need for servers to have a client EKU when initiating outbound MTLS connections. However, AOL still requires this client EKU to be present in the certificate used by Access Proxy servers connecting to AOL via PIC.

Certification Path

The certificate must be issued from a CA that your organization trusts. The CA represents the reliable source that can vouch for the trustworthiness of the certificate. To view the certificate chain leading to its root certificate, select the Certificate Path tab when viewing the certificate, as illustrated in Figure 8-9. If the root certificate or any of its subordinate certificates are not trusted or revoked, the certificate will not be trusted. This is especially useful when validating properties of the issuing CAs to make sure that EKU usage rights of interest have been inherited as well as locally granted.

Figure 8-9. *Certificate properties: certification path*

Summary

Based on our experience in helping customers deploy Live Communications Server 2003 and Live Communications Server 2005 SP1, certificate issues are the most frequent deployment problem encountered by customers. We thought this topic was sufficiently important to warrant a chapter to assist you in understanding how Live Communications Server 2005 SP1 uses these technologies.

If you're experiencing problems where one Live Communications Server is not able to establish a communication session with other Standard Edition Servers and Enterprise pools, it's probably a certificate misconfiguration issue because the other Live Communications Servers are failing to authenticate this server.

CHAPTER 9

Installing Standard Edition

Installing a Standard Edition Server is simple. In fact, you don't need a long-winded chapter on this subject. Just fire up the Setup program, and follow the instructions. You must complete two steps. The first step is to install the software on the local computer. This requires only local administrative rights. The second step is to activate the server. You'll need administrative rights with membership in the RTCDomainServerAdmins group, which is created by Live Communications Server. Of course, being the root domain administrator will suffice as well. You'll be done before you even finish reading this chapter. Therefore, instead of walking you through the process, this chapter will provide you with insights that might not be apparent to help you in your successful deployment.

Preparations

If this is the first time you're deploying Live Communications Server, you must first prepare your Active Directory. Before you can deploy Live Communications Server, you must run through the Active Directory "prep steps" like you would when deploying Exchange Server. Actually, this isn't exactly true—you can install the binaries on the server before even preparing the Active Directory; however, activation will fail until your Active Directory forest is prepped.

How do you tell whether you've completed the Active Directory prep steps? If you can't recall, Setup will automatically detect whether any preparatory steps are missing and will block you from activating your server until you've completed them successfully. We've reserved an entire chapter on the subject of preparing Active Directory for Live Communications Server. Please refer to Chapter 7.

Once your Active Directory forest is prepped for Live Communications Server, you're ready to install and activate your first, second, and so on, Standard Edition Servers. Since installing a Standard Edition Server is confined to a single physical server, this task is straightforward. Make sure you're using at least the minimum hardware required as outlined in Chapter 9. In addition, here are some recommendations:

- Split the location of the log files from the location of the database onto two physical hard drives.

- Increase the minimum recommended random access memory (RAM) because Live Communications Server is memory intensive.

- Make sure to use a high-speed network card with 1GB capacity.

- Turn on TLS.

DON'T PLAN TOO MUCH

It's important to do some planning before deploying your first server. Indeed, planning is a critical task to create the best architecture to fit your organization's infrastructure and needs. However, planning can easily be overdone. In our experiences of helping some of Microsoft's largest customers plan their deployment, some customers attempted to plan so far ahead that they often became paralyzed because they had to make assumptions of their organizations' future needs.

Our advice in those situations is to not plan too much. Live Communications Server is very flexible. For example, say you initially decide to deploy a Standard Edition Server thinking that IM is likely to follow a slow adoption rate, but then you realize that IM is picking up like wild fire and every user in your organization wants to use it. You enable more and more users for Live Communications Server and soon realize your Standard Edition Server is reaching its maximum capacity of 15,000 simultaneous users. What do you do?

You realize you need to trade up to an Enterprise pool. You order the required hardware: two servers and a hardware load balancer. You configure one of the servers as the pool's back-end server and the other server as one of the front-end servers. After successfully installing the Enterprise pool, you simply move the users homed on the Standard Edition Server to the Enterprise pool with a few simple clicks. Live Communications Server 2005 SP1's management console makes the task simple, but you should take some precautionary steps, which we'll cover in Chapter 10.

Once you finish moving your users to the Enterprise pool, you deactivate and uninstall the Standard Edition Server and repurpose it as another front-end server for the newly created Enterprise pool. Of course, you could save yourself the hassle with a bit of forward planning. If you can safely assume that you'll need to enable more than 15,000 users for Live Communications Server, directly plan to deploy an Enterprise pool. The moral of the story is that Live Communications Server is flexible enough not to prevent the future growth of your organization.

Since the "Don't Plan Too Much" sidebar makes a good case for planning, you should strategically select where to deploy your Standard Edition Servers. Cost, high availability, and scale requirements are priorities to factor in your decision. The Standard Edition is a great option for medium-sized companies or a large branch office if survivability is an important criterion in your branch offices.

You should not decide to deploy a Standard Edition Server in a branch office automatically, though. If the availability of a Live Communications Server service to a branch office is important when the WAN connectivity is down, then deploying a Standard Edition Server might be the right solution. Since Live Communications Server is dependent upon Active Directory, deploy Standard Edition Servers in branch offices with a global catalog (GC) present locally. If the branch office has unreliable connectivity to a GC, then deploying a Live Communications Server is not a good choice. The Standard Edition Server will fail to start if it cannot reach the nearest GC, and you might spend a lot of time and energy trying to figure out why. Strategically plan your Standard Edition Server deployments near your GCs in remote locations.

Standard Edition Servers have several advantages that make them a better choice than Enterprise pools in certain situations. Live Communications Server 2005 SP1 Standard Edition targets branch offices and medium-sized businesses. As a single-server installation, Standard Edition is relatively easy to deploy in branch offices by remote administrators who may not be experts in deploying Live Communications Server. Deploying a Standard Edition Server requires a single physical server; by contrast, an Enterprise pool requires a minimum of three physical servers plus a hardware load balancer. Using Standard Edition Servers reduces the number of physical servers needed to service different geographic locations where your organization has a presence. This directly translates into lower hardware cost and total cost of ownership (TCO) for maintaining them.

Live Communications Server 2005 SP1 Standard Edition automatically installs Microsoft SQL Server Desktop Engine (MSDE) to store user data homed on it. If preserving user data is important to your users, then you should regularly back up the MSDE database. Backing it up will allow you to restore the database in the eventuality of a failure, and you would need to create a new Standard Edition Server. Backing up the database is supported in Live Communications Server by the tool `dbbackup.exe`. This tool is available in the `Support` subdirectory of the Live Communications Server installation directory: `C:\Program Files\Microsoft LC 2005\Server\Support`. To perform regular backups, schedule a task to perform this operation at recurring intervals of your choice. The same tool is used to restore the content of the database. For more details, please refer to Chapter 15.

If for whatever reason you need to delete the database, you can use the tool `dbsetup.wsf`, located in the `DBsetup` subdirectory:

```
cscript dbsetup.wsf /drop
```

This knowledge becomes particularly handy if you inadvertently uninstall the server without first deactivating it or if the database gets corrupted. Instead of reinstalling the entire server, you can drop the database and restore it from a backup.

Patching MSDE with software updates becomes important particularly if these are security updates. Since MSDE is a data engine based on core SQL Server technology, it can be susceptible to the same viruses that SQL is vulnerable to, such as the Code Red virus and the Slammer virus. The problem is that unless you're aware that the Standard Edition Servers automatically install MSDE, you might not realize that you have these databases to patch up. It's important to remember and therefore monitor SQL Server updates that also apply to MSDE. If your organization isn't subscribed, it's good practice to subscribe to the Microsoft Security Update Alerts. You can receive notifications of security updates in a variety of convenient ways, such as via email, instant messaging, RSS, and the website, to help you better respond to security threats to your organization. See `http://www.microsoft.com/technet/security/bulletin/notify.mspx` to sign up for these notifications.

■**Note** Microsoft recently announced support for SQL Server 2005 SP1 for the Enterprise Edition. However, support of SQL Server 2005 SP1 for Enterprise Edition does not imply that SQL Server 2005 SP1 Express Edition is supported for Standard Edition. Only MSDE is supported for Standard Edition.

To quickly determine the number of unique active users within the last month without having to crack open a SQL book and start writing SQL queries against the database, run the following command from the `%ProgramFiles%\Microsoft LC 2005\Server\Support` directory:

```
dbreport /report:monthlyactiveusers
```

Advantages and Disadvantages of the Standard Edition

The advantages of Standard Edition Servers are as follows:

Single server deployment: You need to install Live Communications Server Standard Edition on only a single physical server as opposed to Live Communications Server Enterprise Edition, which requires a multiserver deployment.

Easy to install: Setup is straightforward via simple-to-use, step-by-step wizards.

Remote management: This is possible using Live Communications Server's Management Console.

The disadvantages of Standard Edition Servers are as follows:

Single point of failure: You must back up the MSDE database regularly if preserving user data is important.

Use of MSDE as a database: Tracking the number of installed databases within the organization is important for software patching particularly if these are security patches. SQL Server can be more readily tracked than MSDE.

Scalability: Standard Edition Servers do not scale beyond 15,000 simultaneous users.

Active Directory connectivity: Reliable connectivity to the nearest GC is required to start.

To monitor your Standard Edition Server, use the freely available MOM Pack for Live Communications Server 2005 SP1 if your organization already has Microsoft Operations Manager 2005 (MOM) deployed. The MOM Pack for Live Communications Server 2005 SP1 is available on Microsoft's website at `http://www.microsoft.com/downloads/details.aspx?familyid=4C9837E1-1B92-4B98-A09C-BCD8F29B2831&displaylang=en`. If you don't have MOM 2005 (or newer) deployed because of the cost or other reasons, you can still monitor your servers. It will take a bit more effort because you need to know which performance counters and events to monitor. For more details on these performance counters and events to monitor, refer to Chapter 19.

Installation

Installing files on the local computer requires only local administrative rights to complete. The Setup program copies and registers all the necessary files for the Standard Edition Server. To run this step, insert the Standard Edition CD, and select the Standard Edition Server link on the setup screen, as shown in Figure 9-1.

The Setup program will then check your deployment state. To install the files for the Standard Edition Server, click the corresponding link, as shown in Figure 9-2.

Figure 9-1. *Setting up Standard Edition*

Figure 9-2. *Installing a Standard Edition Server*

Once the installation is complete, you will be able to start the Live Communications Server 2005 MMC, available in the `Administrative Tools` folder.

The installation task creates the following domain local security groups. No members are added to these groups until the activation step is complete:

RTC Local Administrators: Members of this group can manage this server.

RTC Local User Administrators: Members of this group can manage only user data on the server.

RTC Server Applications: When deploying server applications running as services, the application must run under a service account that is a member of this group.

RTC Server Local Group: Members of this group have access to the WMI store and RTC database used by the server.

RTC ABS Service Local Group: Members of this group can manage the Address Book Service.

Activation

The tasks performed during activation require you to have Domain Admins or RTCDomainServerAdmins privileges, which is why these tasks are separate from installation. Installation and activation were previously combined in Live Communications Server 2003; however, this was changed based on customer feedback. Organizations, particularly large ones, divide IT operations based on roles. These roles define specific privilege requirements. Splitting the process of deploying a Standard Edition Server into two separate tasks fits better with customers' IT personnel structures.

If you've just completed the installation step, Setup will immediately prompt whether you want to activate the server. It is not required to activate the server immediately, particularly if you do not have the required privileges necessary to successfully complete this step. To navigate to this step, select the Standard Edition Server link in the setup screen from the Standard Edition CD, as shown in Figure 9-3.

The Setup program will then check your deployment state and verify that the Active Directory prep steps were configured successfully and the Standard Edition files have been installed. To activate the Standard Edition Server, click the corresponding link, as shown in Figure 9-4.

Figure 9-3. *Activating from Standard Edition setup*

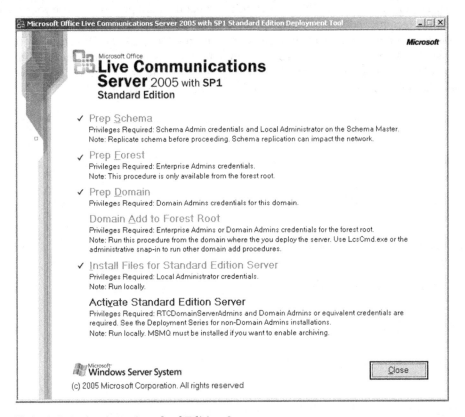

Figure 9-4. *Activating a Standard Edition Server*

Activation performs several tasks:

1. It creates a pool object under the msRTCSIP-Pools container to represent the Standard Edition Server.

2. It creates a trusted server entry by creating a GUID object under the Global Settings container of type msRTCSIP-TrustedServer.

3. It adds the global security groups as members to the corresponding domain local groups:

   - RTCABSDomainServices is added to RTC ABS Service Local Group.

   - RTCDomainServerAdmins is added to RTC Local Administrators.

   - RTCDomainUserAdmins is added to RTC Local User Administrators.

   - RTCHSDomainServices is added to RTC Server Local Group.

Summary

The Standard Edition version is well suited for medium-sized companies or large branch offices that require the Live Communications service even if the WAN link to the corporate office is down. Deploying a Standard Edition Server is a straightforward process. Ensure your server meets the recommended hardware requirements before you install; the installation of files requires no prerequisites. Activating the server requires that the Active Directory forest be prepared for Live Communications Server. For optimal performance, follow the recommended suggestions. As an aid to assist you in installing your Standard Edition Server, the flowchart available at http://www.ruimaximo.com provides a step-by-step guide.

CHAPTER 10

■■■

Installing Enterprise Edition

Installing an Enterprise pool is substantially more involved than installing a Standard Edition Server. This requires using the Enterprise Edition CD. The hardware requirements for an Enterprise pool are also more demanding, and the complexity of the product increases. However, an Enterprise pool provides benefits that are not available in a Standard Edition Server.

Enterprise pools are better suited to deploy in large data centers than in remote branch offices because of the high scalability and reliability they offer but also because of the complexity required to deploy Enterprise pools compared to Standard Edition Servers. An Enterprise pool supports high availability through the redundancy of front-end servers and SQL Server clustering of the back end. An Enterprise pool can have up to eight front-end servers. If a user connected to a front-end server fails, the user should not notice the failure because Office Communicator attempts to immediately reconnect to another front-end server of the Enterprise pool. Messages sent while the user is in the middle of a conversation and the front-end server fails will be lost, and the user will receive a nondelivery receipt. The Enterprise pool's hardware load balancer (HLB) sends the subsequent sign-in request to another front-end server that's available.

By using Microsoft Cluster Services available in Windows Server 2003 Enterprise Edition and Datacenter Edition, you can cluster the Enterprise pool's back-end server. Clustering the back-end server with multiple front-end servers gives the architecture higher availability and reliability across the entire Enterprise pool design. Although SQL Server 2000 and 2005 support four types of cluster topologies (single instance, multi-instance, N+1, N+M), Live Communications Server 2005 SP1 supports only single-instance failover, also commonly referred to as *active/passive clustering*. A two-node cluster is configured to fail over to the standby SQL Server if the primary SQL Server fails.

Microsoft does not recommend reusing an existing SQL Server that is hosting other databases as the Enterprise pool's back end. Enterprise pools also cannot share a common SQL Server as the back-end server. Every Enterprise pool must have a dedicated back-end SQL Server.

Enterprise Edition is an excellent candidate to deploy in large data centers for customers who want high availability across data centers, because an Enterprise pool in one data center cannot fail over to another Enterprise pool in another data center easily.

The advantages of an Enterprise pool are as follows:

- It offers high-availability support with multiple front-end servers.

- Using SQL Server as the back-end server database provides high availability of the database through SQL clustering (active/passive).

- It offers scalability; Enterprise Edition can scale up to 125,000 simultaneous users per Enterprise pool.

- You can use SQL Server tools to remotely manage the back-end server.

- Remote management is possible using Live Communications Server's Management Console.

The disadvantages of an Enterprise pool are as follows:

- It is more complex and expensive to deploy.

- You'll need additional SQL Server license(s).

- It requires more hardware:

  - Multiple servers

  - Hardware load balancer

- You'll need Active Directory connectivity; reliable connectivity to the nearest GC is required to start up.

Creating a Pool

The first step in setting up an Enterprise pool is to create a pool. All Active Directory "prep steps" must be completed beforehand. In addition, before running this step, you must complete some prerequisites:

- The computer to be used as the Enterprise pool back-end server must be installed with Windows Server 2003 (or Windows Server 2000 SP4).

- Do not turn on encryption (EFS) on the %TEMP% directory; otherwise, Setup will fail.

Note An easy way to verify that encryption is not turned on is to start Windows Explorer, type **%temp%** in the address field (as shown in Figure 10-1), and press the Enter key. Right-click anywhere in the empty space of the folder, and select Properties. Click the Advanced button. Verify that the checkbox Encrypt Contents to Secure Data is not checked, as shown in Figure 10-2.

- Install SQL Server on the Enterprise pool back-end server. Both SQL Server 2000 SP3a (or newer) and now SQL Server 2005 SP1 (or newer) are supported versions with Live Communications Server 2005 SP1.

- A 1GB network card (NIC) for the back-end server is recommended.

- Two hard drives with fast access time should be installed on the back-end server.

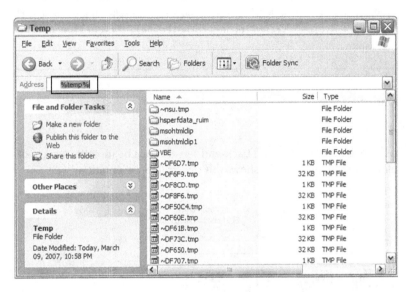

Figure 10-1. *%TEMP% directory*

Figure 10-2. *Checking the encryption properties of the folder*

An Enterprise pool is a logical representation in Active Directory of related physical servers that form a pool. These are servers that compose an Enterprise pool:

- Hardware load balancer

Note You can use Windows Server 2003 Network Load Balancing (NLB) instead of a hardware load balancer; however, NLB is not recommended for production environments. Microsoft already provides a good article on this topic at `http://www.microsoft.com/technet/prodtechnol/office/livecomm/library/nlb/lcsnlb_3.mspx`.

- One or more front-end servers

- One back-end server

Each of these servers (front-end servers and back-end server) must be member servers of the same Active Directory domain. Figure 10-3 shows this physical representation.

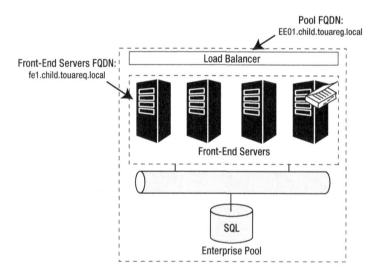

Figure 10-3. *Enterprise pool physical representation*

A pool also has an Active Directory representation, which is created by instantiating an object of class type msRTCSIP-Pool. This object is created under the Global Settings container in the Pools container. Since creating an object in Active Directory requires write access to the global settings, administrators performing this task must be members of the RTCDomainServerAdmins group or the Enterprise Admins group. The Enterprise Admins group is equivalent to the Domain Admins group of the root domain.

In addition to creating a pool object in Active Directory, this step attempts to connect to the SQL Server to create the RTC database tables. In addition to being a member of the RTCDomainServerAdmins group, the administrator must be a local administrator of the local computer. It's recommended that you create the Enterprise pool from the physical computer that will be used as the Enterprise pool's back-end server to avoid getting SQLDMO error messages if you don't have SQL tools installed on the local computer needed to connect the SQL Server. You create a pool by running the step Create/Upgrade Enterprise Edition Pool, as illustrated in Figure 10-4.

You will notice that you can install the Enterprise Edition front-end servers before creating the Enterprise pool; however, you cannot activate the Enterprise Edition front-end servers until you create the Enterprise pool.

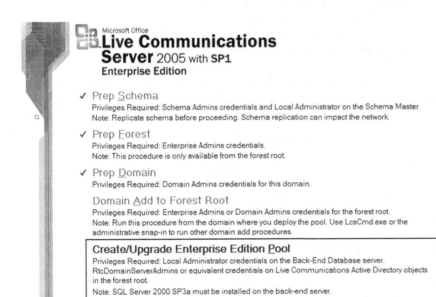

Figure 10-4. *Creating an enterprise pool*

This step configures the Active Directory pool object based on the information requested by the Create Enterprise Pool Wizard. The wizard creates an object of class type msRTCSIP-Pool as defined by the Prep Schema step and populates the object's attributes associated with this class. In addition to creating a pool object, the wizard creates an msRTCSIP-TrustedServer object under the Global Settings container to represent the pool. By adding the pool as a trusted server, other Live Communications Servers will trust it when accepting incoming connections from this pool.

This is the class definition for Pool:

CN = see the later step 1
  msRTCSIP-PoolDisplayName = see the later step 1
  msRTCSIP-PoolType = 2 (specifies Enterprise Edition)
  msRTCSIP-PoolVersion = 131073
  msRTCSIP-BackEndServer = see the later step 3
  msRTCSIP-PoolData = null (reserved)
  Microsoft (class type: container)
    LC Services (class type: msRTCSIP-PoolService)
      msRTCSIP-FrontEndServers (attribute type: multi-valued DN)

This is the class definition for TrustedServer:

CN = {GUID} (generated by the Create Enterprise Pool Wizard)
  msRTCSIP-TrustedServerFQDN = see the later step 2
  msRTCSIP-TrustedServerVersion = 2
  msRTCSIP-TrustedServerData = null (reserved)

After you click past the welcome page of the wizard, the second page prompts you for three pieces of information. These fields are numbered in Figure 10-5 for ease of reference.

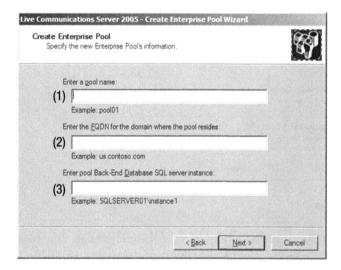

Figure 10-5. *Working with the Create Enterprise Pool Wizard*

Here's how the Create Enterprise Pool Wizard populates these Active Directory attributes:

1. This is the name of the pool. It can be any value you select as long as it doesn't conflict with the name of an existing pool. The pool name gets populated as the name (CN) of the pool object and the value of the msRTCSIP-PoolDisplayName attribute.

2. The domain FQDN is the DNS name of the Active Directory domain, which the back-end server is a member server of. This is used to construct the FQDN of the pool by combining the pool name as defined in (1) and appending the domain FQDN. This pool FQDN is stored in the dnsHostName attribute of the pool object and the msRTCSIP-TrustedServerFQDN attribute of the TrustedServer object.

3. The pool back-end database SQL server instance (that is, serverName\instanceName) is parsed, and the server name portion is stored in the msRTCSIP-BackEndServer attribute. By default if no instance name is supplied, the instances created are called RTC and RTCCONFIG. It's recommended that you leave these fields blank. If you customize the database instances, please refer to KB911996 (http://support.microsoft.com/kb/911996) if you run into problems. The RTC database contains user and pool information synchronized from Active Directory, and the RTCCONFIG database contains pool-level configuration settings specific to the Enterprise pool.[1]

The msRTCSIP-FrontEndServers attribute is populated when the administrator activates the front-end servers associated with this pool object.

The best-practice recommendation is to separate the database from the transaction logs on different hard drives. This will improve the overall performance of the back-end server. By default, the wizard specifies the location of the database and transaction log files to be on the same drive, as shown in Figure 10-6. Be sure to change them to different drives.

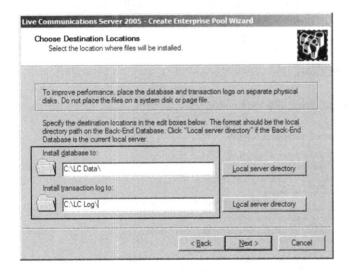

Figure 10-6. *Creating a pool performance recommendation*

---

1. An easy way to poke around the databases created by the Create Enterprise Pool Wizard is to use the sqlwb.exe tool that comes with every SQL Server 2005 installation. You can find it in the %ProgramFiles%\Microsoft SQL Server\90\Tools\Binn\VSShell\Common7\IDE subdirectory. This tool provides a graphical interface to easily connect to the database instances created by the Create Enterprise Pool Wizard without requiring expertise in SQL Server to see the database's tables. Although modifying the database tables directly in SQL is not supported, Live Communications Server exposes three SQL views that can be used to query presence information directly from the database. Each interface exposes a different set of data that might best fit your needs.

After successfully completing the Create Enterprise Pool Wizard, there are still some issues to address. You must configure an HLB, and you must publish the Enterprise pool's FQDN in DNS.

An HLB is required for each Enterprise pool. Once a client's connection is routed by the HLB to a particular front-end server, the HLB must be capable of routing all traffic from that client to the same front-end server for the duration of the user's session.

Microsoft has tested and supports Live Communications Server 2005 SP1 with the following HLBs:

- F5 Big-IP

- CAI Networks WebMux

- Foundry Networks ServerIron

You'll need to configure the HLB with the Enterprise pool FQDN and its IP address for the virtual IP address (VIP) and supply the static IP address of each of the front-end servers of the Enterprise pool. For details on how to configure the specific HLB of your choice, see the Partner Documentation section at http://office.microsoft.com/en-us/FX011526591033.aspx.

Finally, you must publish the FQDN of the Enterprise pool in DNS. An A (Host) record must be defined for the pool FQDN. This FQDN must point to an IP address. You'll need to specify a static IP address that you've reserved for the Enterprise pool's HLB virtual IP address (VIP).

Select Start ➤ Administrative Tools, and select DNS. Right-click your domain's node under the Forward Lookup Zones, and select New Host (A), as shown in Figure 10-7. Enter the Enterprise pool's FQDN in the Name field of the New Host dialog box. The pool's FQDN is composed of the pool name specified in (1) and the domain's FQDN (2) as specified in the Create Enterprise Pool Wizard. Enter the HLB VIP in the IP Address field.

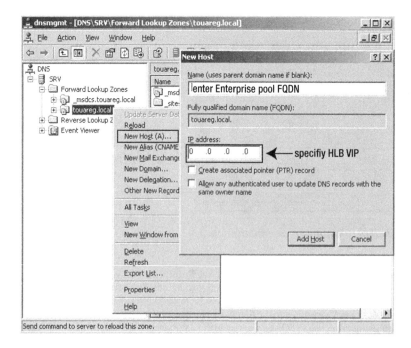

Figure 10-7. *Publishing an Enterprise pool in DNS*

You'll need to configure the HLB with this IP address. Make sure you can resolve the pool's FQDN. You can easily do this by performing a `ping` command. Open a Command Prompt window, and type **ping <pool fqdn>**.

Installing

The next step is to install the front-end servers of your Enterprise pool. For every front-end server, you'll need to run through the step Install Files for Enterprise Edition Server, as shown in Figure 10-8. You'll need to do the same with the activation step.

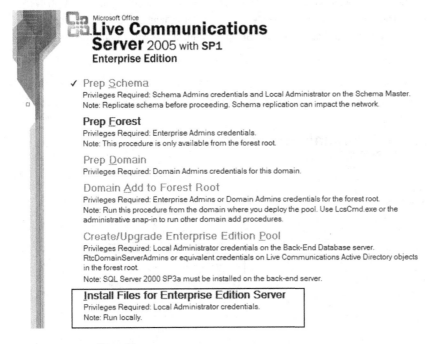

Figure 10-8. *Installing files*

Before running the installation step, you should meet the following prerequisites:

- The computer to be used as the front-end server must be running Windows Server 2003 Standard Edition or newer (or Windows Server 2000 SP4).

- If you intend to configure the front-end server for archiving, then MSMQ must be installed on the front-end server.

- A 1GB network card (NIC) for the front-end server is recommended.

- A static IP address should be allocated for the front-end server.

Local administrative privileges are necessary to run the installation process. This step performs the same tasks as the installation step for a Standard Edition Server:

- Copies the files for the front-end server

- Installs the WMI provider for Live Communications Server

- Creates local groups and configures security permissions

Note   The Live Communications Server WMI provider is the management interface exposed by the server and used by the Live Communications Server MMC. This WMI provider is automatically installed with every server installation. It can also be installed independently on a computer without Live Communications Server installed by clicking the Administration Tools link in the Setup program, as shown in Figure 10-9.

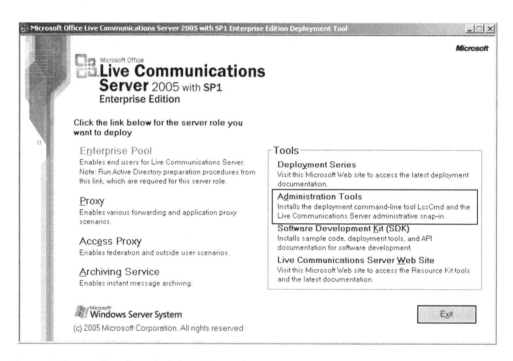

Figure 10-9. *Installing the administration tools*

After completing this step, you are now ready to activate the front-end server.

This WMI interface exposes APIs to perform specific tasks such as enabling users for Live Communications or modifying server or pool configuration settings. This interface incorporates business logic to prevent administrators from misconfiguring these settings. This WMI interface abstracts the different stores (for instance, Active Directory, SQL, WMI) used by Live Communications Server. Active Directory is used to store settings that need to be globally available. SQL stores pool-level settings, and WMI stores server-level settings for the local computer.

Activating

Activating an Enterprise pool is the final step in deploying your front-end server. Activation performs the same tasks as when you activate a Standard Edition Server:

- Creates a service account to run the service unless the administrator selects to use an existing account.[2]

- Configures the service account to access the Live Communications Server objects in Active Directory (that is, global settings, pools, and so on).

- Adds domain global security groups to the corresponding local security groups.

- Creates a trusted server entry for the front-end server under the global settings in Active Directory.[3]

- The computer object is extended with an SCP for registering the computer as a Live Communications Server.[4]

- Modifies the Pool object in Active Directory to associate the front-end server with the pool.[5]

- Registers the service principal name (SPN) for the service, which is required for servers within the pool to perform Kerberos authentication in Active Directory.

- Starts the Live Communications Server service.

---

2. If Live Communications Server creates the service account, verify whether the account's password is set to expire. If the password expires, the service will fail to run until you change the password and restart the Live Communications Server service. An event is logged in the Application Event Log to notify administrators of the root cause of the failure.

3. This step creates a trusted server entry under Global Settings in Active Directory. This allows the front-end server to be trusted by other Live Communications Servers.

4. A service connection point (SCP) is created in the corresponding computer object in Active Directory. This SCP identifies the computer object as a Live Communications Server front-end server and links it to its corresponding pool.

5. Since you must identify which Enterprise pool the front-end server should belong to in the activation wizard (see Figure 10-10), this step modifies the pool object under msRTCSIP-Pools to link it to the front-end server by adding the front-end server's Active Directory computer object DN to the attribute msRTCSIP-FrontEndServers.

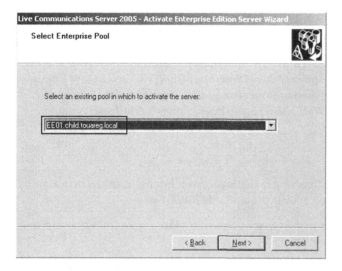

Figure 10-10. *Associating a front-end server to an Enterprise pool*

Each front-end server must be configured with a server certificate; otherwise, server-to-server communications between front-end servers and other Live Communications Servers will fail. An example of when front-end servers of the same Enterprise pool need to communicate with each other is when two or more users homed on the same Enterprise pool and signed in to different front-end servers are conversing with each other. SIP traffic flows between front-end servers over port 5061, and RPC traffic flows over port 135, as shown in Figure 10-11.

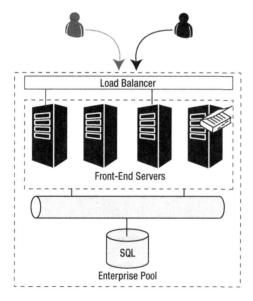

Figure 10-11. *Intrapool communications*

In addition to SIP traffic flowing between front-end servers, these servers communicate via RPC for batch notifications of user presence so every front-end server knows who is online and who isn't. The front-end servers communicate with the back-end server via ODBC.

Each front-end server must be configured with a web server certificate. If your organization has already deployed a Windows Server certificate authority (CA), you can request a certificate using the Web Server Certificate Wizard from any computer running IIS, or you can connect to the CA from a web browser by navigating to http://<server>/certsrv, where <server> is the NetBIOS name of the CA. Using the Web Server Certificate Wizard is more convenient if you do not know the name of the server acting as the CA for your organization. The following steps detail how to request the web server certificate using a web browser.

The first page shown after navigating to http://<server>/certsrv is the certificate server welcome page. Click the link to request a certificate, as shown in Figure 10-12.

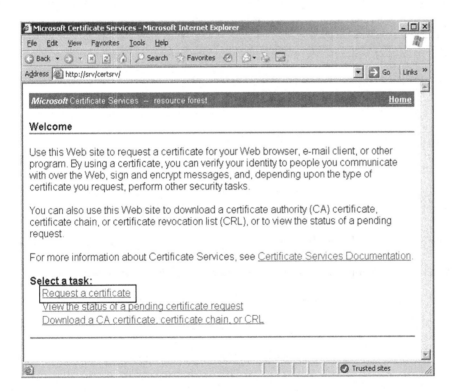

Figure 10-12. *Web certificate request*

On the next page, click the link to submit an advanced certificate request, as shown in Figure 10-13.

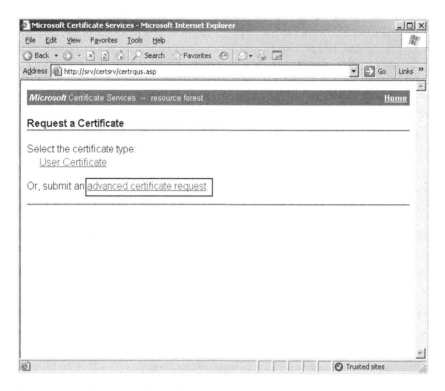

Figure 10-13. *Advanced web certificate request*

Select the Create and Submit a Request to This CA option, as shown in Figure 10-14.

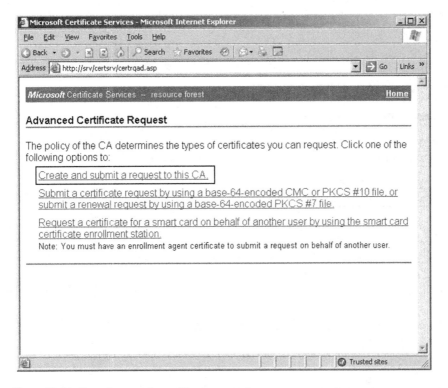

Figure 10-14. *Creating a web certificate request*

On the Advanced Certificate Request page, select the Web Server certificate template; specify the Enterprise pool's FQDN in the Name field, and check the Store Certificate in the Local Computer Certificate Store checkbox, as shown in Figure 10-15. It's recommended that you change the default key size from 1024 to at least 2048 to increase the strength of the key pair used in the certificate. Click Submit to send the request to the CA.

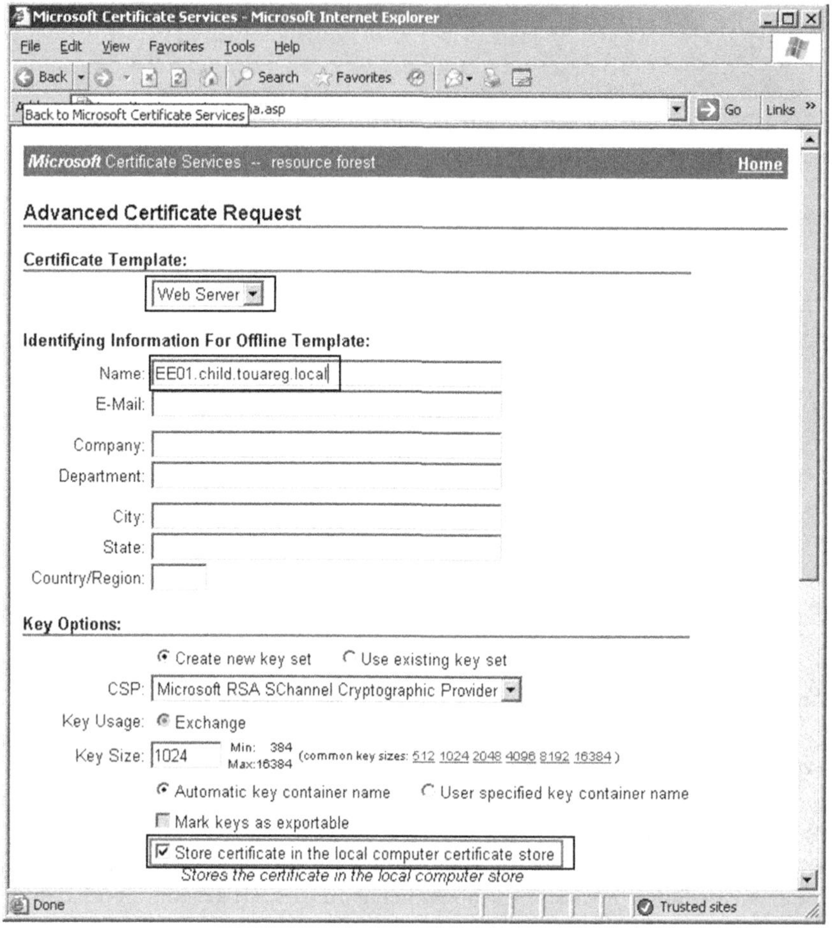

Figure 10-15. *Defining the web certificate request options*

Once the CA issues the certificate, install the certificate in the front-end server's local computer personal store by clicking the Install This Certificate link, as shown in Figure 10-16.

Next, you must configure the web server certificate on the front-end server. To do this, launch the Live Communications Server 2005 MMC from the Administrative Tools link. Drill down to the front-end server you finished installing and activating under the Enterprise pool node in the scope pane. Right-click the front-end server node, and select Properties. Switch to the Security tab, and click the Select Certificate button to configure the front-end server with the recently installed web server certificate, as shown in Figure 10-17.

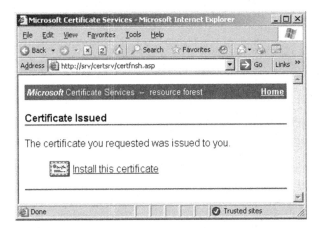

Figure 10-16. *Installing the issued certificate*

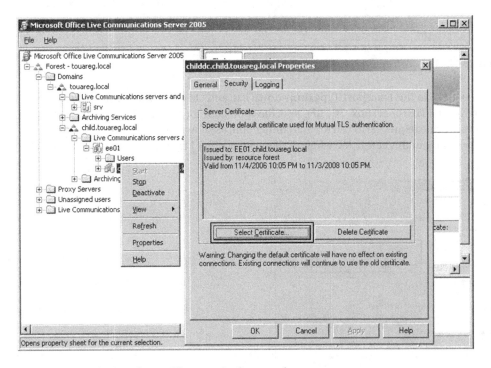

Figure 10-17. *Assigning the certificate to the front-end server*

Switch to the General tab, and configure the front-end server to listen on port 5061 for the MTLS connection. This will allow the front-end server to communicate with other Live Communications Server machines. By default, the front-end server listens on port 5060 only. Click the Add button to add another listening port to the front-end server, as shown in Figure 10-18.

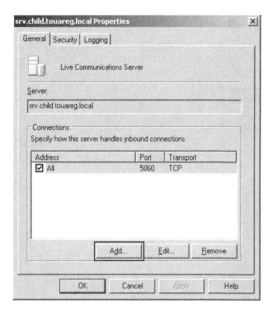

Figure 10-18. *Add the listening port to front-end server*

Select TLS in the Transport Type drop-down list, and check the Authenticate Remote Server (Mutual TLS) checkbox. The RFC specifies port 5061 for secure SIP. Select the same web server certificate requested to use for this connection, as shown in Figure 10-19. The front-end server will present this certificate when challenged by other Live Communications Servers.

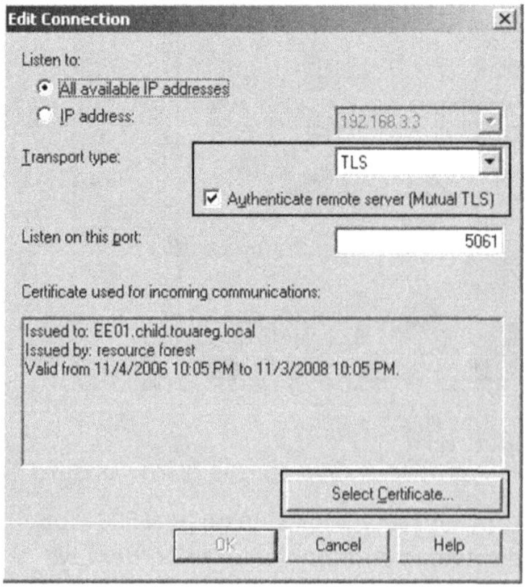

Figure 10-19. *Configuring the front-end server's new listening port*

The front-end server is now configured. Follow the steps in the next section to verify your pool configuration before provisioning additional front-end servers.

Verifying the Configuration

To quickly verify that your Enterprise pool is functional, use the Resource Kit tool, LcsDiag.exe. You can find this tool in the directory %ProgramFiles% \Microsoft LC 2005\ResKit, once you've installed the Live Communications Server 2005 SP1 Resource Kit. To determine whether the Enterprise pool is reachable, select TCP/TLS Connectivity, as shown in Figure 10-20.

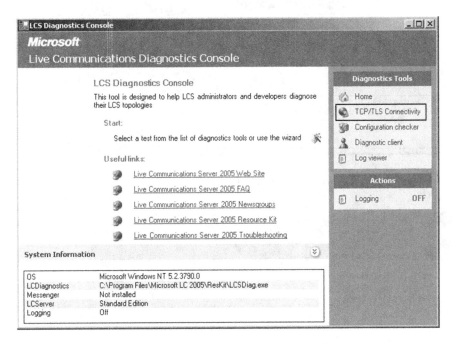

Figure 10-20. *Verifying the front-end server configuration with* LcsDiag.exe

Select the option to check the connectivity to servers in a pool, and click Next, as shown in Figure 10-21.

Enter the Enterprise pool name, and click Start, as shown in Figure 10-22.

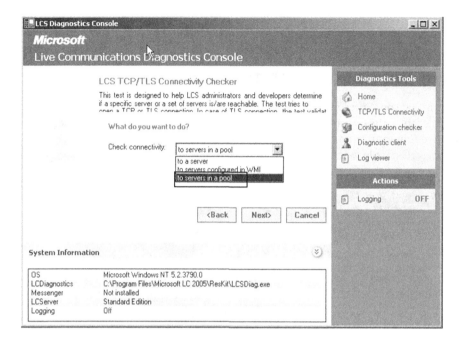

Figure 10-21. *LcsDiag: checking connectivity to a pool*

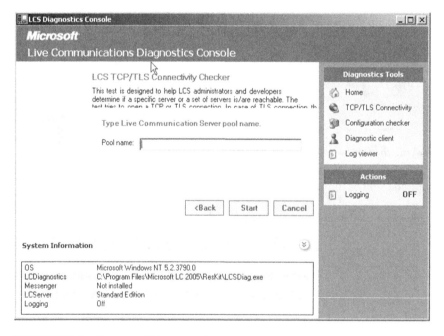

Figure 10-22. *LcsDiag: specifying a pool name*

To determine whether users can sign in to the Enterprise pool without using Communicator, select Diagnostic Client in the Diagnostics Tools section of LcsDiag.exe, as shown in Figure 10-23.

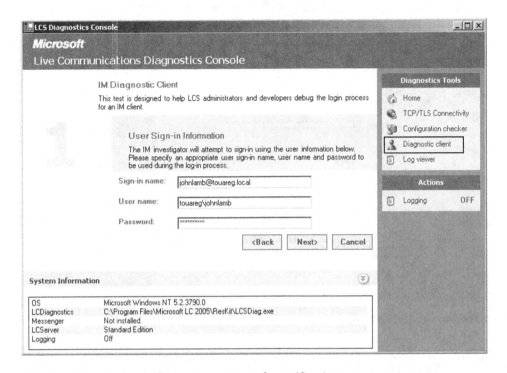

Figure 10-23. *LcsDiag: specifying a user account for verification*

Specify the FQDN of your Enterprise pool in the Server FQDN field. Leave the selection on TLS for the connection type and port number set at 5061, as shown in Figure 10-24.

If your Enterprise pool is properly configured, you should get a report similar to the following output from LcsDiag.exe, as shown in Figure 10-25.

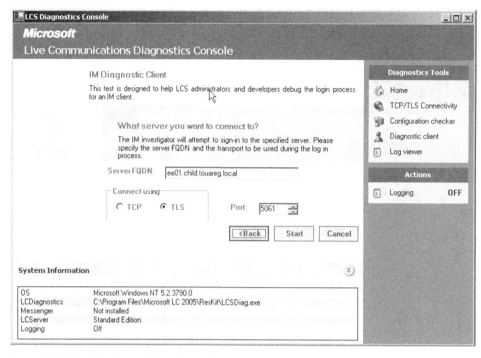

Figure 10-24. *LcsDiag: specifying the pool FQDN*

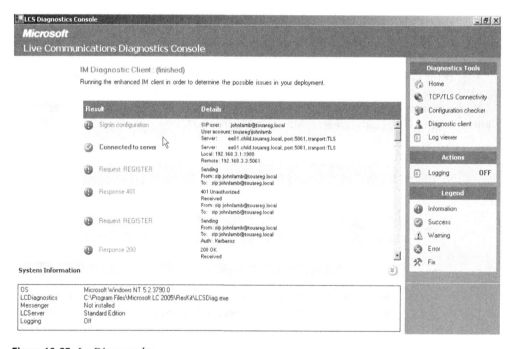

Figure 10-25. *LcsDiag results*

Summary

An Enterprise pool offers higher scalability and availability than a Standard Edition Server; however, the complexity of deploying an Enterprise pool requires a higher degree of expertise. This makes the Enterprise pool best suited for deployments in large data centers. The Enterprise pool is composed of a back-end server running SQL Server and front-end servers abstracted by a hardware load balancer. The Enterprise pool scales by adding multiple front-end servers to the pool. The back-end server can be clustered to achieve high availability of the SQL database.

The higher scalability and availability of the Enterprise pool comes at a higher hardware and software cost. One of the advantages of the Enterprise pool is that the scalability of your pool can grow along with your organization by adding more front-end servers. As an aid to assist you in installing your Enterprise Edition Server, the flowchart available at http://www.ruimaximo.com provides a step-by-step guide.

PART 3

■ ■ ■

Configuring Live Communications Server

So, Live Communications Server 2005 is now installed . . . what do you do next? Well, this part of the book will guide you through configuring users to be able to log in to and use the various features of Live Communications Server. We will then cover the Address Book Service, which is a valuable service for publishing your contact information from Active Directory, and explain how to install and configure it. We will then cover how to configure federation in order to securely work with users in other domains. You might need to securely communicate with partners, suppliers, or customers who don't use Live Communications Server but do use a public instant messaging provider such as MSN, AOL, or Yahoo!. We will explain all about this feature and how to set it up for use in your environment. Lastly, we will cover how to back up and restore your Live Communications Server environment.

CHAPTER 11

■■■

Configuring Users

Live Communications Server 2005 SP1 extends the Active Directory schema of the user class with additional attributes that define new properties. These properties must be configured to enable users for Live Communications. In addition to being enabled for Live Communications, users can be configured for federation, public IM connectivity, remote access, archiving, and remote call control. Only administrators of the RTCDomainUserAdmins group can configure these settings. These properties are configurable using the Active Directory Users and Computers MMC (DSA.MSC) and the Live Communications Server MMC (WRTCSNAP2.MSC) and are scriptable using the Live Communications Server WMI interface. The main difference between the Active Directory Users and Computers MMC and the Live Communications Server MMC is that users can be enabled for Live Communications only from DSA.MSC. Once enabled, they become visible from WRTCSNAP2.MSC.

To enable a user for Live Communications, launch DSA.MSC. Locate the user account, right-click the user, and select Properties (see Figure 11-1).

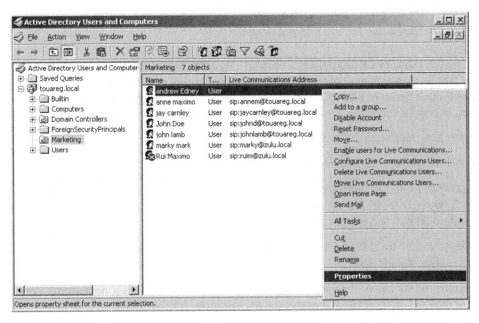

Figure 11-1. *Active Directory Users and Computers user properties*

Navigate to the Live Communications tab, and select the checkbox Enable Live Communications for This User. Once this checkbox is selected, the other settings become configurable (see Figure 11-2).

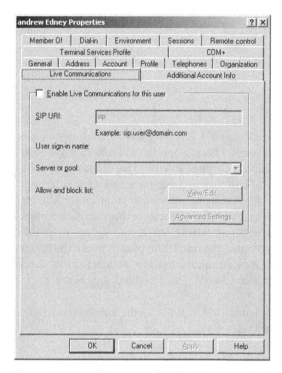

Figure 11-2. *Enabling a user for Live Communications*

Before you can click OK or Apply, you must specify a SIP URI and a home server or pool for the user. The home server or pool option is a drop-down list that makes it easy to select a valid Standard Edition Server or Enterprise pool to assign the user. Enabling a user for Live Communications affects the following Active Directory attributes on the user's object:

msRTCSIP-UserEnabled: TRUE

msRTCSIP-PrimaryUserAddress: A unique SIP URI

msRTCSIP-PrimaryHomeServer: DN (for example, `CN=LC Services,CN=Microsoft,CN=`
`<pool name>,CN=Pools,CN=RTC Service,CN=Microsoft,CN=System,DC=<domain DN>`) of a
Standard Edition Server or Enterprise pool

proxyAddresses: Includes a entry for the user's SIP URI in the format
`sip:ruim@microsoft.com`

Defining the SIP URI of the user can be prone to manual errors. If the administrator does not know the valid SIP domain names that the organization is authoritative for and defines an invalid SIP URI, the user will not be able to sign in.

The list of SIP domains that your deployment of Live Communications Server 2005 SP1 is authoritative for appear on the General tab under Domains, as shown in Figure 11-3.

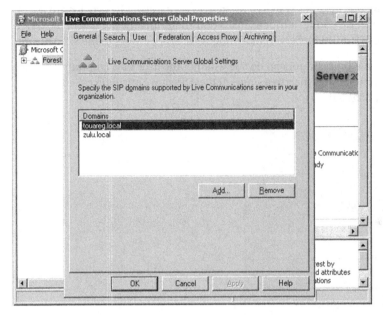

Figure 11-3. *Configuring your organization's SIP domains*

In this example, the SIP domains that one of our deployments is authoritative for are touareg.local and zulu.local. Specifying a SIP URI for the user Andrew Edney of sip: andrew@bogus.com would be invalid. Valid SIP URI options are sip:andrew@touareg.local and sip:andrew@zulu.local. Notice that specifying sip: before the SIP URI is required.

Once these three settings, enabled for Live Communications, SIP URI, and home server or pool, are specified, the user can begin signing in to Live Communications Server from her Office Communicator client. You can configure other settings by clicking the Advanced Settings and Allow and Block List buttons.

Figure 11-4 shows the user properties configurable after clicking Advanced Settings:

Enable Federation: This setting enables the user to add users from other organizations with which you've established an IM and presence federation trust. This setting corresponds to the Active Directory attribute msRTCSIP-FederationEnabled.

Enable Public IM Connectivity: This allows users to communicate over IM with friends, partners, and customers who do not have an Active Directory account in their organization. This setting corresponds to a bit flag (bit #0) in the Active Directory attribute msRTCSIP-OptionFlags.

Enable Remote User Access: This setting allows users to sign in to Live Communications Servers in your organization across your firewalls from anywhere with connectivity to the Internet. This setting corresponds to the Active Directory attribute msRTCSIP-InternetAccessEnabled.

Enable Remote Call Control: This setting makes it possible for the user to control their desktop PBX phone from Communicator. This setting corresponds to a bit flag (bit #4) in the Active Directory attribute msRTCSIP-OptionFlags. You'll notice that two additional fields inside the group box become available when RCC is enabled. These fields are the device URI of the user's PBX phone (attribute: msRTCSIP-Line) and the SIP URI of the CSTA gateway (attribute: msRTCSIP-LineServer) that bridges the PBX network to the SIP network.

Archiving Settings: The administrator can decide whether the user's IM communications should be logged. These settings map to a single Active Directory attribute called msRTCSIP-ArchivingEnabled.

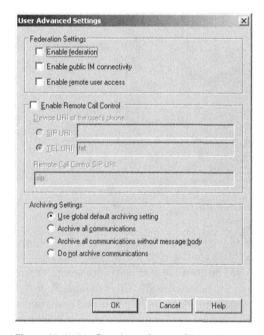

Figure 11-4. *Configuring advanced Live Communications settings*

Configuring these settings manually for one or even five users is fine. Doing this task for ten or more users becomes tedious, but configuring hundreds to thousands or tens of thousands of users becomes unpractical at best. It would be valuable to configure these settings in one place and apply them globally. The only setting that can be configured at a global level is archiving. However, if the administrator changes this configuration at the user level, it overwrites the global-level setting. Figure 11-5 displays this global archiving setting.

Since it's not possible to configure these user settings at a global level, WRTCSNAP2.MSC provides wizards to perform operations on users. These wizards can be applied on a set of users selected by the administrator, an organizational unit (OU), or all users homed on a particular Standard Edition Server or Enterprise pool. These wizards cannot be used on security groups. Live Communications Server offers four wizards to simplify the management of multiple users without going into the property settings of each user.

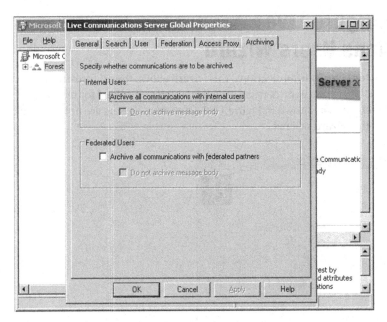

Figure 11-5. *Configuring global archiving settings*

These wizards are as follows:

- Enable Users for Live Communications Wizard

- Configure Live Communications Users Wizard

- Delete Live Communications Users Wizard

- Move Live Communications Users Wizard

Using the Enable Users for Live Communications Wizard

This wizard is available only in DSA.MSC. This wizard can enable one or more users for Live Communications. It configures each user individually by performing the equivalent of selecting the checkbox Enable Live Communications for This User, defining a unique SIP URI for each user, and homing the users on the Standard Edition Server or Enterprise pool selected by the administrator. Since each user must have a unique SIP URI, the wizard uses the user's email address as the SIP URI. If the user is not configured with an email address, the wizard will fail to configure the user.

Using the Configure Live Communications Users Wizard

Once users are configured for Live Communications, this wizard allows the administrator to change their configuration. Using this wizard, users can be enabled or disabled for federation, PIC, remote access, and archiving, as shown in Figure 11-6. Of course, if users are not enabled for Live Communications, the wizard will fail.

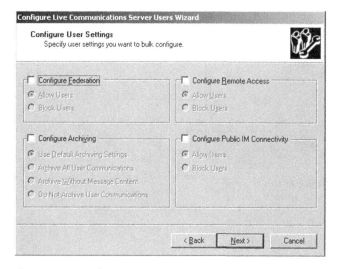

Figure 11-6. *Configure Live Communications Users Wizard*

Using the Delete Live Communications Users Wizard

This wizard is the counterpart to the Enable Users for Live Communications Wizard. Really, it should be called the Disable Live Communications Users Wizard; however, the use of the word *disable* might be confused with disabling users, which prevents users from logging on. Therefore, the design team opted to use the word *delete*. This wizard disables users from Live Communications. After running this wizard successfully, users will no longer be able to sign in to Live Communications Server.

Using the Move Live Communications Users Wizard

This wizard, as its name implies, moves users from their respective home servers or pools to Standard Edition Servers or Enterprise pools selected by the administrator. A possible reason why this move operation might fail for certain users is that the current home server or pool is down or unavailable or the destination server or pool is down. Although a move operation is composed of seven separate atomic steps, a user could become orphaned, which is the state where a user is enabled for Live Communications but is no longer homed on a server or pool. So, how can you determine which users are orphaned? You can locate these orphaned users under the Unassigned Users node in the Live Communications Server MMC, as shown in Figure 11-7.

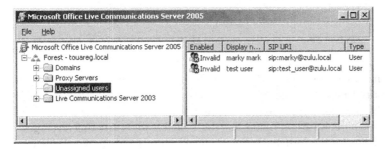

Figure 11-7. *Finding users unassigned to a home server/pool*

If you find orphaned users, you can resolve the user's state in several ways. You can open the user's properties and assign a home server or pool, you can try the move user operation again, or you can disable the user from Live Communications.

When a user is orphaned, all their persistent data (SIP URI, contact group names, contacts, and permissions) is lost. Once they are reenabled on another server or pool, their contact list will be blank when they sign in. If it's important to prevent this loss of data, the administrator can export the user's information using the tool dbimpexp.exe before performing the move operation. This tool is available in the Support subdirectory of the Live Communications Server installation directory. You can export only the user's data instead of the entire database into a file in XML format, which is human readable. You can then use the same tool to import the user's data to their newly assigned server or pool in case the move operation failed and the user became orphaned.

Windows Management Instrumentation (WMI)

If the management tools available with Live Communications Server 2005 SP1 do not meet your administrative needs, Live Communications Server 2005 SP1 provides a WMI interface that offers the flexibility to script tools for your needs. The WMI class to manage these user settings is MSFT_SIPESUserSetting. You can find details about this class on MSDN at http://msdn2.microsoft.com/en-us/library/aa202602(office.11).aspx. The WMI attributes available to the MSFT_SIPESUserSetting class are as follows:

```
class MSFT_SIPESUserSetting
{
  string ArchivingEnabled;
  string DisplayName;
  boolean Enabled;
  boolean EnabledForFederation;
  boolean EnabledForInternetAccess;
  string HomeServerDN;
  [key] string InstanceID;
```

```
    string LineServerURI;
    string LineURI;
    string PrimaryURI;
    boolean PublicNetworkEnabled;
    boolean RemoteCallControlTelephonyEnabled;
    string TargetServerDNIfMoving;
    string UserCategory;
    string UserDN;
};
```

Using this interface makes it possible to script solutions such as enabling and configuring users belonging to a security group or changing the SIP domain name portion of the user's SIP URI without modifying the alias portion or other solutions that you might think of.

LcsSolutions.com offers a freeware command-line tool called LcsUtil.exe that leverages Live Communications Server's WMI to provide more advanced actions, such as the ability to change the SIP domain name of everyone's SIP URI or a select group of users using the /domain option. This option comes in handy in scenarios such as in a merger where you need to migrate users from an acquired company to your Live Communications infrastructure. LcsUtil.exe offers the capability to configure users who are members of a group or container using the /group and /container options. These options complement Live Communications Server's management features. You can find this tool on the Internet at http://lcssolutions.com/Downloads/tabid/58/Default.aspx. LcsUtil.exe provides help when passed the parameter /?. The various options available are as follows:

```
LCS Utility

command-line arguments:
        /users:<name>           - list of users separated by commas
        /group:<name>           - group name
        /container:<name>       - container DN

        Modifiers:
        /append:<string>        - append to username portion of user's SIP URI
        /server:<fqdn>          - server name (fqdn) to home users
        /domain:<string>        - modify domain portion of user's SIP URI

        Operations:
        /lcs:y|n                - enable or disable user for LCS
        /fed:y|n                - enable or disable user for federation
        /remote:y|n             - enable or disable user for remote access
        /pic:y|n                - enable or disable user for public IM
```

Tracking Service Account Passwords

Chapters 12 and 13 discuss that installing a Standard Edition Server or Enterprise pool front-end server creates a service account. By default, the password of this service account will comply with your organization's password policy and will expire. For security reasons, Live Communications Server does not set the service account's password to not expire. Letting the service account password expire before changing it will cause the service to fail. To prevent the service from failing, the administrator can set the password to never expire or track when the password is about to expire and change it before the expiration date.

A handy way to track when a service account such as LCService or CWAService has a password that is about to expire is to use the Account Lockout and Management Tools to troubleshoot account lockouts. ALTools.exe is a set of tools available at http://www.microsoft.com/downloads/details.aspx?FamilyId=7AF2E69C-91F3-4E63-8629-B999ADDE0B9E&displaylang=en. After downloading this toolbox, register the DLL, AcctInfo.dll, by running the following command from a Command Prompt window:

```
Regsvr32 acctinfo.dll
```

The next time you open the administrative tool Active Directory Users and Computers (DSA.MSC) and right-click a user to view its properties, you'll notice two new tabs. Select the Additional Account Info tab (see Figure 11-8). You'll be able to view when the password was last set and, more important, when it will expire. You'll be able to be more proactive by changing the password before it expires, instead of waiting for the Live Communications Server service to fail, which can result in support calls because users are no longer able to sign in to the server with their Communicator clients.

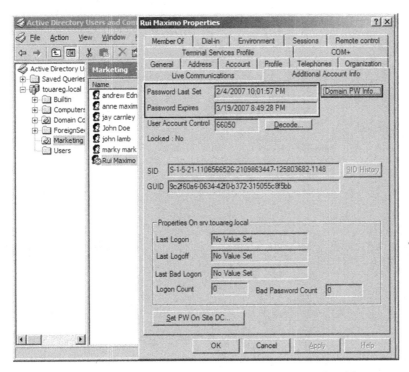

Figure 11-8. *Checking for expired passwords using the AcctInfo add-in to DSA.MSC*

To track how long ago passwords were changed for all accounts on a particular server, use the tool `aloinfo.exe`:

```
aloinfo /expires /server:<name>
```

This gives you an easy way to determine how old each account's password is.

Summary

Live Communications Server 2005 SP1 extends the Active Directory schema of the user class with additional attributes that define new properties. To make configuring multiple users at the same time simpler, wizards available in the Active Directory Users and Computers MMC and the Live Communications Server MMC provide an administrative experience to perform these tasks. For more complex automation tasks that are specific to your organization, Live Communications Server provides a WMI interface that can be called from Windows applications and scripts for further customization. You can also conveniently check for expired passwords and additional configuration solutions using `LcsUtil.exe`, a command-line tool provided by LcsSolutions.com.

CHAPTER 12

■ ■ ■

Address Book Service

The Address Book Service is a new feature that was introduced with Live Communications Server 2005 SP1. It was introduced to provide two important functions: to provide global address list information from your Active Directory to Office Communicator 2005 and to perform phone number normalization for Office Communicator telephony integration.

So what does this actually mean to you and your organization?

Well, the main idea behind the Address Book Service is to have a single route into Active Directory that provides a local copy of the address list so that your network and your Active Directory do not become overrun with requests from Office Communicator clients for global address list information. You might not think this is a real problem if you have a small number of users, but imagine if you had thousands or tens of thousands of users.

"How does it work?" you ask. Well, the Address Book Service, as it sounds, is a Windows service that runs daily, retrieving contact information from a Live Communications Server Standard Edition MSDE database or an Enterprise Edition SQL Server database and creating a local copy of that information within an NTFS folder that is then accessible by the client. And again, to reduce the amount of bandwidth that is used, after a full copy of the contact information is created, the deltas are captured, and on top of this the files are compressed to keep the amount of disk space used to a minimum.

The Address Book Service has three components:

- The Address Book Service

- The service account for the Address Book Service

- The Address Book file store

With regard to the phone number normalization, the Address Book Service can normalize any phone numbers that are stored in Active Directory user and contact objects. Microsoft recommends converting phone numbers to the E.164 international standard for compatibility, but this is not a Communicator requirement. E.164 is an ITU-T recommendation that defines the international public telecommunication numbering plan used in phone and some data networks. It also defines the format of those telephone numbers. E.164 numbers can have a maximum of 15 digits and are usually written with a + prefix. The Address Book Service contains two standard normalization rules that can be used to normalize the entries within Active Directory; however, the preferred method is actually to follow the standard within Active Directory. If you want to normalize phone numbers within Active Directory, you can use the Phone Normalization utility that ships with the Live Communications Server 2005 SP1 Resource Kit.

Address Book Files

The Address Book Service is a Windows service called ABServer, with its display name being Microsoft Office Live Communication Server 2005 Address Book Service.

The default setting for the Address Book Service is to run at 1:30 a.m. each night. When the service starts, it connects to the RTC SQL table and reads the user and contact data. It then creates a set of data files that are stored in a shared directory. These data files include the following:

- A full file containing all contacts

- The deltas between the current full file and the previous full file

These data files are kept for 30 days, and this setting cannot be changed. So at the end of the 30-day period, there will be 30 full data files and 435 delta files—465 files total. If you look in the Address Book file store, you will see that the files beginning with *F* are the full files and the ones beginning with *D* are the deltas.

The Address Book file store can be on the local server, a SAN, or anywhere else as long as the Address Book Service and the clients can access it. Because the data is compressed, the storage requirements are minimal. Microsoft has published some guidelines for file sizes and number of users, as shown in Table 12-1. (These are just guidelines and are not necessarily the same for your environment.) Also, a single Address Book Service can support up to 500,000 users and contacts from Active Directory.

Table 12-1. *Address Book File Store Sizing Guidelines*

Number of Users	Full File Average Size
15,000	1.526 MB
60,000	6.098 MB
100,000	10.155 MB
400,000	40.623 MB

When Communicator logs on to either a Live Communications Server 2005 Standard Edition Server or an Enterprise pool, it will receive the URL to the Address Book file store and will then connect to that file store and download either a full copy of the Address Book file if it does not have one or the delta files for each day since the last full file (up to a maximum of 30 days at which point it will attempt to download a full copy again). Figure 12-1 shows the process in more detail.

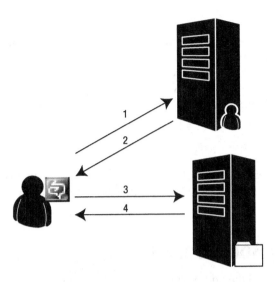

Figure 12-1. *The Address Book Service download process in Communicator*

Here's the process:

1. Communicator logs on to either a Live Communications Server 2005 SP1 Standard Edition Server or an Enterprise pool.

2. Communicator then receives the URL of the Address Book file store.

3. Communicator then connects to the Address Book file store.

4. Communicator then downloads either the full data file or the relevant delta files.

The Address Book file store URL is a standard file URL (file://server/share) and points to the Address Book file store that contains all the files. If you want remote users, branch office users, or remote sites to access the Address Book file store, then you will need to use IIS 6.0 to publish the file store via HTTP (or HTTPS if you want it secured). This obviously requires that you have an IIS 6.0 server available and also certificates installed and configured. This chapter will walk you through setting up and configuring the Address Book Service and publishing to a file store for internal users only. If you want to see more information about how to set up and configure remote access, then take a look at Microsoft Office Live Communications Server 2005's Address Book Service Planning and Deployment Guide, which you can download from http://www.microsoft.com/downloads/details.aspx?FamilyId= 80C7A511-36B4-4E34-9330-88922C7BA72B&displaylang=en.

Supported Topologies

You can install the Address Book Service on either a Live Communications Server 2005 Standard Edition Server or an Enterprise pool, as we have already mentioned. You can deploy it in any of the supported Active Directory topologies, such as the following:

- A single forest

- A resource forest

- A central forest

You can also install the Address Book Service on a dedicated server. If you want to do this, you will need to install a Live Communications Server 2005 SP1 Standard Edition Server followed by the Address Book Service.

Installing the Address Book Service

You need to follow a number of steps to install the Address Book Service. These steps are the same for either Live Communications Server 2005 Standard Edition or Enterprise Edition servers.

1. On the server you want to install the Address Book Service on, ensure you are logged in as a member of the Administrators group. If you are planning on activating the Address Book Service after installation (and these steps assume you are), you will also need to ensure that account is a member of both the Domain Admins group and also the RTC-DomainServerAdmins group.

2. Run ABSSETUP.EXE from the \SETUP\I386 folder from the Live Communications Server 2005 CD or from a different location if you stored the installation files online to launch the Microsoft Office Live Communications Server 2005 Address Book Service Deployment Tool window.

3. Click Install Files for Address Book Service, as shown in Figure 12-2.

4. On the Welcome to the Setup Wizard for Live Communications Address Book Service screen, click Next to continue (as shown in Figure 12-3).

5. Read the license agreement, accept the terms in the license agreement, and click Next to continue.

6. Choose the destination location of the files either by accepting the default location or by clicking Change and choosing a location yourself. Then click Next to continue.

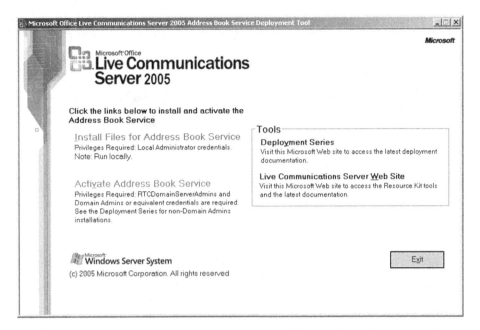

Figure 12-2. *The Live Communications Server 2005 Address Book Deployment Tool window*

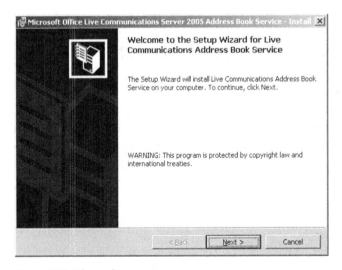

Figure 12-3. *The welcome screen*

7. On the Ready to Install the Program screen, you can confirm the settings (as shown in Figure 12-4). If the settings are incorrect, click Back to make any changes. Click Install to start the installation process.

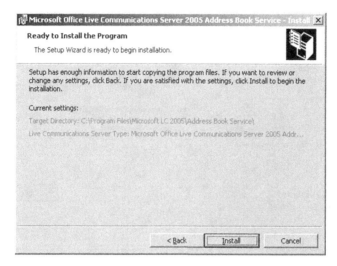

Figure 12-4. *Ready to install*

8. At the end of the installation process, click Finish.

Activating the Address Book Service

The next step in the process is to activate the Address Book Service, as follows:

1. You will then be offered the opportunity to activate the service (as shown in Figure 12-5). If you want to active the service now, click Yes. Otherwise, you can do it later by choosing the Activate Address Book Service option from the Deployment Tool window.

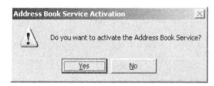

Figure 12-5. *Starting the activation sequence*

2. On the Welcome to the Activate Address Book Service Wizard screen, click Next to start the wizard, as shown in Figure 12-6. Remember, to perform this task, you need to be a member of both the Domain Admins group and the RTCDomainServerAdmins group.

Figure 12-6. *The Welcome to the Activate Address Book Service Wizard screen*

3. Before going any further with the Address Book Service activation, you will need to create the NTFS folder that you want to use as the Address Book file store and share it out, assuming you have not done so already. The Address Book file store can be located anywhere as long as it is shared out with the correct permissions for Office Communicator clients to be able to gain access to it.

4. On the Select Location for File Share screen, enter the UNC share name of the Address Book file store you created and shared in step 3, as shown in Figure 12-7. Then click Next to continue.

5. Select the pool in which you want to activate the service from the drop-down list, as shown in Figure 12-8, and then click Next to continue.

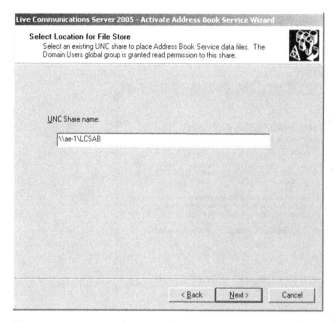

Figure 12-7. *Entering the UNC share name to the Address Book file store*

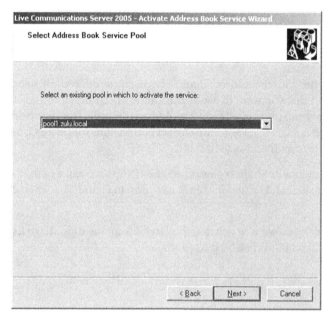

Figure 12-8. *Selecting the pool in which to activate the Address Book Service*

6. You now have the option to either create a new service account, which by default is called LCABService, or use an existing account, as shown in Figure 12-9. We recommend you create a new service account and, unless your organizational naming policy prohibits its use, leave the default account name as it is displayed. Enter the password and confirm it; then click the Next button.

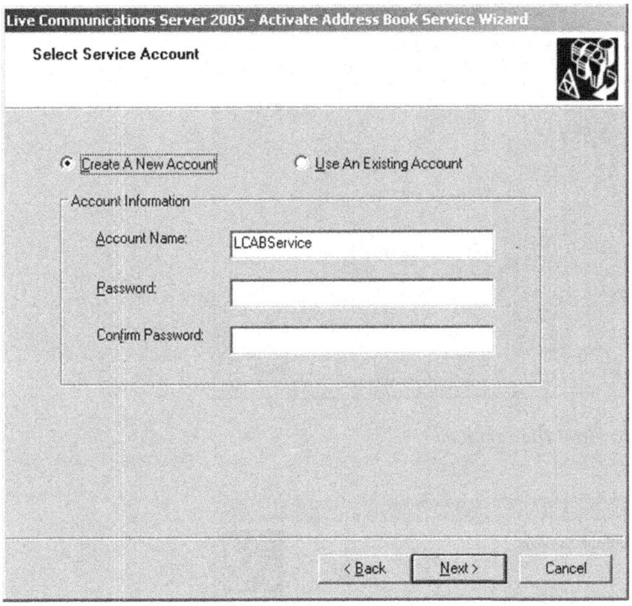

Figure 12-9. *Creating or selecting the Address Book Service account*

7. By default, the service will be started (or attempted to be started) at the end of the process. If for whatever reason you do not want this to happen, just clear the Start the Service After Activation check box, as shown in Figure 12-10. Click Next to continue.

8. The next screen allows you to confirm all your settings, as shown in Figure 12-11. If you need to change anything, click Back, and make the relevant changes. Click Next to continue.

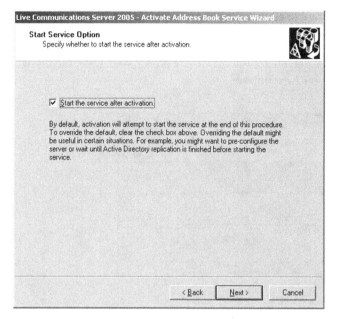

Figure 12-10. *Option to start the service*

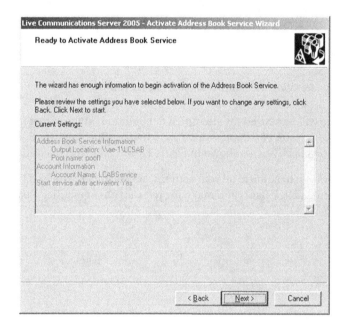

Figure 12-11. *Confirming your settings and selections*

9. The Address Book Service will then be activated, and you should see the successful completion screen, as shown in Figure 12-12.

10. Click the View Log button to review all the actions that took place, as shown in Figure 12-13.

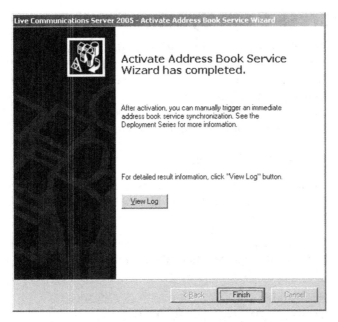

Figure 12-12. *Address Book Service activation completed successfully*

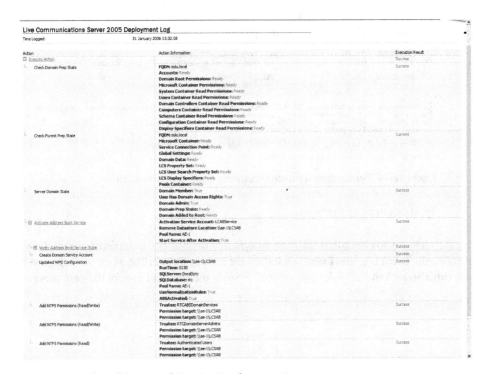

Figure 12-13. *The Address Book Service Deployment Log*

11. Click Finish on the wizard screen and then Exit in the Deployment Tool window.

Forcing an Address Book Synchronization

As mentioned, the Address Book Service will perform synchronization every night at 1:30 a.m. The first synchronization after you have installed and activated the service will take place at 1:30 a.m. the following night, so rather than wait for it to see whether the service is running as expected, you can perform a manual synchronization.

Unfortunately, there is no nice whizzy graphical interface for performing a manual synchronization—you need to perform it from the command prompt:

1. Click Start ➤ Run, and type **CMD** in the Open box.

2. Change the directory path to the location of the Address Book Service files; if you accepted the default location, it will be C:\Program Files\Microsoft LC 2005\ Address Book Service.

3. Type **abserver –syncnow** (as shown in Figure 12-14). This will pause the ABServer service and start it again, which will force a manual synchronization.

```
C:\WINDOWS\system32\cmd.exe                                                    _ |□| x|
C:\Program Files\Microsoft LC 2005\Address Book Service>dir
 Volume in drive C has no label.
 Volume Serial Number is ECEF-3281

 Directory of C:\Program Files\Microsoft LC 2005\Address Book Service

31/01/2007  16:22    <DIR>          .
31/01/2007  16:22    <DIR>          ..
24/04/2005  23:33           101,064 ABServer.exe
02/04/2005  08:21             3,681 Generic_Phone_Number_Normalization_Rules.txt
24/04/2005  23:02           348,160 msvcr71.dll
02/04/2005  08:21             2,496 Sample_Company_Phone_Number_Normalization_Ru
les.txt
24/04/2005  23:32            20,680 UrtHelper.dll
               5 File(s)        476,081 bytes
               2 Dir(s)  107,982,483,456 bytes free

C:\Program Files\Microsoft LC 2005\Address Book Service>abserver -syncnow
Pausing 'ABServer' service....paused successfully.
Continuing 'ABServer' service....continued successfully.
Synchronization pass initiated.

C:\Program Files\Microsoft LC 2005\Address Book Service>
```

Figure 12-14. *Performing a manual Address Book synchronization*

4. Type **exit** to close the window.

A quick way to check that the manual synchronization has completed successfully is to examine the Event Log. The Event Log ID you are looking for is 21010, as shown in Figure 12-15. You can also look in the folder you created to store the files and ensure they are there.

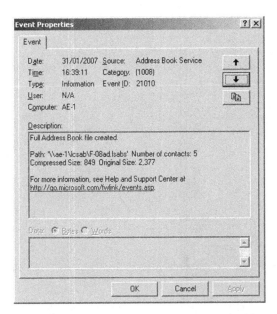

Figure 12-15. *Event Viewer confirmation of Address Book creation*

Configuring Communicator

The last step in the process is to configure Communicator to connect to and download the newly created Address Book files in order to be able to search and use them. The simplest way of doing this is to add the Address Book URL to the Standard Edition Server or the Enterprise pool. This way when the Communicator client logs into the Live Communication Server, it is directed to the Address Book file store and will download either a full copy of the Address Book or the relevant delta files, depending on what is needed.

The following steps are the process for adding the Address Book URL to an Enterprise pool:

1. Launch the Microsoft Office Live Communications Server 2005 administration tool.

2. Expand your Forest node, expand the Domains node, and then expand your domain.

3. Expand the Live Communications Servers and Pools node, and select the pool you want to administer.

4. Right-click the pool, and select Properties.

5. Click the Address Book tab, as shown in Figure 12-16.

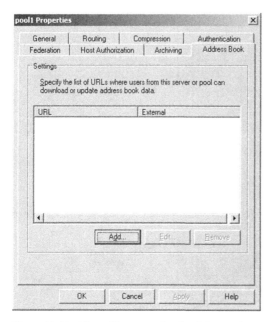

Figure 12-16. *The Address Book tab of the pool*

6. Click the Add button.

7. Enter the URL of the Address Book file store share you created, as shown in Figure 12-17. An important thing to note here is that you *must* type the word **file:** before the share name; otherwise, it will not work. The documentation says to just enter the share name, but if you do this, the Communicator download will fail every time with an error about the administrator not having configured the feature.

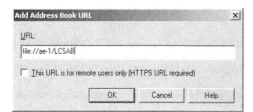

Figure 12-17. *Adding the Address Book file store URL*

8. If the file store URL is only for internal and nonremote users, make sure you uncheck the This URL Is for Remote Users Only (HTTPS URL Required) check box.

9. Click OK to close the Properties dialog box.

If you look at the Enterprise Pool information pane now, you will see that the URL is showing in the Address Book Links section and a check mark shows that it is an internal URL, as shown in Figure 12-18.

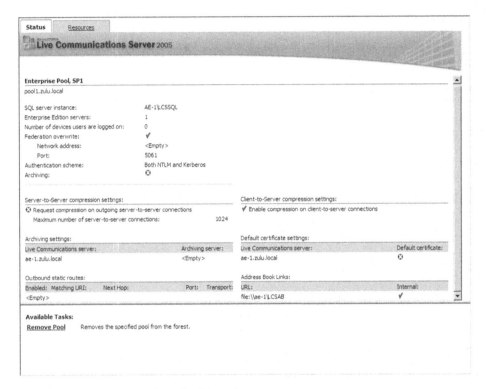

Figure 12-18. *The Enterprise Pool information pane*

Adding Users

And that's it—everything should now been installed, activated, and configured. The only thing left to do is to log in to Communicator and search for a user who is not in your contact list. You might notice that it takes slightly longer to log in now; this is because the Address Book is downloading.

After you have logged in, enter the name of someone in the Find box who is not in your contact list. That someone should now appear listed, and you will have the option to contact them, see whether they are online, and use all the other usual features of Communicator. If you hover over the person's name, you will see additional information, as shown in Figure 12-19. As you can see from this example, Rui is offline, but the contact information is taken from the corporate Address Book.

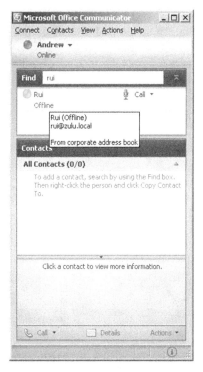

Figure 12-19. *Searching for a user in the corporate Address Book*

Fixing Problems with the Download

Sometimes you might have problems downloading the Address Book to Communicator. These problems could be anything from network issues to the service being unavailable. Communicator will try the download again with time intervals that double for each subsequent failure (for example, one minute, two minutes, four minutes . . . all the way to a maximum of 64 minutes). If any data was downloaded, it is discarded, and a clean copy is then attempted to be downloaded.

If there is a problem, you will notice a new icon that appears at the bottom of the Communicator box, as shown in Figure 12-20.

If you click the icon, you will see information about that error, as shown in Figure 12-21. Use this information to help troubleshoot and correct the error. In this example, the Address Book URL was incorrect, so Communicator could not find or download the Address Book.

Figure 12-20. *Address Book problem in Communicator*

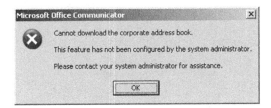

Figure 12-21. *An Address Book download error*

Summary

As you read in this chapter, the Address Book Service is a useful addition to your Live Communications Server 2005 environment. It enables you to provide local copies of the global address list and reduce the amount of unnecessary network traffic within your environment. You also learned how install and configure it and how to enable Communicator to use the Address Book Service. You also learned how to deal with a common problem with the Address Book Service—download problems.

CHAPTER 13

Configuring Federation

Federation is a feature introduced in Live Communications Server 2005 SP1 that allows users from one organization to communicate with users from another organization. Federated users can view each other's presence information and initiate instant messages once they mutually add each other to their contact lists. This provides the benefit of not having to use a different IM client to interoperate. Users from different organizations maintain their corporate identity while communicating securely. Federating with other companies assumes that those organizations also have Live Communications Server 2005 SP1 deployed and that their infrastructure is configured for federation.

From a user perspective, before a user can communicate over IM with a user from a different organization, the user needs to add the federated user as a contact. The user can do this by running the Add a Contact Wizard. Since this contact is from a different organization, it cannot be searched in Active Directory. Users can discover each other's SIP URI by exchanging business cards, for example. Most organizations make the user's SIP URI the same as the user's email address for simplicity. Once added to the contact list, users can view their federated contacts' presence status and initiate IMs with them.

Introducing Federation

Live Communications Server 2005 SP1 supports various flavors of federation. Deciding which one is appropriate will often require input from your project manager because you need to consider your business's needs. The different variations of federation are as follows:

- Direct federation

- Enhanced federation

- Clearinghouse

- Default route

Direct federation provides the greatest level of control. Your organization decides which companies to federate with and establishes a direct federation upon mutual agreement with each individual company. This type of federation is manually intensive. Organizations must exchange root certificate authorities if using private Certificate Authorities (CAs) and FQDNs of their respective Access Proxy servers. The administrator must configure the Access Proxy servers to specifically federate with each specific organization. Figure 13-1 illustrates this type of federation.

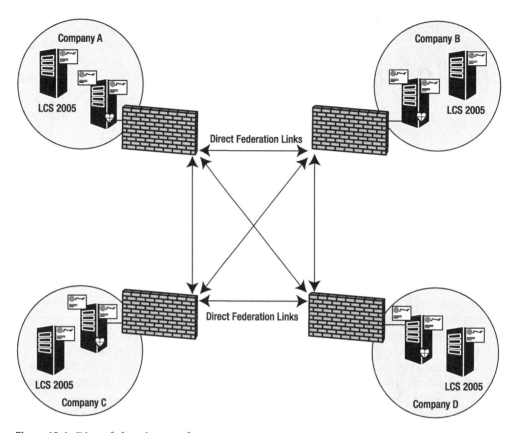

Figure 13-1. *Direct federation topology*

Explicitly establishing a direct federation with each company your organization partners with is time-consuming and tedious. Users have to wait until the administrator configures the Access Proxy servers to federate with a specific company before they can initiate IM conversations with those users. The list of companies with direct federation trust can quickly grow quite large, which makes it difficult to maintain and keep up-to-date. For example, if company A changes the FQDN of its Access Proxy, it must notify all the other companies it has a direct federation with of this change; otherwise, direct federation with these companies will fail.

Companies that do not have policy restrictions preventing employees from communicating with users from other organizations will find enhanced federation a more practical option. This is similar to how users today can send email to anyone outside the organization.

Enhanced federation automates the discovery process of locating (that is, resolving the address) the Access Proxy servers that are authoritative for a SIP domain. You can accomplish this through DNS publishing. Organizations that publish an external DNS SRV record for the SIP domain it is authoritative for in the form _sipfederationtls._tcp.<sip domain> make it possible for other organizations to resolve where to route SIP traffic automatically. By leveraging DNS, no manual configuration is required to route IMs outside the organization.

Organizations using enhanced federation have the option to restrict IM communications with specific companies. This restriction is specified in the Block list. However, this Block list can grow large if the organization has a policy to limit communications to only those companies belonging to a specific industry (such as financial, medical, and so on) or are members of a partnership or clearance level (such as the military). Such a Block list must be maintained and kept updated by the administrator of the Access Proxy servers every time a new SIP domain is published by adding it to the Access Proxy's Block list. This quickly becomes a full-time job! In these cases, enhanced federation is probably not the right choice. Using a *clearinghouse* is better suited for companies that want to allow IM communications with only those members of a professional association. When the clearinghouse accepts a new member, all existing member companies can immediately start IM conversations with users of the new entrant organization without further configuration by the existing member companies. The clearinghouse is responsible for approving membership and maintaining the membership roster. Figure 13-2 illustrates this scenario.

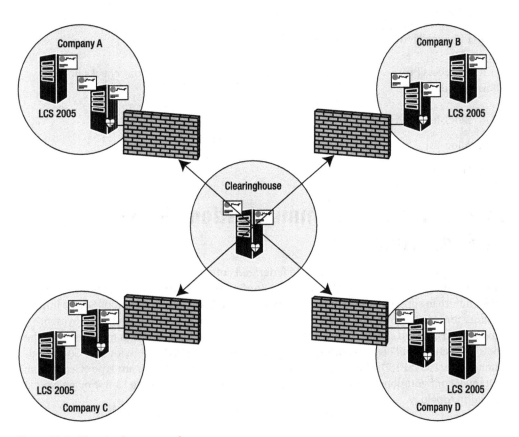

Figure 13-2. *Clearinghouse topology*

The last federation option is configuring your Access Proxy servers with a *default route*. When the Access Proxy attempts to resolve the SIP domain name in the To URI, it first checks the Block list before checking the Allow list. If no match is found, then the Access Proxy checks the enhanced federation partner list. If still no match is found and enhanced federation is not configured, the Access Proxy routes the SIP message to the default route, assuming one is specified. The Access Proxy MMC enforces this restriction imposed when configuring an Access Proxy for different federation types: if an Access Proxy is configured for enhanced federation, it cannot be simultaneously configured with a default route or act as a clearinghouse.

When resolving the destination of an outgoing SIP message to a federated contact, the Access Proxy performs validation differently depending on the type of federation configured.

If the Access Proxy is configured for enhanced federation, the Access Proxy checks in the following order:

1. Block list

2. Allow list

3. Enhanced federation partner list

If the Access Proxy is configured with a default route, the Access Proxy checks in the following order:

1. Block list

2. Allow list

3. Default route

Configuring Live Communications Server for Federation

Before users in your organization can add federated contacts to their contact lists and start communicating with them over IM, you must configure the Live Communications Server infrastructure to support this scenario. Configuring your Live Communications Server infrastructure for federation can be fraught with configuration errors. The series of deployment steps is nontrivial and can introduce problems that later become difficult to troubleshoot. The following sections will help you through the perils of deploying federation for Live Communications Server 2005 SP1. The following configuration steps are applicable for any type of federation; we'll cover configurations specific to the type of federation desired. Figure 13-3 shows a typical federation topology.

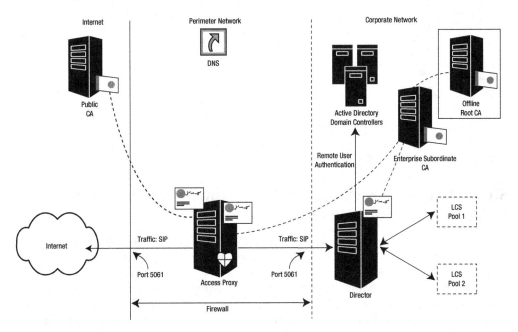

Figure 13-3. *Federation topology*

Step 1: Install an Access Proxy on a Server Machine with Two Network Interfaces

Select a physical server with hardware specifications that meet or exceed the minimum requirements specified for an Access Proxy. The physical server must have two NICs, with one NIC connected to the internal network and the other NIC connected to the external network (in other words, the Internet).

Note If you're planning to deploy more than one Access Proxy for redundancy and high availability, you must deploy a hardware load balancer in front of both ends of the Access Proxy servers. Logically, Figure 13-4 shows how it would look.

Instead of specifying the FQDN of the Access Proxy NICs in the following steps, you should specify the virtual IP address (VIP) of the hardware load balancer corresponding to the NIC.

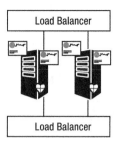

Figure 13-4. *Bank of Access Proxy servers*

Step 2: Request a Server Certificate from Your Private CA for the Private Network Interface

Each NIC of the Access Proxy must be associated with a certificate. A Server Authentication certificate is needed for the private network interface so internal Office Communications Servers (that is, the Directors) connecting to that interface can verify the Access Proxy's identity. By verifying the certificate's issuing authority is a trusted entity, the Director(s) can trust that it is not connecting to a rogue Access Proxy. To make sure that the certificate the Access Proxy presents to the Director was properly issued to the Access Proxy, the Director verifies that the FQDN specified in the certificate matches the FQDN of the internal network interface.

If your organization uses an internal CA, then the certificate for the private NIC can be issued from this CA. This certificate must be a Server Authentication certificate.

Note If you're deploying multiple Access Proxy servers in a bank configuration abstracted by a hardware load balancer, then the certificate should be marked as exportable. By marking the certificate's private key as exportable, you can use the same certificate and corresponding private key across the Access Proxy servers in that bank. Instead of specifying the FQDN of the Access Proxy when requesting the certificate, you must specify the FQDN of the VIP.

We'll now go through the steps for requesting this certificate from Microsoft's Certificate Server. These instructions use the Web Server Certificate Wizard to request the certificate from your internal CA. Since the Access Proxy is deployed in your network perimeter, it is unlikely that it will have network access to your internal CA. Therefore, you need to run these steps from a server within your organization with access to your private network to request this certificate.

From a computer with Internet Information Services (IIS) installed, click Start, right-click My Computer, and select Manage. This will launch the Local Computer Management MMC. Expand the Services and Applications node in the scope pane. Expand the IIS Manager node. Alternatively, you can find the IIS Manager under the Administrative Tools folder. Expand the Web Sites node. Right-click the Default Web Site node, and select Properties, as shown in Figure 13-5. Any website without a certificate already installed will do the trick. We just know this node will always exist in any IIS installation.

Select the Directory Security tab from the property page, as shown in Figure 13-6. Click the Server Certificate button to launch the Web Server Certificate Wizard, as shown in Figure 13-7.

■**Note** Although the welcome page of the wizard refers to itself as the Web Server Certificate Wizard, the title bars of subsequent pages say IIS Certificate Wizard.

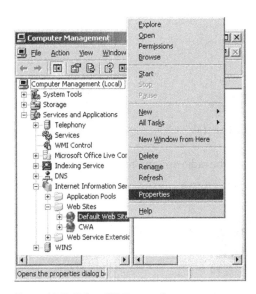

Figure 13-5. *Select IIS Properties*

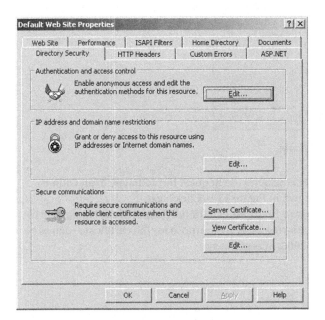

Figure 13-6. *Launching the Web Server Certificate Wizard*

Figure 13-7. *Working with the Web Server Certificate Wizard*

After passing the welcome page of the wizard, leave the radio option Create a New Certificate selected, as shown in Figure 13-8. Click Next.

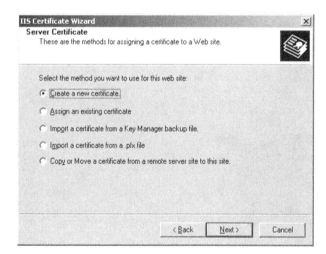

Figure 13-8. *Wizard: creating a new certificate*

On the next page of the wizard, select the Send the Request Immediately to an Online Certificate Authority radio option, as shown in Figure 13-9. Click Next.

On the following page, shown in Figure 13-10, enter a friendly name in the Name field to make it easily recognizable. Best practice is to specify the purpose for the certificate such as by entering **Live Communications Server 2005, Access Proxy**.

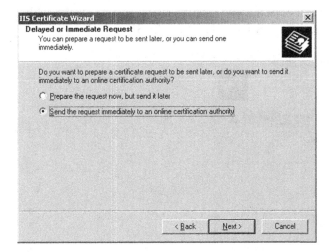

Figure 13-9. *Wizard: sending the certificate request to the CA*

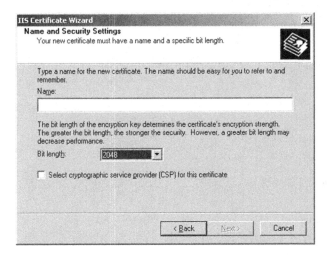

Figure 13-10. *Wizard: entering a friendly name*

On the page shown in Figure 13-11, specify your organization name and organization unit.

■**Note** If deploying a bank of Access Proxy servers, you should enter the FQDN of the VIP for the exterior hardware load balancer facing the extranet (in other words, the Internet), as depicted in Figure 13-12.

It is critical to specify the correct FQDN on the next page. You must enter the FQDN of your Access Proxy in the Common Name field, as shown in Figure 13-13.

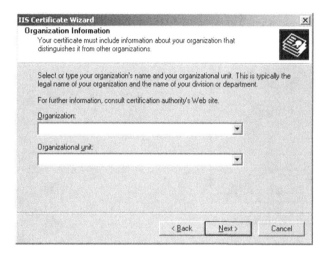

Figure 13-11. *Wizard: entering organization information*

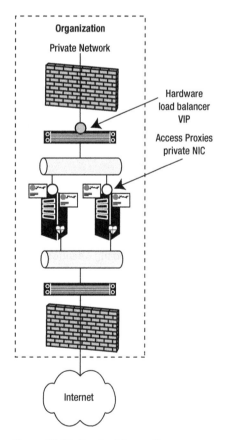

Figure 13-12. *Bank of Access Proxy servers private interface*

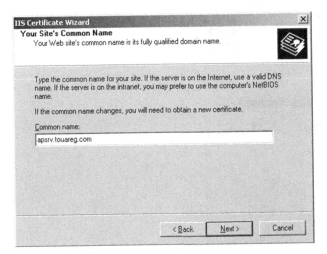

Figure 13-13. *Wizard: entering a certificate common name*

Specify port 5061 on the next page, as shown in Figure 13-14.

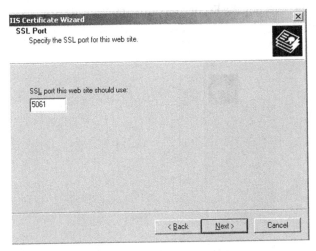

Figure 13-14. *Wizard: entering port information*

The advantage of using the Web Server Certificate Wizard to request a certificate for your Access Proxy is that you do not need to figure out how to contact your Enterprise CA. Certainly, this certificate could be requested via the web enrollment pages, but it would require knowing what the URL is to connect to it if you don't already know it. The Web Server Certificate Wizard automatically discovers the Enterprise CAs available in your organization that can issue a Server Authentication certificate, which you need to select, as indicated in Figure 13-15.

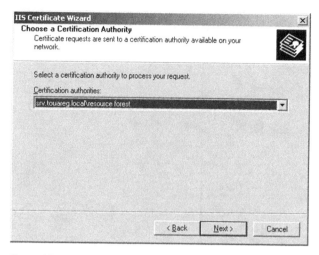

Figure 13-15. *Wizard: selecting the CA*

Complete the wizard to request the certificate.

Once the certificate is generated, you'll need to export it to the Access Proxy. Rerun the Web Server Certificate Wizard, this time selecting the Export the Current Certificate to a .pfx File option, as shown in Figure 13-16.

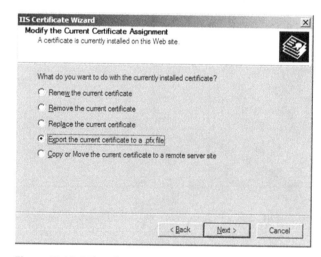

Figure 13-16. *Wizard: exporting the issued certificate*

Specify where to save the .pfx file, as shown in Figure 13-17. This file will contain both the certificate and its associated private key.

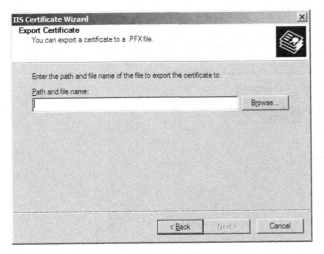

Figure 13-17. *Wizard: exporting the file location*

Since this file will contain the certificate's private key, the wizard will prompt you to specify a password to protect the file, as shown in Figure 13-18.

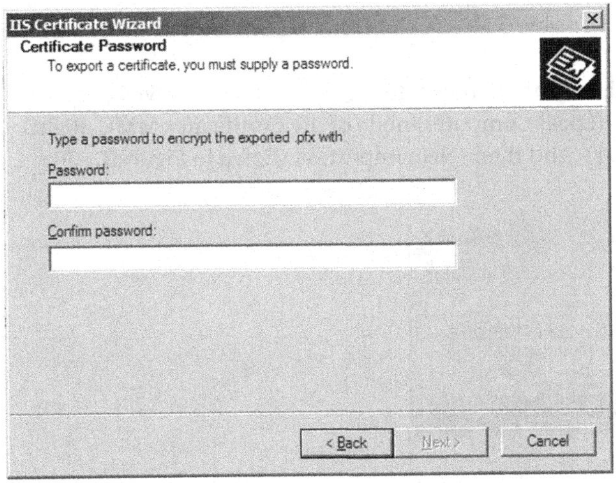

Figure 13-18. *Wizard: password protecting the private key*

Complete the wizard. Next, copy the .pfx file to your Access Proxy, and install it in the local computer's Personal store, as instructed next.

From the Access Proxy, click Start ➤ Run, and type **MMC**. Select File and Add/Remove Snap-in. Click the Add button. Find and select the Certificates snap-in from the available list, and click Add. The snap-in will prompt for the account to use. Select Computer Account since this is the account the Access Proxy uses, as shown in Figure 13-19.

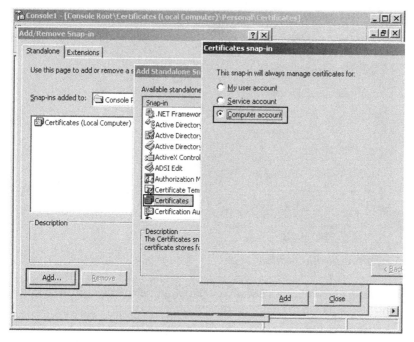

Figure 13-19. *Certificate Manager*

After clicking Next and OK multiple times to return to the main window, navigate to the Personal node under the Certificates (Local Computer) node of the Certificates MMC. Right-click the Personal node, select All Tasks, and then select Import, as shown in Figure 13-20.

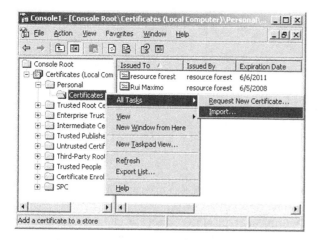

Figure 13-20. *Importing the issued certificate to the local computer*

This will launch the Certificate Import Wizard, as shown in Figure 13-21.

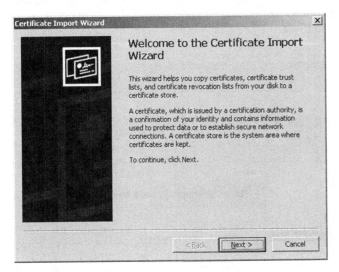

Figure 13-21. *Certificate Import Wizard*

Provide the path to the *.pfx file created from the Certificate Export Wizard to import the certificate to the Access Proxy's local computer Personal store.

Step 3: Configure the Private Interface of the Access Proxy with Your Certificate

In this step, the Access Proxy's private interface is configured. You configure these settings by navigating to the Private tab of the Access Proxy's property page, as shown in Figure 13-22. You must specify the IP address of the NIC connected to the corporate private network, and you must associate the certificate requested in step 2 to this interface. Leave the listening port number configured at 5061. This is the standard port number for SIP.

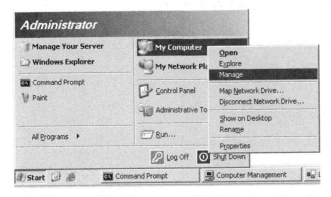

Figure 13-22. *Access Proxy's private NIC configuration*

The Access Proxy's property page is accessible by right-clicking My Computer and selecting Manager, as shown in Figure 13-23. Once the Computer Management MMC appears, navigate to the Microsoft Office Live Communications Server 2005 node. Right-click this node, and select Properties, as shown in Figure 13-24.

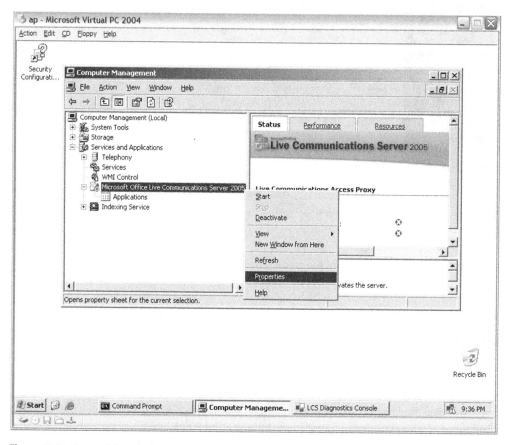

Figure 13-23. *Launching the local computer's Management Console*

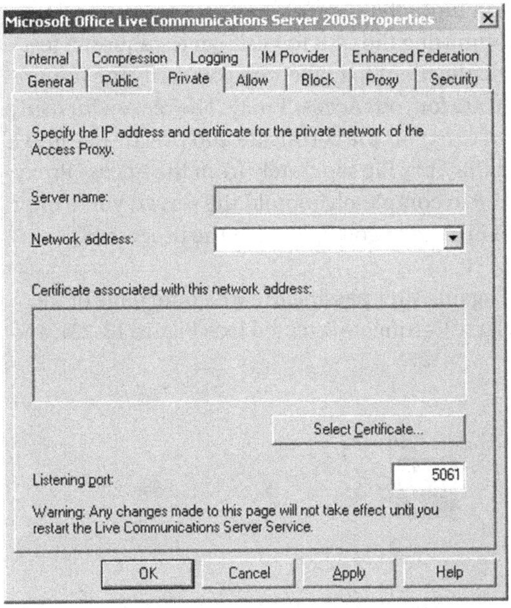

Figure 13-24. *Accessing the management Access Proxy's properties*

Step 4: Request a Server Authentication Certificate from a Public CA for the Public Network Interface

It's recommended that the certificate for the public NIC be issued by a public (also referred to as an *external* or *third-party*) CA. A public CA is a CA that issues certificates to the public. VeriSign, Entrust, and GeoTrust are examples of companies that offer this type of service. You'll need to request a certificate with both Server and Client Authentication EKUs for the public interface of your Access Proxy. This type of certificate is commonly referred to an *SSL certificate*.

The following link by VeriSign provides directions for generating the certificate-signing request (CSR) necessary before submitting the certificate request to VeriSign: http:// www.verisign.com/support/ssl-certificates-support/page_dev020182.html. We'll walk you through the process of generating a CSR in this section. Alternatively, the Live Communications Server 2005 Resource Kit also provides a tool called LcsCertUtil.exe, which is similar in function to the Web Server Certificate Wizard for generating a CSR and configuring your Access Proxy with the generated certificate. If you plan to support more than one SIP domain namespace (for example, zulu.com, touareg.com, nomad.com), then it's best to use the LcsCertUtil.exe tool because the Web Server Certificate Wizard will not allow you to specify multiple SIP domains in the subject alternative name (SAN), whereas the LcsCertUtil.exe tool will. For an understanding of how Live Communications Server 2005 SP1 uses SANs in Access Proxy certificates, please refer to Chapter 10.

The instructions in this section will walk you through the process of generating the CSR using the Web Server Certificate Wizard and submitting the CSR to VeriSign to request a test certificate. You can use this certificate in a lab deployment to make sure you verify the requirements needed before purchasing the real certificate for your Access Proxy. The reason for using the Web Server Certificate Wizard is to be forced to export the certificate and private key into a .pfx file. It's recommended that you safeguard this .pfx file separately from the Access Proxy. In a disaster situation where you might be forced to completely rebuild the server, you'll only need to import the certificate from the .pfx file instead of going through the process of requesting new certificates.

Launch the Web Server Certificate Wizard again. After passing the welcome page of the wizard, leave the default radio option Create a New Certificate selected (see Figure 13-25), and click Next.

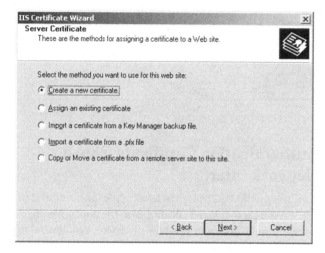

Figure 13-25. *Creating a certificate*

On the next page of the wizard, leave the default radio option Prepare the Request Now, but Send It Later selected (as shown in Figure 13-26), and click Next.

On the page shown in Figure 13-27, enter a friendly name in the Name field to make it easily recognizable. Best practice is to specify the purpose for the certificate such as by entering **Live Communications Server 2005, Access Proxy**.

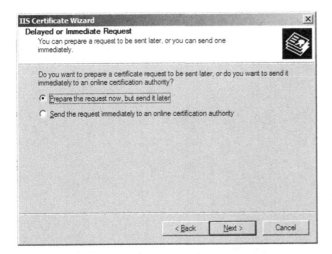

Figure 13-26. *Submitting the certificate request to CA*

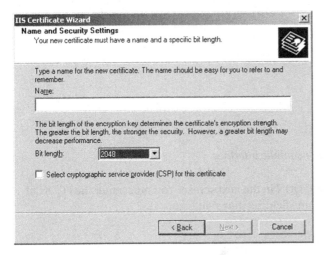

Figure 13-27. *Specifying a friendly name for your certificate*

■**Note** If deploying a bank of Access Proxy servers, you should enter the FQDN of the VIP for the exterior hardware load balancer facing the extranet (that is, the Internet), as depicted in Figure 13-28.

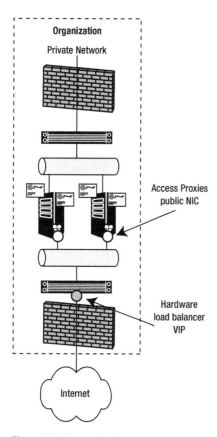

Figure 13-28. *Bank of Access Proxy servers public interface*

It is critical to specify the correct FQDN in the next screen. You must enter the FQDN of your Access Proxy in the Common Name field, as shown in Figure 13-29.

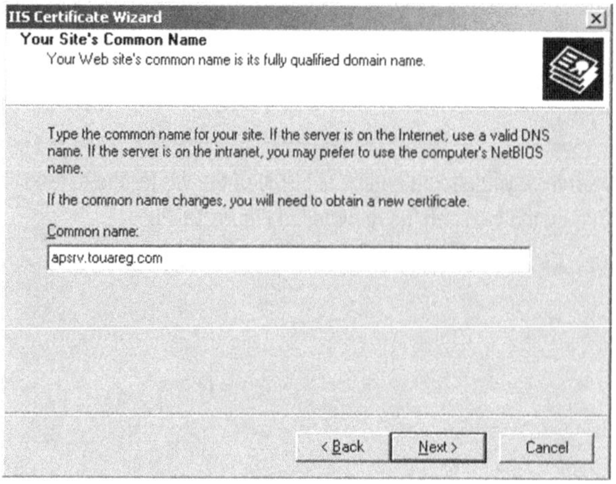

Figure 13-29. *Specifying the FQDN for the common name of the certificate*

On the page shown in Figure 13-30, make sure to type the full name of your state. For example, instead of WA, type **Washington**. VeriSign will not accept two-letter abbreviations for states when submitting your CSR.

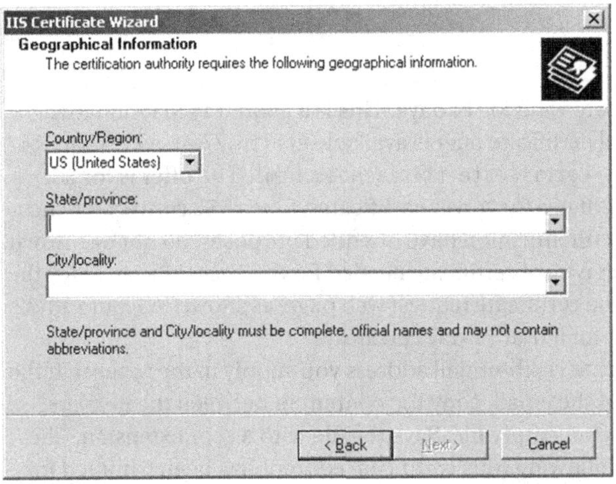

Figure 13-30. *Specifying your location in the certificate request*

Save the certificate request to a text file, as shown in Figure 13-31. You'll use the content of this file to submit your request to VeriSign.

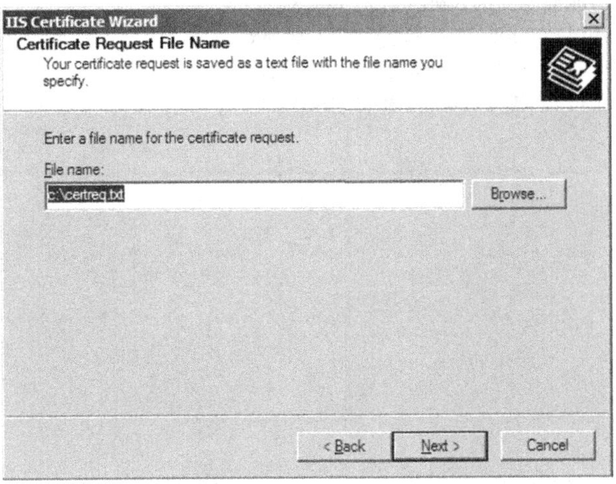

Figure 13-31. *Saving certificate request in a text file*

Next, open the file where the certificate request is stored. This is the CSR that you'll use to submit your certificate request for the public interface of your Access Proxy. The request will look like this (this certificate request has been trimmed for illustration purposes):

```
-----BEGIN NEW CERTIFICATE REQUEST-----
MIIDXDCCAsUCAQAwgYAxCzAJBgNVBAYTAlVTMQswCQYDVQQIEwJXQTERMA8GA1UE
BxMISXNzYXF1YWgxEDAOBgNVBAoTBONvbnRvc28xIzAhBgNVBAsTGkxpdmUgQ29t
qTEn15OBtruEdcoVu1kxvh5wtDsJCGhdQWVKR/F4SSR5O4waqVP8KyxLjGtN5nfH
-----END NEW CERTIFICATE REQUEST-----
```

VeriSign offers a free trial certificate valid for 14 days. This is a good way to familiarize yourself with the process. The free trial certificate offer is available at http://www.verisign.com/ssl/buy-ssl-certificates/free-ssl-certificate-trial/index.html. The offer is for SSL certificates, which is the most prevalent use for server certificates. Since SSL certificates such as Server Authentication and Client Authentication have intended purposes, do not be thrown off by the name SSL. This is the correct type of certificate needed for the Access Proxy. Copy the content of the CSR, and paste it into the certificate request web page, as shown in Figure 13-32. The figure shows a certificate request for a trial 14-day certificate.

VeriSign will send you the certificate via the email address you supply in the request. If the certificate is sent to you in the body of the email, copy the content in between the headers, including the header, and paste it into an empty file. Save the file with a .cer extension. The certificate content will resemble the following (this certificate content has been trimmed for illustration purposes):

```
-----BEGIN CERTIFICATE-----
MIAGCSqGSIb3DQEHAqCAMIACAQExADALBgkqhkiG9w0BBwGggDCCBVgwggRAoAMC
AQICEAwfuIvn50/kaFuBwHPmyJAwDQYJKoZIhvcNAQEFBQAwgcsxCzAJBgNVBAYT
dmVyIFRlc3QgUm9vdCBDQYIQIKiXrtuCAt7BNqBOJr2HczANBgkqhkiG9w0BAQUF
AAOBgQBLPm/yzf9KPNG9jaUqp/bfhhE6IvnVlLXXWhRnYwA2nYfhuLDiK1+wbmyc
MOXBJGaIfcFb9JToQTMP2iICL1Ne9EhwPmrSYH6fIr18HZoHM6JqIdKIhbMAl5CO
6oD5D3eM17D6l66PgCF28Y2f8or/7Vi/rXDf7uDq6QUwBFUE2AAAMQAAAAAAAA=
-----END CERTIFICATE-----
```

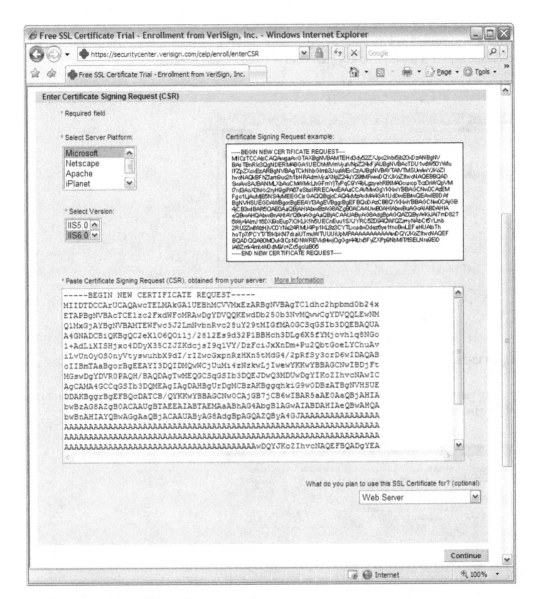

Figure 13-32. *VeriSign trial certificate example*

Now that VeriSign has issued the certificate, you must install it, as shown in Figure 13-33. Return to the same IIS website used to generate the certificate request, and run through the same wizard, the Web Server Certificate Wizard. This time it will prompt you whether you want to process the pending request or delete it. Select the option to process the pending request. Supply in the wizard the *.cer file containing the certificate. This will complete the process of installing the certificate.

Note It's important that you install the certificate on the same computer on which you generated your certificate request. If you fail to do this, you'll have to rerequest your certificate.

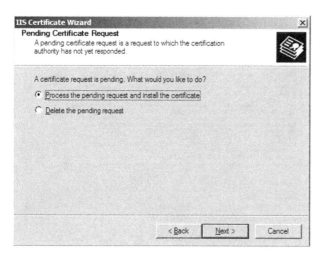

Figure 13-33. *Installing the certificate issued by VeriSign*

To view the certificate, select the View Certificate button on the Directory Security tab, as shown in Figure 13-34. This will launch the Certificate page.

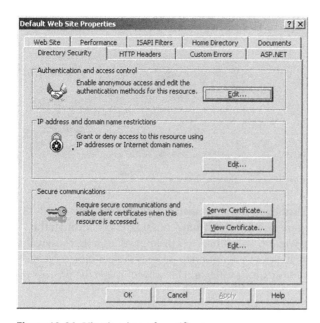

Figure 13-34. *Viewing issued certificate*

If you've requested the certificate from a different computer other than the Access Proxy or you plan to deploy a bank of Access Proxy servers, then you need to export the certificate and its private key so you can import it to the other Access Proxy servers. If you've generated the CSR from the Access Proxy, then the certificate and private key are now installed in the Personal store of the Computer account. Even if you plan to deploy only a single Access Proxy, it's recommended that you export the certificate and its private key for safekeeping because it might come in handy at a later time.

To export the certificate, navigate to the Details tab of the Certificate page, and click the Copy to File button. The Certificate Export Wizard will appear and help you through the process of exporting the new certificate, as shown in Figure 13-35.

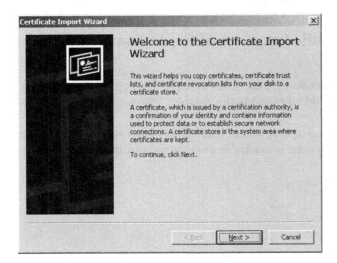

Figure 13-35. *Launching the Certificate Export Wizard*

Make sure to specify to export the private key, as shown in Figure 13-36.

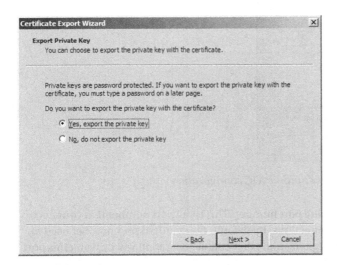

Figure 13-36. *Exporting the certificate's private key*

Copy the *.pfx file generated by the Certificate Export Wizard to the Access Proxy. Now you must install the certificate and private key on the Access Proxy. You can easily do this with the Certificate MMC.

Make sure the certificate's root CA certificate is imported into the Access Proxy's local computer Trusted Root Certification Authorities certificate store. If you're using VeriSign's free trial certificate, the corresponding root CA certificate is provided as a URL link in the email received from VeriSign. You can find the root CA certificate at http://www.verisign.com/support/verisign-intermediate-ca/Trial_Secure_Server_Root/index.html. Follow the same procedures used to import the trial server certificate to import the root CA certificate to the Trusted Root Certification Authorities node.

You're now ready to proceed to the next step.

Step 5: Configure the Public Interface of the Access Proxy with Your Certificate

You'll configure the Access Proxy's public interface in this step. You must specify the IP address of the NIC facing the public network (in other words, the Internet). The certificate requested in step 4 is associated to this interface.

You configure these settings by navigating to the Public tab of the Access Proxy's property page, as shown in Figure 13-37. Directions to reach this property page are described in step 3.

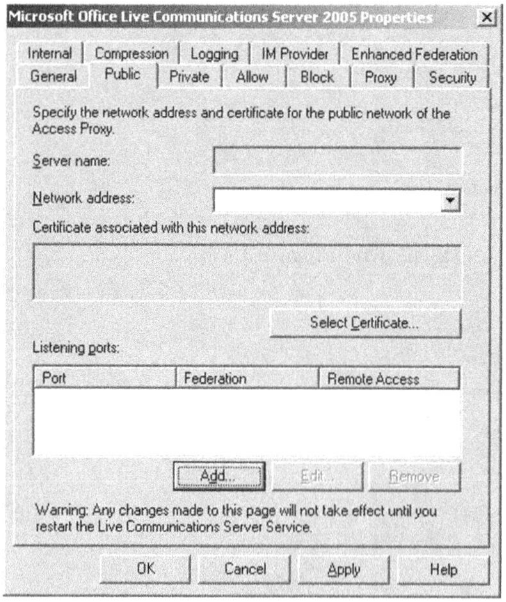

Figure 13-37. *Accessing the Access Proxy's public NIC configuration*

You must also configure a listening port number. This is the port number that your Access Proxy will listen on for incoming connections. By default, the standard port number used for SIP federation is 5061. Since other organizations that enable federation will be using this port number, it's recommended that you don't modify it; otherwise, you'll need to communicate to your federated partners your port number used.

The checkbox Allow Server Connections for Federation or Branch Office should be selected to enable federation, as shown in Figure 13-38.

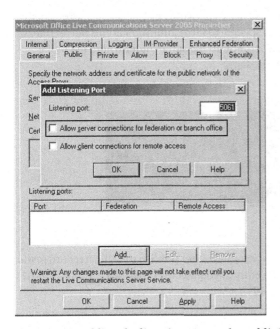

Figure 13-38. *Adding the listening port to the public NIC of the Access Proxy*

Step 6: Configure Your External DNS to Resolve the Access Proxy's Public FQDN

For federated partners to be able to route SIP traffic to your Access Proxy, their Access Proxy servers need to be able to resolve your Access Proxy's FQDN into an IP address. You do this by publishing your Access Proxy's public IP address on your external DNS server. Please follow your organization's policy for publishing servers to the Internet.

Step 7: Configure the Access Proxy to Allow Connections Originating from Your Director

In this step, you should specify the FQDN of the Director inside your corporate network as the next hop. The Access Proxy needs to know what SIP domains are authoritative to your organization. For example, if your organization is contoso.com and all employees have a SIP URI of the form name@contoso.com, then the Access Proxy needs to know to route all SIP requests with a To URI of <name>@contoso.com to the next hop. Finally, the Access Proxy needs to know which internal Live Communications Servers are allowed to connect to it. It is recommended that the only server authorized to connect to the Access Proxy is the same Director specified as the next hop server. Leave the port number at 5061.

Since your organization may have a firewall separating servers in the network perimeter from servers inside your organization, make sure the FQDN of the Director is resolvable from the Access Proxy. A simple `telnet.exe` test run from a `cmd.exe` window can verify that the Access Proxy can access the Director. The Live Communications Server 2005 SP1 resource kit provides a tool similar to `ping.exe` called `LcsPing.exe` that performs a TCP query instead of an ICMP query, which may be blocked for security reasons. This test using `LcsPing.exe` is more effective because it will target the ports and it transports specific to Live Communications Server. Please refer to the Resource Kit documentation, `LcsPing.htm`, in the same folder where the tool is available. Figure 13-39 shows an example of its usage.

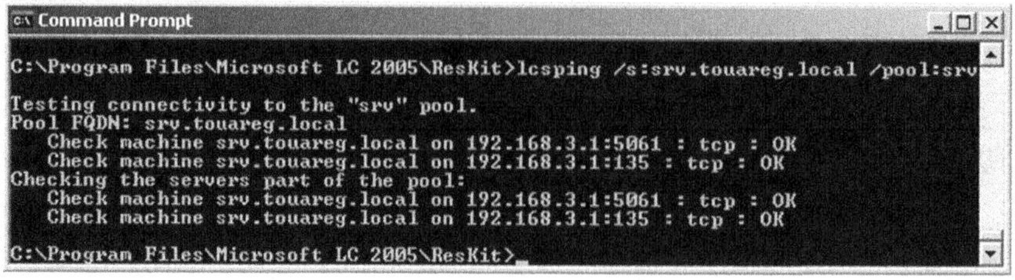

Figure 13-39. `LcsPing.exe`

If the FQDN of the Director cannot be resolved, then either publish the A host record in the DNS server in your network perimeter or add an entry to your Access Proxy's `%windir%\system32\drivers\etc\hosts` file, as shown in Figure 13-40.

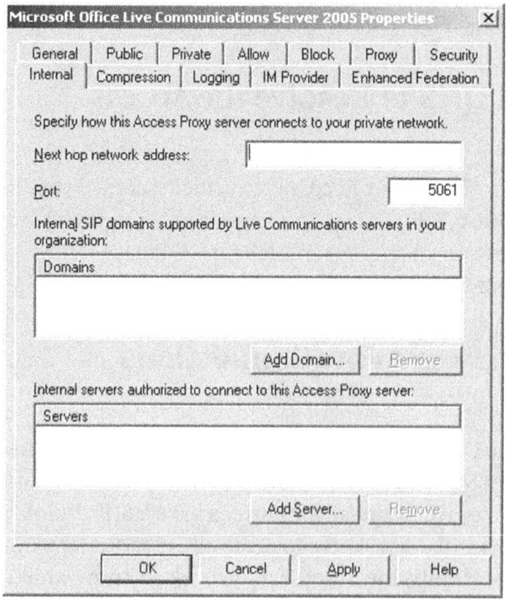

Figure 13-40. *Access Proxy internal configuration*

Step 8: Configure the Director to Route Outgoing SIP Messages to Your Access Proxy

After configuring the Access Proxy to route incoming traffic for your organization to your Director, you need to configure the Director to route outgoing traffic from your organization; otherwise, messages from your users will not reach their federated contacts. You do this by configuring the Director.

Navigate to the property settings of the Director by starting the administrative tool Live Communications Server 2005. You can find this MMC snap-in by clicking Start ▶ Administrative Tools from any computer where Live Communications Server 2005's Administration Tools are installed. Click the Federation tab, as shown in Figure 13-41. This property page is very simple.

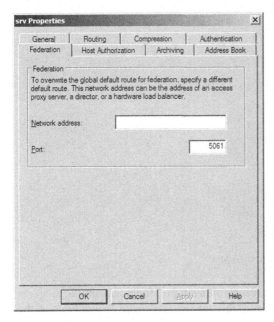

Figure 13-41. *Configuring the Director to route federated traffic to the Access Proxy*

You specify the FQDN of the Access Proxy and the port number to use. The FQDN to specify is that of the Access Proxy's private NIC. It's recommended that you leave the default set to port 5061. If you decide to change it, make sure the port number specified on the Access Proxy in step 6 is the same; otherwise, the connection between the Access Proxy and Director will fail.

Note In the case where a bank of Access Proxy servers is used, the FQDN specified should be the VIP of the interior hardware load balancer, as shown in Figure 13-42.

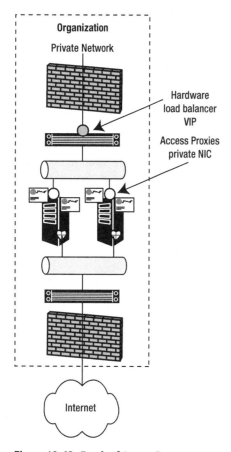

Figure 13-42. *Bank of Access Proxy servers private interface*

Make sure the FQDN of the Access Proxy is resolvable from the Director. A simple `ping.exe` test run from a `cmd.exe` window will verify that the Director can access the Access Proxy. If the FQDN of the Access Proxy cannot be resolved, then either publish the A host record in the DNS server or add an entry to your Director's `%windir%\system32\drivers\etc\hosts` file.

Step 9: Configure the Access Proxy for Federation

Before you can configure the Access Proxy for any form of federation, you must select the general setting Federate with Other Domains. You can find this setting on the General tab of the Access Proxy's property page, as shown in Figure 13-43. If this setting is unchecked, all forms of federation are disabled. Once this setting is checked, you can configure your Access Proxy for direct federation, enhanced federation, clearinghouse, or default route.

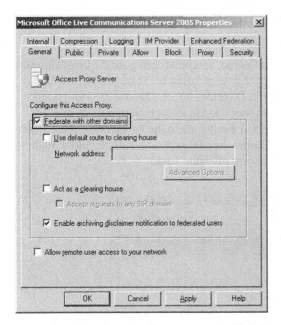

Figure 13-43. *Configuring the Access Proxy for federation*

It is prudent to also begin by specifying those SIP domains that you want to block before enabling federation access. You can easily do this by selecting the Block tab, as shown in Figure 13-44. After clicking the Add button, specify the SIP domain to block. The more difficult question to answer is to determine which SIP domains should be blocked.

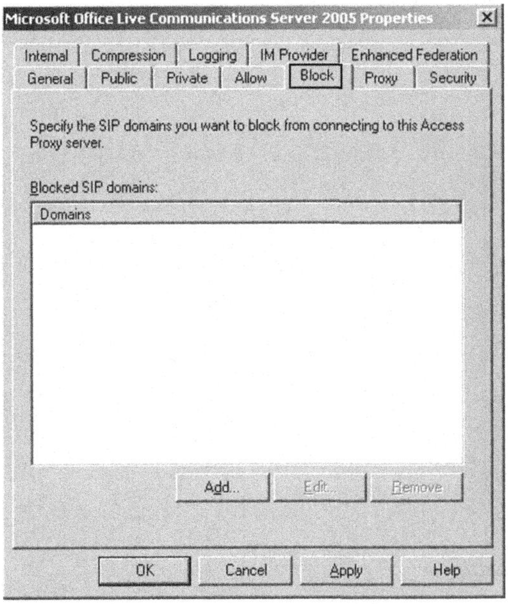

Figure 13-44. *Configuring the Block list*

Step 10: Configure the Live Communications Server Infrastructure for Federation

Now that the Access Proxy and Director are configured, you must configure the Live Communications Server infrastructure for federation. By this we mean all the Standard Edition Servers and Enterprise pools deployed within your Active Directory forest. These servers and pools need to be aware that federation is allowed, and they need to know how to route federated traffic out of the organization. You configure this by navigating to the Forest node of the MMC tool called Live Communications Server 2005, under the `Administrative Tools` folder. Right-click the forest node, and select Properties, as shown in Figure 13-45.

Figure 13-45. *Global Live Communications Server settings*

To configure your Live Communications Server infrastructure for federation, click the Federation tab, as shown in Figure 13-46. Select the Enable Federation and Public IM Connectivity checkbox, and specify the FQDN of the Director. Leave the port number set at 5061.

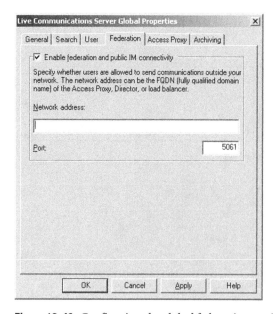

Figure 13-46. *Configuring the global federation settings*

Next, navigate to the Access Proxy tab, as shown in Figure 13-47. Specify the FQDN of the Access Proxy. In the case of a bank of Access Proxy servers, specify the FQDN of each Access Proxy. This is a measure of security to make sure that the Standard Edition Servers and Enterprise pools within your organization authorize traffic only with your Access Proxy servers. An Access Proxy is configured as a stand-alone workstation computer and is not joined to your organization's Active Directory forest. Since the Access Proxy servers deployed in your organization cannot be discovered via Active Directory, you must publish them manually.

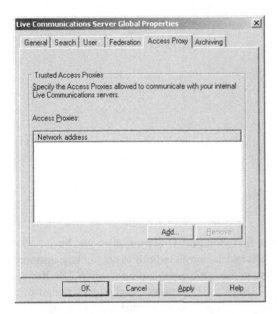

Figure 13-47. *Configuring trusted Access Proxy servers*

This completes your deployment of federation for your organization. The next step is to configure the type of federation you want to set up. Federation traffic is not authorized into your organization until you configure which SIP domains are allowed.

Step 11: Configure Users for Federation

Users now need to be configured for federation before they can start IM conversations with federated contacts. You can configure users one at a time or in bulk. You'll now explore the different ways you can do this.

You can configure users from Active Directory Users and Computers or Live Communications Server 2005 available in the Administrative Tools folder. To configure users individually, right-click the user, and select Properties. Navigate to the Live Communications tab if using Active Directory Users and Computers. Click the Advanced Settings button. Select the Enable Federation checkbox, as shown in Figure 13-48, and click OK twice.

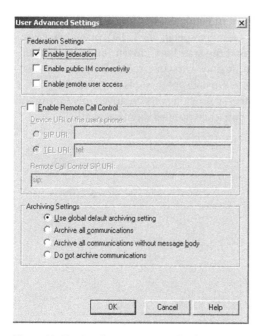

Figure 13-48. *Configuring a user for federation*

These steps will configure one user at a time for federation. However, when you have 1,000 or 10,000 or 30,000 or more users to configure, this task becomes tedious to do. Luckily, options exist. If the users to enable for federation belong to the same organizational unit (OU), then simply right-click the OU from Active Directory Users and Computers, and select Configure Live Communications Users. This will launch the Configure Users Wizard. After passing the welcome page, select the Configure Federation checkbox, and select the radio option Allow Users. Similarly, the same procedure applies when you select a number of users.

Another option to automate this process is to use the WMI interface defined by Live Communications Server. The WMI class to use is MSFT_SIPESUserSetting, as defined by MSDN at http://msdn.microsoft.com/library/default.asp?url=/library/en-us/lcs2005/rtc/msft_sipesusersetting.asp. The resource kit offers several WMI samples written in VBScript for reference. See the LcsEnableConfigureUsers.wsf sample. LcsSolutions.com offers a free trial tool called LcsUtil.exe that offers the ability to configure users for federation (and more) based on any query criteria.

For convenience, instead of trying to figure out which parts of the WMI sample addresses configuring users for federation, the following C# sample code isolates this task:

```
// Define user query to configure for federation.
// <insert identifier> should be replaced with the
// identifier to query the desired set of users.
sQuery = "select * from MSFT_SIPESUserSetting where <insert identifier> = '";
// <attr> should be replaced with the value of the attribute to match.
ManagementObjectSearcher oSrch = new ManagementObjectSearcher(sQuery+<attr>+"'");
ManagementObjectCollection oCollection = oSrch.Get();
foreach(ManagementObject user in oCollection)
```

```
{
    // Configure user for federation
    user["EnabledForFederation"] = TRUE;

    try
    {
        // Commit changes
        user.Put();
        Console.WriteLine(user["DisplayName"].ToString() + ": success");
    }
    catch(Exception e)
    {
        Console.WriteLine(e.Message);
        Console.WriteLine();
    }
}
```

Before continuing, it's helpful to verify that your federation setup is functional. The easiest and best tool to use to verify your configuration is the Live Communications Diagnostic Tool (LcsDiag.exe). You can find this tool in the Live Communications Server 2005 SP1 Resource Kit. After installing the resource kit, you can find LcsDiag.exe under %ProgramFiles%Microsoft LC 2005\ResKit. It's not immediately obvious how to start the diagnostic test, but you can find it by clicking the icon circled in Figure 13-49.

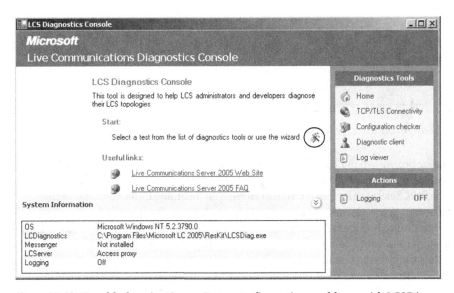

Figure 13-49. *Troubleshooting Access Proxy configuration problems with LCSDiag*

Direct Federation

For a partner company to begin communicating over IM with your organization using Live Communications Server 2005 SP1, you'll need to add its SIP domain and specify the FQDN of its Access Proxy to the Allow list. For every partner company you want to enable IM traffic, you must repeat this procedure. This process can quickly become work intensive if your list of federated partners grows. If it does, you'll want to consider using enhanced federation or going with a clearinghouse if available.

To reach the federated partner's Allow list, open the Access Proxy's property page, and navigate to the Allow tab, as shown in Figure 13-50.

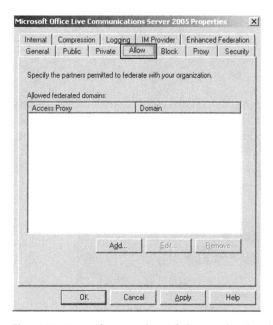

Figure 13-50. *Configuring direct federation's Allow list*

In the dialog box shown in Figure 13-51, specify the FQDN of the partner's Access Proxy in the Federated Partner Access Proxy field, and specify the SIP domain in the Federated Partner Domain Name field. Select the level of filtering to enforce on incoming traffic from this partner.

The first option, Allow Communications Only from Users on Recipient's Contact List, implies that users from the federated partner cannot initiate IM conversations with users from your organization until your users add them to their contact list as contacts. This is the most restrictive policy that you can establish between two federated partners.

The second option, Allow Communications Only from Users Verified by This Federated Partner, is similar to the third option as long as messages are tagged as verified by the federated partner's Access Proxy. By default, the Access Proxy will tag all outgoing messages as verified. It is possible, however, for the Access Proxy to tag messages as unverified.

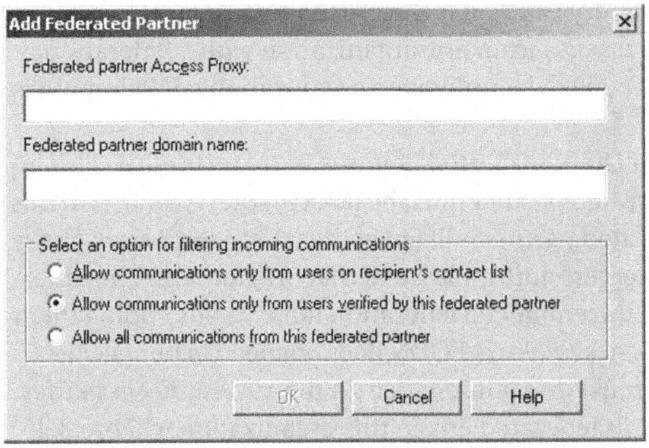

Figure 13-51. *Adding a direct federation partner*

The third option, Allow All Communications from This Federated Partner, allows users from the federated partner to initiate IM conversations to users in your organization without first being added as contacts to the contact list of users in your organization. This is the highest degree of freedom.

Enhanced Federation

To configure enhanced federation, open the Access Proxy's property page, and navigate to the Enhanced Federation tab. Click the Enable Enhanced Federation checkbox. The two radio options become enabled, as shown in Figure 13-52.

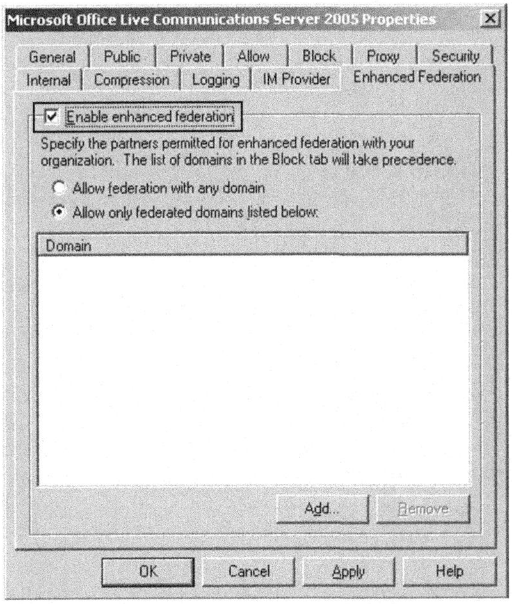

Figure 13-52. *Configuring enhanced federation*

The radio option Allow Federation with Any Domain is the most permissive. This option implies that your Access Proxy will allow messages from any organization with a federation deployment of Live Communications Server 2005 SP1 unless the organization's SIP domain is explicitly listed in the Block list.

The radio option Allow Only Federated Domains Listed Below is more restrictive. This is similar to direct federation where each federated partner must be listed in the Allow list. In this scenario, unless the SIP domain of the federated partner is listed in the table, your Access Proxy will drop messages from the Access Proxy servers authoritative of that SIP domain. The difference between adding federated partners to the enhanced federation table versus adding them to the Allow list is that the federated partner's Access Proxy FQDN does not need to be specified. This is convenient if the federated partner must do maintenance on the current Access Proxy and replace it with a new one. Suddenly, your federated link to this organization will break if this federated partner is listed in the Allow list. With enhanced federation, the federated link no longer breaks from maintenance changes to the partner's Access Proxy.

For companies to discover your Access Proxy and establish a federation link, a resource record of type Service Location (SRV) must be defined in your external DNS. This SRV record to publish should be of the form _sipfederationtls._tcp.<SIP domain>, where <SIP domain> is the domain name for which your Live Communications Server infrastructure is authoritative.

If your external DNS is using Windows Server 2003 DNS service, Figure 13-53 and Figure 13-54 show how to create such a record.

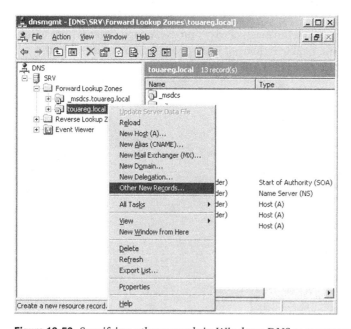

Figure 13-53. *Specifying other records in Windows DNS management console*

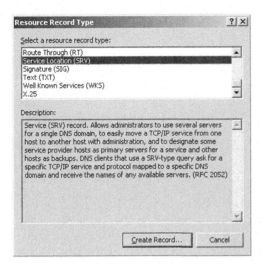

Figure 13-54. *Creating a DNS SRV record for federation*

Once the _sipfederationtls._tcp.<domain> DNS SRV record is published, other organizations can discover your Access Proxy by performing a DNS query for this SRV record. The record will return the Access Proxy's FQDN. A subsequent DNS query for the FQDN's A host record returns the Access Proxy's IP address. When the partner's Access Proxy connects to your Access Proxy, it will challenge for your server's certificate. Your Access Proxy presents the certificate associated to its public interface. Since a public CA issued this certificate, the partner's Access Proxy validates that your Access Proxy's certificate chains up to a trusted root authority and that the server's FQDN matches the certificate's common name. Once verified, federated traffic can flow across the two Access Proxy servers.

Clearinghouse

Most organizations will not set up a clearinghouse. A clearinghouse is a specialized form of federation for companies that offer it as a business service to other companies that do not want to manage the membership of federated partners. We won't cover this type of federation in detail.

To configure your Access Proxy as a clearinghouse, open the Access Proxy's property page, and navigate to the General tab, as shown in Figure 13-55.

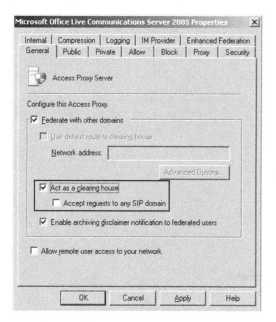

Figure 13-55. *Configuring a clearinghouse*

Default Route

You can use the default route in conjunction with direct federation. In a dynamic environment where the number of direct federated partners your organization needs to interact with is constantly changing, a default route to a clearinghouse is an alternative to constantly updating the Allow list. Federated traffic not explicitly defined in your Access Proxy's Allow list is routed to the default route. This default route sends federated traffic to a clearinghouse. The clearinghouse determines whether the traffic should be routed and where to route it. When selecting a clearinghouse, determine whether the clearinghouse meets your organization's security policy. Before you can use a default route, all entries on the IM Provider tab must be deleted, and enhanced federation must be turned off.

To configure your Access Proxy as a clearinghouse, open the Access Proxy's property page, and navigate to the General tab. Check the Use Default Route to Clearing House checkbox, and specify the FQDN of the clearinghouse in the Network Address field. You can specify the filtering options by clicking the Advanced Options button, as shown in Figure 13-56.

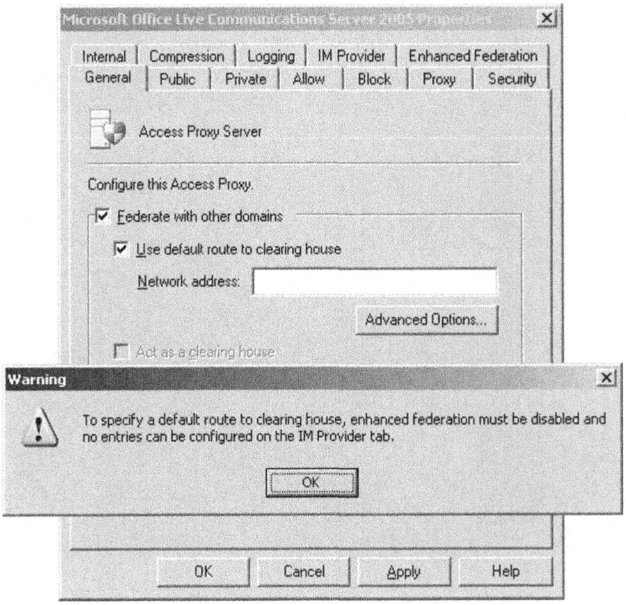

Figure 13-56. *Configuring default route*

Summary

Federation support was introduced in Live Communications Server 2005 SP1. Federation provides the ability for users in your organization to securely communicate with users from other companies or public IM providers. Enabling federation requires configuring the Access Proxy server role in the network perimeter, configuring your Active Directory forest, and configuring users for federation. Live Communications Server 2005 SP1 provides different types of federation to best meet your corporate needs: direct federation, enhanced federation, clearinghouse, and default route. The Access Proxy controls outside access to your Live Communications Server infrastructure.

■■■

CHAPTER 14

Public Instant Messaging Connectivity

If you need to provide secure connections to external parties, such as business partners (who you are not federating with), customers, and others, you can now do so without using a separate instant messaging client that does not provide the security or traceability that Live Communications Server 2005 provides. This could be because the instant messaging traffic is effectively in clear text and because conversations cannot be captured in order to meet corporate or legal policies.

You can connect to and configure secure and auditable communications with users who are homed on systems provided by public service providers such as AOL, Yahoo!, and MSN using a feature of Live Communications Server 2005 called Public Instant Messaging Connectivity (PIC).

Introducing PIC

The way PIC works is to effectively expand federation to encompass those service providers using a Live Communications Server 2005 Access Proxy server in order to act as an intermediary between your Live Communications Server 2005 environment and the service provider's environment, as shown in Figure 14-1 (which extends the figure you might remember from Chapter 4).

This obviously means you must have a correctly configured and functioning Access Proxy server in place prior to connecting and configuring this new connection. If you have already set up an Access Proxy for federation purposes, you don't have to install another one; you can use that one as long as it does not currently have a default route to a clearinghouse. If it does, you will need to set up an additional Access Proxy to use for this function. And as with federated partners, you can archive instant messaging conversations that take place with users of public service providers in order to meet any corporate or legal policies that your organization might have.

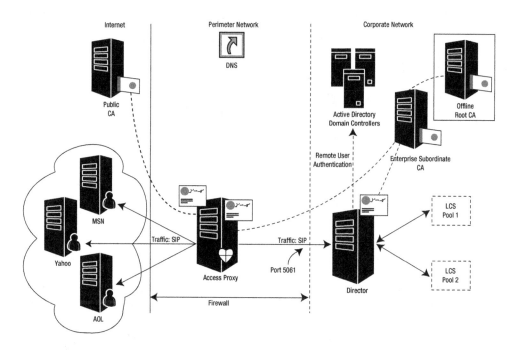

Figure 14-1. *PIC topology*

Once the connection has been made and configured, users within your organization can use either Office Communicator 2005 (or later) or Windows Messenger 5.1 (or later) to communicate with any internal and external users (either federated partners or public instant messaging users) who have been configured. This now means that users no longer need multiple clients to communicate with both internal and external users; in addition, this greatly reduces the risks associated with using external communications providers. In fact, your organization might have a policy of not allowing external communication through "public" instant messaging clients and services because of the inherent security and privacy issues that exist, including concerns about viruses.

Users will not get the full functionality of Live Communications Server when they use PIC; however, they will be able to do the following:

- Add and remove contacts on their contact lists

- Share their presence information with users outside the organization

- Communicate with users of public service providers

You can wield a significant amount of control over PIC; it's not just a case of enabling it and everyone getting to use it. As an administrator, you can specify which user has the ability to use PIC. However, you cannot specify which provider can be connected to; you can specify only that a user can use PIC, which means that if you have configured PIC with all three service providers (MSN, Yahoo!, and AOL), then that user could communicate with anyone using those providers. The best solution is to configure PIC to use only those service providers that you need to, although there is a good chance that before long you will have configured access to all three!

When deciding what users to give access to PIC, you should consider the additional licensing costs. Additional licenses are required for each user who you want to enable for PIC; also, these charges are monthly, so this could potentially get quite expensive. Therefore, give access only to those users who really have a business need for the service. The charge does include access to all three public service providers, so you won't need to buy licenses for each one. You can add these licenses to a current Select License, Enterprise Agreement, or Open Value License. Pricing and licensing details for Public IM Connectivity are available through Microsoft Volume Licensing programs. For more information, refer to `http://www.microsoft.com/office/livecomm/howtobuy/default.mspx`.

According to Microsoft, the average cost, depending on a number of factors, including volume licensing discounts, is approximately $1–$2 per user per month. So for a small number of users, this cost can be quite manageable; however, the more users you give it to, the higher the cost!

Note Microsoft is also in the process of developing a Public IM Connectivity Partner Site that will contain value-added services. This site is at `http://office.microsoft.com/en-us/products/FX011960751033.aspx`.

As mentioned when you read about federation in Chapter 13, all instant messaging traffic between your organization and your federated partners uses Mutual Transport Layer Security (MTLS) to provide an encrypted connection so that all communications are protected. The same is true when you use PIC to connect to public service providers. As mentioned earlier, you should think of PIC as just an extension of federation. A certificate is required from a public certification authority (CA) that is on the list of trusted CAs; you cannot use an enterprise certificate you created yourself.

Setting Up and Configuring PIC

You need to complete several steps to successfully set up and configure PIC:

- Provisioning PIC

- Configuring DNS

- Adding certificates

- Configuring the Access Proxy

- Enabling users for PIC

In the following sections, we will go through these steps in order to give you a better understanding of the process. However, because you have already seen some of these steps in earlier chapters, we won't go into too much detail on those specific ones again.

Provisioning PIC

You must initiate the provisioning process with the public service providers to which you want to be able to communicate. So if you want to communicate with all three of them, you must initiate the provisioning process with all three of them.

Before you go any further, decide how many PIC licenses you will need, and purchase them from Microsoft. You need to do this before the provisioning process because you will need some information from Microsoft that is provided when you buy the licenses.

Once you have these additional licenses, you can begin the provisioning process.

Point your browser to `https://www.livemeeting.com/LCSVL/` to display the Live Communications Server Public IM Connectivity Provisioning Request for Volume Licensing Customers website. Then follow these steps:

1. Select your preferred language from the drop-down list (as shown in Figure 14-2).

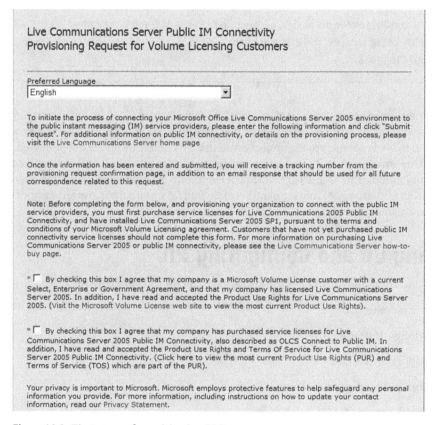

Figure 14-2. *First stage of provisioning PIC*

2. Read the information displayed on the page, and check the box to agree that your company is a Microsoft Volume Licensing customer with a current agreement and a licensed Live Communications Server 2005 and that you have read and accepted the product use rights.

3. Check the box to agree that your company has purchased service licenses for Live Communications Server 2005 PIC and that you have read and accepted the product use rights.

4. Complete the Profile and Product Information section (as shown in Figure 14-3). You will need the following information:

   • Your organization's name

   • Your organization's master business agreement number

   • Your organization's agreement enrollment number

   • Your organization's license agreement type (either Select License, Enterprise Agreement, Open Value Licensing, or Other)

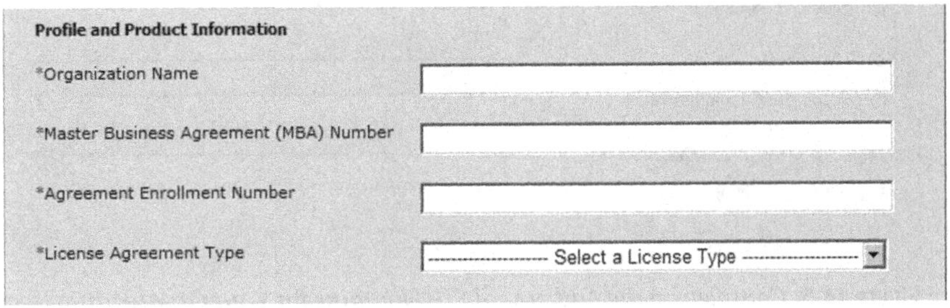

Figure 14-3. *Completing the Profile and Product Information section*

5. Complete the Connectivity Information for Your Organization section (as shown in Figure 14-4). You will need the following:

   • Your organization's primary SIP domain name

   • The email address for the administrator (probably you!)

   • The FQDN of the Access Proxy you will be using

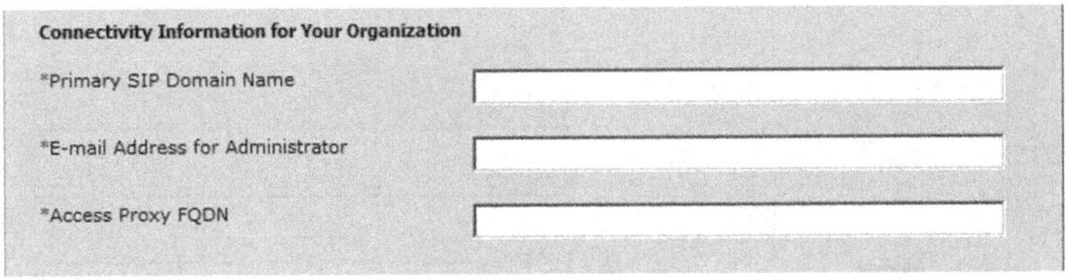

Figure 14-4. *Completing the Connectivity Information for Your Organization section*

6. Complete the Additional SIP Domains for Your Organization section, if required (as shown in Figure 14-5). You will need the following:

   • Your organization's secondary SIP domain name

   • The email address for the administrator (probably you again!)

7. Add all the other SIP domain names before you continue.

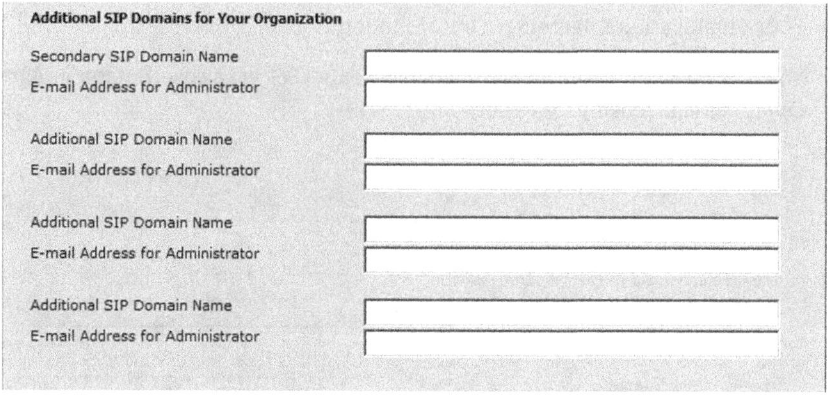

Figure 14-5. *Completing the Additional SIP Domains for Your Organization section*

8. Complete the Administrator Contact Information section (as shown in Figure 14-6). This is most likely your contact information if you are the administrator for your organization. You will need the following:

   • Your last name

   • Your first name

   • Your email address

   • Your phone number

Figure 14-6. *Completing the Administrator Contact Information section*

9. The last section to complete is the Public IM Service Providers section (as shown in Figure 14-7). Here you must select which public IM service providers you want to provision. You can select any or all of them as needed.

Figure 14-7. *Completing the Public IM Service Providers section*

10. Check all the information you have entered on this website, and then click the Submit button.

You should then receive an email confirming that your provision request has been received and is being validated. Once the request has been validated, you should receive another email advising you that your details have been passed to the relevant public IM service providers, and you should also be given an approximate time of how long the process should then take.

The public IM service providers you want to communicate with will provision their routing tables to forward any instant messages aimed at your SIP domain to your Access Proxy. When this has been completed, you should receive a final email message advising you that the process is complete and that you can now communicate with those providers.

Configuring DNS

For this section, we will assume that you already have a functioning DNS server or servers; if you do not, you must ensure that you have one before continuing. Then follow these steps:

1. You must publish a DNS SRV record for your SIP domain, so create a DNS SRV record of _sipfederationtls._tcp.<domain> where <domain> is your SIP domain.

2. Ensure that a DNS A record exists for your Access Proxy. If one doesn't exist, you will need to add one.

3. Point the DNS SRV record you created in step 1 to the DNS A record of your Access Proxy.

Adding Certificates

As we mentioned earlier in this chapter, MTLS is required in order to encrypt the connection between your Live Communications Server environment and that of the public service providers, and MTLS requires the use of certificates.

This is the same requirement that you had for setting up federation, but for PIC you need to use a certificate from a trusted public certification authority, and that certificate also needs to be installed on your Access Proxy.

You need to make sure you use a certificate from a trusted public certification authority rather than just a Windows Server 2003 CA. A simple way of ensuring that you are obtaining a certificate from a trusted authority is to check whether Windows lists it in its Trusted Root Certificate Authorities list (as shown in Figure 14-8).

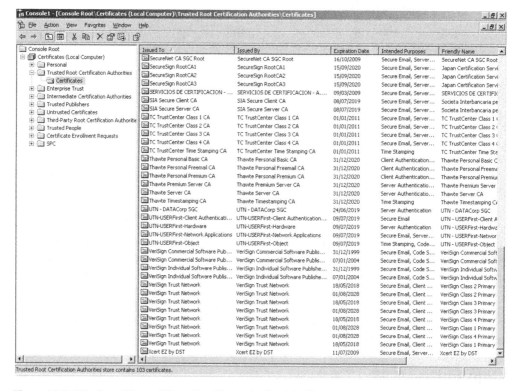

Figure 14-8. *Windows Trusted Root Certificate Authorities list*

To display this list, perform the following steps:

1. Select Start ➤ Run.

2. Type **mmc**, and click OK; this will launch the MMC console.

3. Select File ➤ Add/Remove Snap-In, and then click Add.

4. Scroll through the list of available stand-alone snap-ins until you come to Certificates, and then click Add.

5. Ensure Computer Account is selected, and click Next.

6. Ensure that the Local Computer check box is selected, and click Finish.

7. Expand Certificates (Local Computer).

8. Expand Trusted Root Certification Authorities.

9. Click Certificates to display the list.

Choose one of the trusted certification authorities, generate a certificate signing request as you did before, and then submit the certificate signing request to your chosen trusted certification authority in order to receive your certificate. If you are unsure about how to generate the certificate signing request, then you can always check with your chosen certification authority because they often will have step-by-step guides to help you. We have assumed that you are comfortable in doing this task already.

This certificate must then be installed on your Access Proxy or your Access Proxy array, and again we have assumed you are comfortable doing this task.

If for whatever reason you are unsure of what to do or want some further information on using and configuring certificates with Live Communications Server, then there is a useful document produced by Microsoft that you can download from http://www.microsoft.com/downloads/details.aspx?FamilyId=779DEDAA-2687-4452-901E-719CE6EC4E5A&displaylang=en.

Configuring the Access Proxy

The next step in the process is to configure the Access Proxy to allow PIC, including specifying the public service providers with which your organization can communicate.

To do this, you need to perform the following steps on the Access Proxy:

1. Click Start ➤ All Programs ➤ Administrative Tools, and then click Computer Management.

2. Expand Services and Applications.

3. Right-click Microsoft Office Live Communications Server 2005, and then click Properties.

4. Click the IM Provider tab (as shown in Figure 14-9).

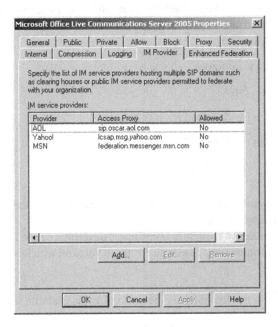

Figure 14-9. *The IM Provider tab*

As you can see, all three of the public service providers are displayed, along with the Access Proxy addresses. They are all configured, by default, to *not* allow communication.

5. Select the provider you want to configure, and click Edit (as shown in Figure 14-10).

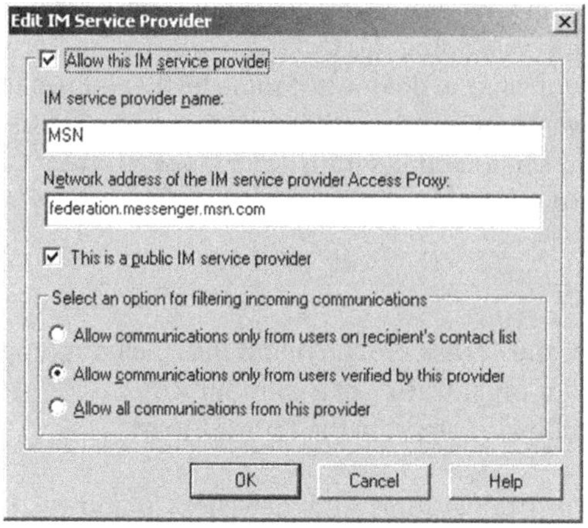

Figure 14-10. *Editing a service provider*

6. Check the Allow This IM Service Provider box.

You can add another layer of security by selecting filtering options for the provider. These options include allowing communications only from those users on a recipient's contact list, only those users who have been verified by the provider, or all communications from the provider. It is important to note that the Allow All Communications from This Provider option can mean that users will receive spam instant messages (SPIM), so be careful when setting these options.

7. Select which filtering option you want to use.

8. Click OK to return to the IM Filter tab.

9. Repeat steps 5 through 8 for each provider you want to enable.

10. Click Apply and then OK to finish this part of the provisioning.

Enabling Users for PIC

The last stage is to actually enable users so that they can start communicating with other users who are based on a public service provider's system.

To enable users, you can use either Active Directory Users and Computers or the Live Communications Server 2005 Administrative tool. The choice is up to you and whichever you are most comfortable using.

1. Open whichever tool you want to use to configure the users (for this example we are using Active Directory Users and Computers).

2. Select the user, and right-click Properties.

3. Click the Live Communications tab.

4. Click Advanced Settings.

5. Check the Enable Public IM Connectivity box, as shown in Figure 14-11.

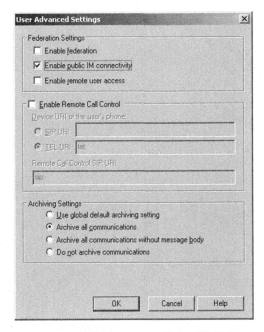

Figure 14-11. *Enabling a user for public IM connectivity*

6. Click OK.

7. Repeat steps 3 through 6 for each user you want to enable. If you plan on enabling a large number of users, consider using the bulk administration tool.

Summary

This chapter has given you some insight into exactly what PIC is and what it can do for your organization. You learned what you need to do in order to set up and configure PIC, and you saw a step-by-step walk-through of the provisioning process. If you want to have secure instant messaging conversations with your business partners, customers, or other users, you need to use PIC.

PART 4

###

Getting the Most from LCS

This final part of the book will demonstrate how to get the most out of Live Communications Server. We'll cover logging and archiving, two separate functions that people often confuse as the same task. Then we'll give you some tips for troubleshooting problems in your environment and also show how to monitor your environment using tools such as the Microsoft Operations Manager. For developers, we'll briefly explore the Live Communications Server 2005 software development kit (SDK) and the applications that come with it. Then to finish the book, we'll highlight some of the additional resources, such as newsgroups and online help, that are available for Live Communications Server.

CHAPTER 15

■■■

Backup and Restore

It is extremely important that you back up your Live Communications Server environment and that you can restore it if that fateful time ever arrives where you have to restore it because of either data loss or hardware failure, or worse. It is also extremely important that you test those backups—there is nothing worse than having to restore a backup only to find that the backup does not actually work. Now, we're not suggesting that you perform a restore every day or even every week, but you should perform regular restores to ensure that they are working. And don't forget to test your restore on a spare server and not on your live production server!

If you are used to performing backups, then you will already be familiar with terms such as full backups and incremental backups. A *full backup* is where you back up everything, and an *incremental backup* is where you back up only what has changed since the last backup. Live Communications Server supports only full backups. This is because the database file that needs to be backed up is quite small—certainly smaller than the transaction log files and definitely a lot smaller than what most system administrators are used to having to back up for typical applications.

Different tools are provided for backing up Live Communications Server, depending on what version you are using (Standard Edition or Enterprise Edition), and you can also buy third-party backup software that can provide additional functionality over and above what the built-in tools can provide. If you are planning on buying additional backup software, make sure it is compatible with Live Communications Server. One particular software product that is compatible with Live Communications Server is Backup Exec 10 from Veritas. You can download a whitepaper entitled "Protecting Live Communications Server 2005 with Veritas Backup Exec Software" from `http://office.microsoft.com/search/redir.aspx?AssetID=XT011613731033&CTT=5&Origin=HA011526621033`. To download this whitepaper, you will need to register with Symantec; however, this takes only a few minutes.

In this chapter, you will look at how you can back up both Live Communications Server 2005 Standard Edition and Enterprise Edition with the tools provided out of the box (for both Live Communications Server 2005 and SQL Server 2000). This chapter also includes a brief section on best practices for both backing up and restoring your Live Communications Server environment.

Standard Edition

If you have a Live Communications Server 2005 Standard Edition that you want to back up, you must ensure you back up the following:

- Forest configurations

- Server configurations

- Pool configurations

- MSDE database

Backing Up the Configurations

You can use a single tool to back up and restore the forest and server configurations. This tool is called LcsCmd.exe and is installed as part of Live Communications Server.

It is run from a command prompt and has the following syntax specific to backup and restore operations:

- LcsCmd.exe /? (this displays all the parameters and help information)

- LcsCmd.exe /batch:{input file} [/l:{log file}]

- LcsCmd.exe /forest[:{FQDN} /action:{action name} {Parameter 1} ... {Parameter N}

- LcsCmd.exe /server[:{FQDN} /action:{action name} {Parameter 1} ... {Parameter N}

LcsCmd.exe has a lot of functionality, so it is worth looking at it for other uses apart from backing up and restoring your Live Communications Server environment.

Forest Actions

The following are the forest actions:

- ExportGlobalConfig is a forest action that is used to export the global-level configuration into an XML file.

- ImportGlobalConfig is a forest action that is used to import the global-level configuration into an XML file.

- ExportPoolConfig is a forest action that is used to export the pool configuration that is used by all front-end servers into an XML file.

- ImportPoolConfig is a forest action that is used to import the pool configuration into an XML file.

Obviously, the ExportPoolConfig and ImportPoolConfig actions are needed only if you have front-end servers in a pool.

A useful switch to use is /configFile:{file name}, which specifies the file that is exported to or imported from. You must this switch with both the ExportGlobalConfig and ImportGlobalConfig commands.

Server Actions

The following are the server actions:

- ExportServerConfig is a server action that is used to export the server configuration to an XML file. You must use the /role and /configFile switches.

- ImportServerConfig is a server action that is used to import the server configurations to an XML file. You must use the /role and /configFile switches, and there is also an optional /restore switch.

To back up the forest configuration, do the following:

1. Ensure you are logged in as an administrator of the Live Communications Server 2005 Standard Edition server you want to back up.

2. Open a command prompt by clicking Start ➤ Run. Then type **cmd**, and click OK.

3. From the command prompt, type the following, as shown in Figure 15-1:

   ```
   LcsCmd.exe /forest /action:ExportGlobalConfig ➥
   /configFile:c:\GlobalConfig.xml
   ```

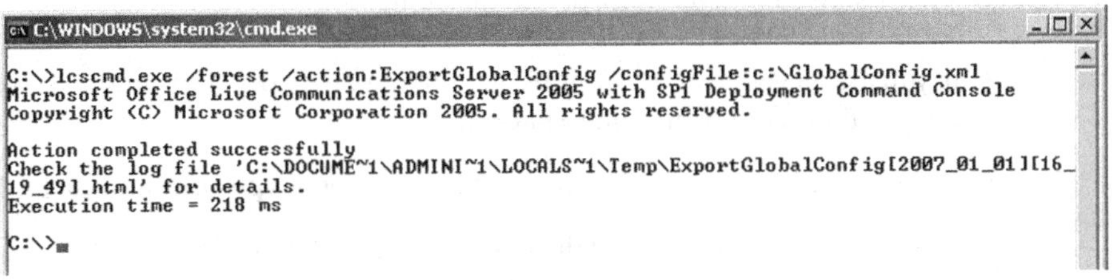

Figure 15-1. *Backing up the forest configuration*

4. You can then check the log file to ensure that the backup was successful by going to the directory that is listed and double-clicking the .html file to view it (as shown in Figure 15-2).

5. Take a copy of the GlobalConfig.xml file, and store it in a safe location. If you are familiar with XML, you can examine the file to see what is stored within it.

Figure 15-2. *The forest configuration backup log file*

To back up the server configuration, do the following:

1. Ensure you are logged in as an administrator of the Live Communications Server 2005 Standard Edition server you want to back up.

2. Open a command prompt by clicking Start ➤ Run. Then type **cmd**, and click OK.

3. From the command prompt, type the following, as shown in Figure 15-3:

```
LcsCmd.exe /server /action:ExportServerConfig ➥
/role:SE /configFile:c:\HSconfig.xml
```

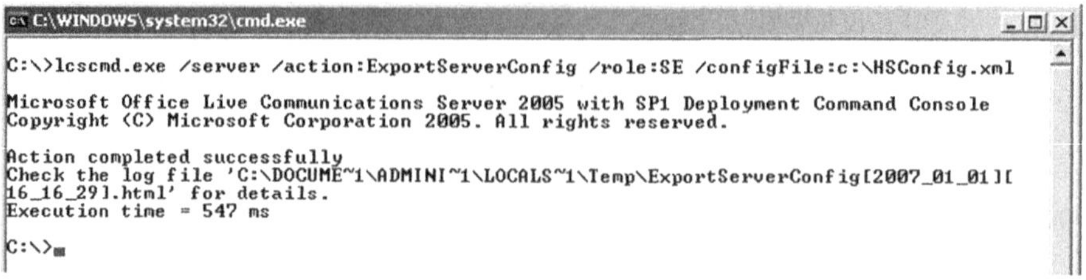

Figure 15-3. *Backing up the server configuration*

4. You can then check the log file to ensure that the backup was successful by going to the directory that is listed and double-clicking the .html file to view it (as shown in Figure 15-4).

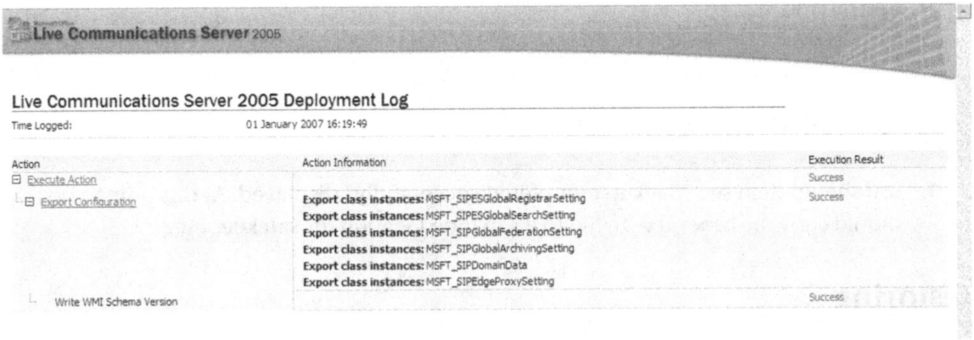

Figure 15-4. *The server configuration backup log file*

5. Take a copy of the HSconfig.xml file, and store it in a safe location. If you are familiar with XML, you can examine the file to see what is stored within it.

Backing Up the MSDE Database

MSDE does not have a whizzy front end, so you need to carry out all backup and restore operations from a command prompt.

The tool you can use is called Dbbackup.exe; you can find it in the \Support directory within the Live Communications Server directory on the server. You use this tool to back up the user contacts and allow/block lists that are stored in the MSDE database. Follow these steps:

1. Ensure you are logged in as an administrator of the Live Communications Server 2005 Standard Edition server you want to back up.

2. Create a folder at the root of the C drive called Backup.

3. Ensure the new Backup folder is shared, and grant read permissions to the Domain Admins group in your domain.

4. Open a command prompt by clicking Start ➤ Run. Then type **cmd**, and click OK.

5. From the command prompt, go to the C:\Program Files\Microsoft LC 2005\Server\ Support folder (or wherever the folder is if you installed it into a different location).

6. To back up the MSDE database, type the following, as shown in Figure 15-5:

```
Dbbackup /backupfile:c:\backup\home-srv-in
```

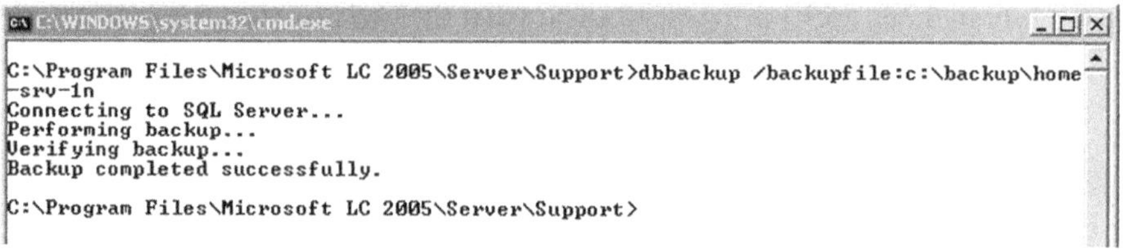

Figure 15-5. *Backing up the MSDE database*

7. You should then see "Backup completed successfully" displayed. At this point, you should copy the home-srv-1n file to a separate location for safekeeping.

Restoring

If you need to perform a restore, perform the following steps on the Live Communications Server 2005 Standard Edition server prior to restoring the configuration files and the MSDE database:

1. Deactivate the corrupt Live Communications Server 2005 Standard Edition server.

2. Uninstall the corrupt Live Communications Server 2005 Standard Edition server.

3. Reinstall Live Communications Server 2005 Standard Edition server.

4. Restore the forest, server, and pool configurations (see the following section).

5. Restore the MSDE database (see the "Restoring the MSDE Database" section).

If you have had to build a completely new server, you can obviously skip steps 1 and 2 and move straight to step 3.

Restoring the Configurations

To restore the various configuration files, perform the following steps:

1. Ensure you are logged in as an administrator of the Live Communications Server 2005 Standard Edition server you want to back up.

2. Copy the XML files from their stored location back to the server you want to restore.

3. Open a command prompt by clicking Start ➤ Run. Then type **cmd**, and click OK.

4. From the command prompt, type the following for the server and pool configurations:

```
LcsCmd.exe /server /action:ImportServerConfig ➥
/role:SE /configFile:c:\HSconfig.xml
```

5. From the command prompt, type the following for the server configuration:

```
LcsCmd.exe /forest /action:ImportGlobalConfig ➥
/configFile:c:\GlobalConfig.xml
```

Restoring the MSDE Database

Restoring the MSDE database is just as simple as backing it up:

1. Ensure you are logged in as an administrator of the Live Communications Server 2005 Standard Edition server you want to back up.

2. Create a folder at the root of the C drive called Backup (assuming it doesn't already exist from when you backed up the MSDE database).

3. Locate the backup file you want to recover, and then copy the home-srv-1n file to the Backup directory.

4. Open a command prompt by clicking Start ➤ Run. Then type **cmd**, and click OK.

5. From the command prompt, go to the C:\Program Files\Microsoft LC 2005\Server\ Support folder (or wherever the folder is if you installed it into a different location).

6. To restore the MSDE database, type the following, as shown in Figure 15-6:

   Dbbackup /restore /backupfile:c:\backup\home-srv-in

```
C:\WINDOWS\system32\cmd.exe                                           _ □ ×

C:\Program Files\Microsoft LC 2005\Server\Support>dbbackup /restore /backupfile:c:\ba
ckup\home-srv-1n
Connecting to SQL Server...
Stopping Live Communications Server...
Restoring database...
Backing up restored database...
Verifying backup...

C:\Program Files\Microsoft LC 2005\Server\Support>
```

Figure 15-6. *Restoring the MSDE database*

7. You should then see "Verifying backup . . ." displayed. The restore is now complete.

Enterprise Edition

Live Communications Server supports only a simple backup for backing up and restoring SQL clusters. Remember that if you have to perform a restore, you can restore only up to the point that the backup was taken—anything that has happened since that point will be lost, which is why it is extremely important to perform nightly backups so that the worst case will be a single day's loss of data (which in itself is still a potentially bad situation).

Backing Up the Databases

Live Communications Server uses two separate SQL databases called rtc and rtcconfig. Both of these databases need to be backed up in order to have a complete set:

1. Open Enterprise Manager on the SQL Server.

2. Expand the server group, and then expand the server on which the Live Communications Server databases reside.

3. Expand Databases (as shown in Figure 15-7).

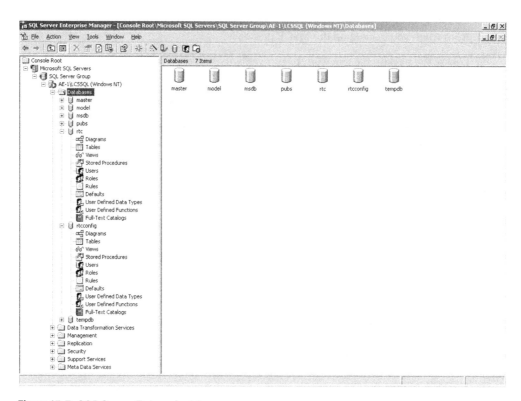

Figure 15-7. *SQL Server Enterprise Manager*

4. Right-click the rtc database, and then select All Tasks ➤ Backup Database (as shown in Figure 15-8).

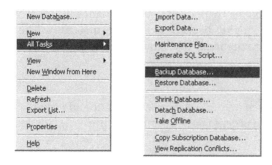

Figure 15-8. *Selecting All Tasks ➤ Backup Database*

5. Enter a name for the backup in the Name box, and enter a description in the Description box.

6. Under Backup, ensure Database – Complete is selected (as shown in Figure 15-9).

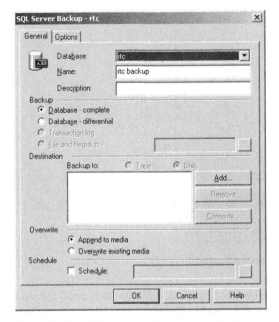

Figure 15-9. *SQL Server Backup – rtc dialog box*

7. In the Destination section, select either Tape or Disk, or if nothing is displayed, click Add.

8. Select an existing location, or click the file location icon (as shown in Figure 15-10).

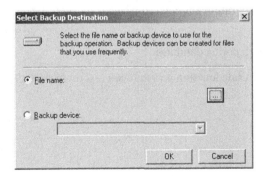

Figure 15-10. *Selecting the backup destination*

9. Either type the location or select it from the list, and then click OK (as shown in Figure 15-11) if you want to back up the databases to disk.

Figure 15-11. *Setting the backup device location*

10. In the Overwrite section, choose between Append to Media (to append the backup to any existing backup) or Overwrite Existing Media (to overwrite any existing backup).

11. You can also use the Schedule box to schedule your backups if you want.

12. On the Options tab you can select a number of additional options including Verify Backup Upon Completion, which is a useful box to select to ensure your backup is successful (as shown in Figure 15-12).

13. Click OK to start the backup. When the backup has completed, you should see a dialog box advising you that the backup operation has been completed successfully (as shown in Figure 15-13).

14. Repeat steps 4 through 13 for the rtcconfig database.

15. Ensure you store your backups in a safe location and that you test them periodically.

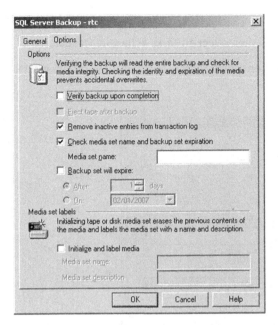

Figure 15-12. *Setting SQL Server backup options*

Figure 15-13. *Successfully completed backup*

Restoring the Databases

To restore the databases, you will need to complete the following steps:

1. Ensure you have your backups available.

2. Open Enterprise Manager on SQL Server.

3. Expand the server group, and then expand the server on which the Live Communications Server databases reside.

4. Expand Databases.

5. Right-click the rtc database, and then select All Tasks ➤ Restore Database.

6. In the Restore As Database box, ensure the database you want to restore is selected (as shown in Figure 15-14).

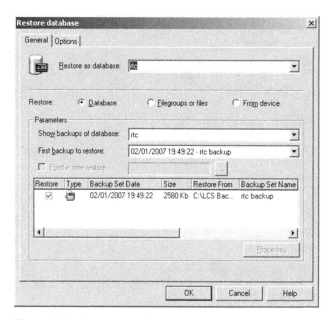

Figure 15-14. *Restoring a database*

7. Ensure that Database is selected under Restore.

8. In the First Backup to Restore list, select the backup to restore.

9. On the Options tab, you can select additional options if required (as shown in Figure 15-15).

10. Click OK to restore the selected database.

11. Repeat steps 5 through 10 for the rtcconfig database.

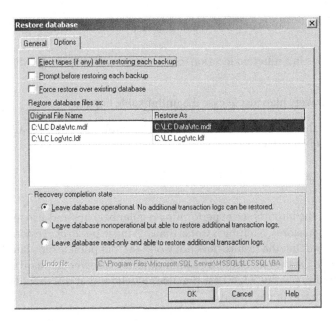

Figure 15-15. *Restoring database options*

Best-Practice Guidelines

This section has some brief best-practice guidelines to help you with the backup and restore processes. Most, if not all, are common sense, but sometimes we can forget even the simplest of tasks when we are busy or under pressure (we have all been there!), so we hope the following tips will help remind you of a few issues:

- Always back up your environment on a nightly basis; that way if something does go wrong and you need to perform a restore, you should have all your data up to the previous night's backup available to you.

- Try to perform your backups during a period of least activity (such as early or late evening).

- Don't forget that online database maintenance is performed from 1 a.m. to 5 a.m., and therefore you should not perform your backups during this four-hour time period.

- Check the logs of the backup software to ensure that the backups were successful, and examine any alerts that are generated.

- Test your backups by performing a restore onto a nonproduction server on a regular basis.

- Store your backup tapes in a different location to your servers, preferably in a different building.

- Develop a disaster recovery plan just in case the unthinkable happens.

- Always have copies of the software and any service packs, hotfixes, or patches available in case you need them in a hurry.

Summary

We hope now you have seen the importance of performing regular backups and also testing those backups by performing restores. Nothing is worse than having to perform a restore in the event of a problem only to find that the restore does not work—at that point it's too late! You also learned how and what to back up for both Live Communications Server Standard Edition and Enterprise Edition. Finally, you saw a few best-practice guidelines that you should try to adopt; they will certainly help you in the long run.

CHAPTER 16

■ ■ ■

Logging

Logging is the process of recording the SIP traffic within a log file. You can then use these logs to produce reports that can help you debug and troubleshoot problems that you might be experiencing in your environment with routing or security. In addition, you can use these logs to provide some patterns of usage for all your users (or even just specific ones if you need) and to provide an audit trail.

This is not to be confused with *archiving*, which is the process of taking copies of the IM conversations, which we'll cover in the next chapter. Logging records only the SIP headers, not the actual instant messages.

Each of the logs created by Live Communications Server are stored in a readable text format within a flat file rather than in a database. You can enable logging on a per-server basis, and you can choose to have only certain servers perform logging rather than having them all do it.

Logging Levels

There are four separate logging levels, levels 1 through 4. Level 1 is the minimum logging level that you can set (apart from no logging), and as each level increases, so does the amount of information that is logged because each additional level just adds to the previous level (for example, level 3 includes levels 1 and 2 as well as the specific information within level 3). Here are the specifics:

Level 1: Critical security information

Level 2: Client logons and session initiations

Level 3: Presence changes and contact management

Level 4: Verbose information for all SIP messages that pass through the server

Information that is logged falls under three particular types:

- Metadata related to the start, stop, and modification of logging

- Protocol information related to incoming and outgoing SIP messages

- Critical server event information

Critical server event information is the same information that is written to the Windows Application Event Logs and can be included in the Live Communications Server logs for consistency.

However, it is far easier to read that information directly from the Windows Application Event Log and keep the Live Communications Server logs for specific Live Communications Server–related information. You can always look up information in the Event Logs if you need to do so. This will also keep the size of the logs down. Be aware that the maximum size for a single log file is 2GB, but really you never want to let it get that high because it becomes difficult to interpret the data when it is that large.

Obviously, the higher the level of logging, the more information that is actually logged. Level 1 can be left on continuously if needed, whereas level 4 should be used only when necessary because it quickly will consume disk space. For example, enabling level 4 logging on a single server and just having a client log in and start an IM conversation with another user increased our log file by 60KB. The total amount of time that process took was less than two minutes and was for only one user; therefore, if you have several hundred or even thousand users and level 4 is enabled all the time, you can see that you will quickly run out of disk space. One of the ways to ensure you don't run out of disk space is to either archive the log files or move them to another location on a regular basis. Live Communications Server does not do this for you, so make sure you get into the habit of doing this!

Tables 16-1, 16-2, and 16-3 detail what is included with each logging level.

Table 16-1. *Logging Levels for SIP Method*

SIP Method	Level 1	Level 2	Level 3	Level 4
INVITE		✓	✓	✓
ACK		✓	✓	✓
CANCEL		✓	✓	✓
BYE		✓	✓	✓
REFER		✓	✓	✓
INFO				✓
MESSAGE				✓
SERVICE			✓	✓
REGISTER		✓	✓	✓
SUBSCRIBE				✓
NOTIFY				✓
BENOTIFY				✓
NEGOTIATE				✓

Table 16-2. *Logging Levels for SIP Header*

SIP Method	Level 1	Level 2	Level 3	Level 4
To		✓	✓	✓
From		✓	✓	✓
Call-ID		✓	✓	✓
CSeq		✓	✓	✓
Contact		✓	✓	✓
Via		✓	✓	✓
Route		✓	✓	✓
Record-Route		✓	✓	✓
Expires		✓	✓	✓
Content-Type		✓	✓	✓
Content-Length		✓	✓	✓
Max-Forwards		✓	✓	✓
All other headers			✓	✓

Table 16-3. *Logging Levels for Other*

Other	Level 1	Level 2	Level 3	Level 4
Windows Application Events	Errors	Errors, Warnings	Errors, Warnings, Information	Errors, Warnings, Information
Security	All	All	All	All
DNS		All	All	All
Connection	Severity 1	Severity 1 and 2	Severity 1 and 2	Severity 1 and 2
Diagnostic	Errors	Errors, Warnings	Errors, Warnings	Errors, Warnings, Information

Enabling Flat-File Logging

By default, flat-file logging is disabled on every instance of Live Communications Server, be it Standard Edition or Enterprise Edition.

To enable flat file logging, perform the following steps:

1. If it's not open already, start the Live Communications Server administrative snap-in (click Start ➤ All Programs ➤ Administrative Tools, and then click Live Communications Server 2005).

2. Expand Microsoft Office Live Communications Server 2005.

3. Expand Forest.

4. Expand Domains, and then expand the domain you want to administer.

5. Expand everything underneath that domain until you have either the pool and server or just the server displayed (as shown in Figure 16-1).

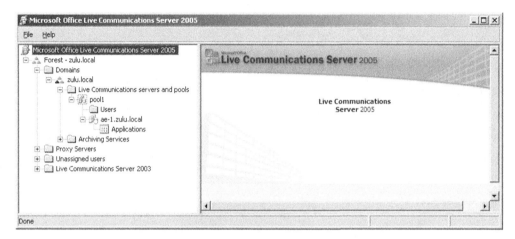

Figure 16-1. *Live Communications Server 2005 administrative snap-in*

6. Right-click the FQDN of the server, and select Properties from the menu.

7. Select the Logging tab on the Properties box, and check the Enable Logging box (as shown in Figure 16-2).

8. Select the logging level you want for this server (from 1 to 4).

9. If you want Windows Application events to be logged to the flat file, select Duplicate Application Event.

10. Select the location of the log file folder (as shown in Figure 16-3). If you do not already have one, create a folder now.

11. In the Create New Log When File Size Reaches box, enter the size (in megabytes) when the new log file should be created. This can be from 1MB to 2047MB. Depending on the level of logging you selected in step 8, the log files might fill up quickly.

12. In the Stop Logging When Disk Usage Reaches box, enter the percentage of the disk capacity at which stage the logging will stop. This can be from 25 percent to 100 percent. This is important so your server does not run out of disk space and stop working, such as if you are storing your logs on the system partition (which really is not a good idea, and you should avoid doing that if you can).

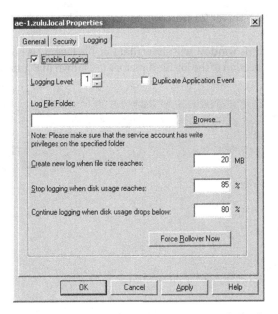

Figure 16-2. *Logging tab of the Properties dialog box*

Figure 16-3. *Selecting the log file folder*

13. In addition to that setting, the Continue Logging When Disk Usage Drops Below box enables logging to resume. This can be from 0 percent to 100 percent. Enter the percentage of the disk capacity to allow logging to continue.

14. The last item is Force Rollover Now. If you click this button, it will stop logging to the current file and start logging to a new one. This is useful if you want to take the current log to analyze. Don't worry about selecting this for normal operations because the log file is automatically rolled over either at midnight or when the size of the log file reaches what you set in step 11.

15. When you have made all the changes you want, click Apply and then OK.

16. Repeat steps 6 through 15 for each server for which you want to enable logging.

If you select that server now, the status window will show that flat-file logging is enabled, the level of logging you selected, and the location of the log file directory (as shown in Figure 16-4).

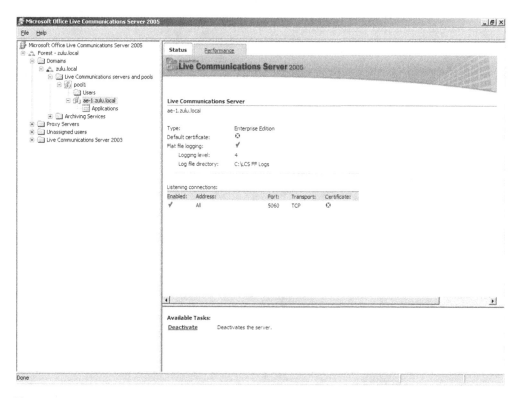

Figure 16-4. *Server status*

Disabling Flat-File Logging

To disable flat-file logging, perform the following steps:

1. If it's not open already, start the Live Communications Server administrative snap-in (click Start ➤ All Programs ➤ Administrative Tools, and then click Live Communications Server 2005).

2. Expand Microsoft Office Live Communications Server 2005.

3. Expand Forest.

4. Expand Domains, and then expand the domain you want to administer.

5. Expand everything underneath that domain until you have either the pool and server or just the server displayed.

6. Right-click the FQDN of the server, and select Properties from the menu.

7. Select the Logging tab on the Properties box, and uncheck the Enable Logging box.

Using the Logs

As mentioned earlier, the logs are stored in such a way that you can open them with any text editor or word processor. You could even import them into an application such as Microsoft Operations Manager (MOM). For more about MOM, take a look at Chapter 19, which is about monitoring Live Communications Server.

Figure 16-5 shows an example of part of a log file and is a single record created within a level 4 log.

```
$$begin_record
LogType: protocol
Date: 2007/01/03 22:48:33
Direction: Incoming
Peer: 192.168.0.1:1402
Message-Type: Request
Start-Line: REGISTER sip:zulu.local SIP/2.0
To:  <sip:andrew@zulu.local>
From:  <sip:andrew@zulu.local>;tag=e51583af08;epid=9def7b1c5b
Call-ID:  9dfe750c32524f609f580a11b5434378
CSeq: 1 REGISTER
Contact:  <sip:192.168.0.1:11341;transport=tcp>;methods="INVITE, MESSAGE,
INFO, SUBSCRIBE, OPTIONS, BYE, CANCEL, NOTIFY, ACK, REFER,
BENOTIFY";proxy=replace
Via:  SIP/2.0/TCP 192.168.0.1:11341
Max-Forwards:  70
Content-Length:  0
Other-Headers: User-Agent:  LCC/1.3.5371 (Microsoft Office Communicator
2005 1.0.559.0)
Other-Headers: Supported:  com.microsoft.msrtc.presence, adhoclist
Other-Headers: Supported:  ms-forking
Other-Headers: ms-keep-alive:  UAC;hop-hop=yes
Other-Headers: Event:  registration
Other-Headers: Allow-Events:  presence
$$end_record
```

Figure 16-5. *A record in a level 4 log file*

Although that information on its own could be quite useful, the log file could contain thousands of lines of data, so using a text editor might not be the best way to review the logs. Fortunately, a tool called SIPView can help you review the logs.

SIPView

SIPView is an application that is included as part of the Live Communications Server 2005 Resource Kit.

If you don't already have the resource kit installed, you should download it and install it now from `http://www.microsoft.com/downloads/details.aspx?FamilyID=d21c38e5-5d8f-44c7-ba17-2cc4f85d8b51&DisplayLang=en`. Then follow these steps:

1. To launch SIPView, browse to the location of the resource kit, which if you accepted the defaults will be `C:\Program Files\Microsoft LC 2005\ResKit`.

2. Open the `SIPView` folder.

3. Double-click `SipView.exe` to launch it.

4. Click File ➤ Open File, select the location of your log files, and then choose a specific log file to open.

The log file is then opened and processed into a readable format (as shown in Figure 16-6). This particular record is the same one as shown earlier in Figure 16-5.

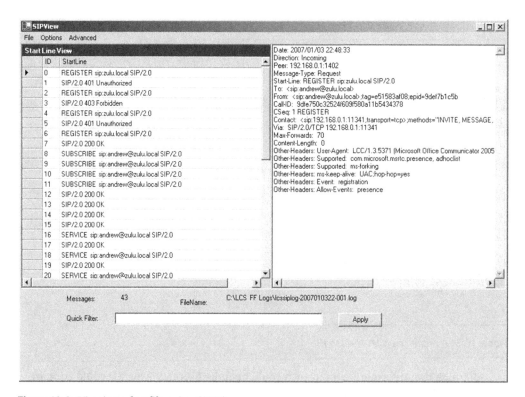

Figure 16-6. *Viewing a log file using SIPView*

As you can see, the log file is processed, and each record is collated into a single line with an ID number.

You can quickly filter the log file by using the Quick Filter box. Enter a filter search in the box, and then click Apply to filter the log. You can also use wildcards such as *SERVICE*. If your filter search does not display any results, just remove the test, and click Apply again to restore the full log view.

You can also specify additional filters by selecting Options ➤ Filter (as shown in Figure 16-7).

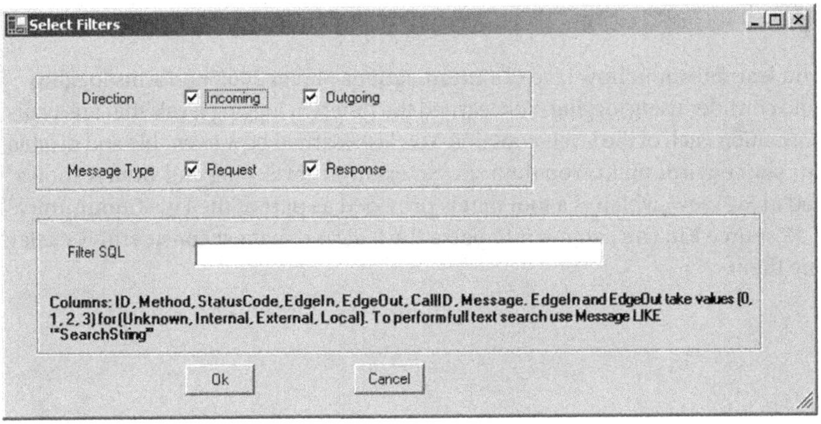

Figure 16-7. *The filter options*

From here you can filter the direction of the traffic (either incoming or outgoing), filter the message type (request or response), or even use simple SQL queries to filter the log.

There is also an Advanced menu (as shown in Figure 16-8).

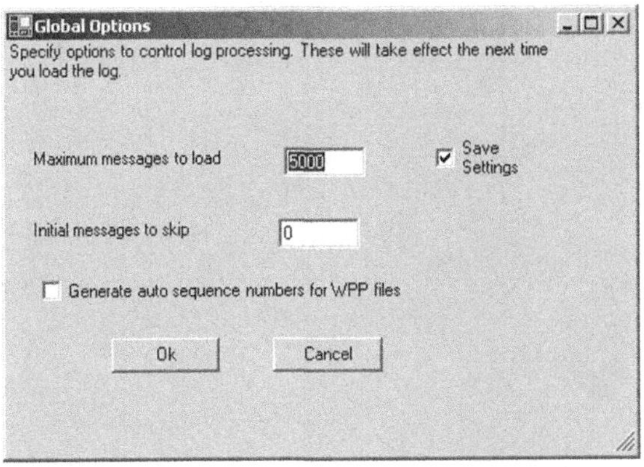

Figure 16-8. *Advanced options*

From here you can specify the maximum number of messages to load. By default only the first 5,000 records will be displayed. Depending on the level of logging you're using, this might be sufficient, but if you are using something like level 4 logging, you might need to increase that number. Don't forget that these settings take effect only the next time you open the log file, so make sure you close the current log file and open it again if you want to see the changes immediately.

Another file that is included in the resource kit is called LCSError.exe; this application allows you to enter an error code that might have been displayed in the logs and have it then displayed into something that you can understand rather than just an error code that might not mean anything to you. For more information about LCSError.exe, the LCSErrorReadme.htm file has additional details on its usage. This is a useful tool when troubleshooting issues in your Live Communications Server environment.

Summary

In this chapter, you learned about how Live Communications Server 2005 performs logging and why you should consider using logging. You learned the different logging levels that are available and what information each of the levels contains. You also learned how to enable and disable flat-file logging for your environment. You then saw an example level 4 log and what it shows. Finally, you looked at SIPView, which is a tool that is provided as part of the Live Communications Server 2005 Resource Kit; you can use it to parse the logs and make it considerably easier for you to examine them.

CHAPTER 17

■■■

Archiving

Now that you have looked at logging, it's time to look at archiving. *Archiving* is the process of taking copies of instant message conversations and keeping them for any number of reasons, including auditing conversations, ensuring that corporate policies are maintained, and even complying with regulations (such as HIPPA or Sarbanes-Oxley), depending on where you are in the world and what business your company is in. It is important to note, however, that Live Communicators Server archiving is not certified to meet regulatory auditing requirements—it is merely a tool that an organization can use to help it to meet its requirements. One of the reasons for this is that the archive is not considered to be "tamper-proof," and as such it might not meet certain compliance requirements. Make sure you completely understand what the requirements are if you have to comply with any regulations.

When enabled, the Archiving Service will archive all instant messaging conversations by default. Archiving provides a great deal of granularity, which means you can archive conversations from everyone or even a single user if you want. You can also archive conversations with federated partners. Note that only the conversations are archived. File transfers and multimedia (audio and video) are not archived. Also, for each domain you want to enable archiving in, the Archiving Service must be installed because it cannot archive messages across domains.

The Archiving Service requires the following in order to function correctly:

- The archiving agent, which records the content of the message (this is actually installed by default for each Live Communications Server machine, but it requires configuring and activating before it can be used).

- The archiving back-end server (which includes an archiving back-end queue and a back-end database). The back-end database is a SQL database and so requires SQL Server 2000 SP3a or newer to be installed and available.

A simple walk-through of how archiving works is as follows:

1. Archiving agents installed on the Live Communications Server record the instant message conversations and write them to the archiving back-end queue.

2. The Archiving Service will then read the contents of the back-end queue and write them to the archiving back-end database.

Best practice dictates that the Archiving Service should be installed on its own dedicated server; however, you can install it on any Live Communications Server if you need to do so. For examples of the different types of archiving topologies that are supported, see the Microsoft Office Live Communications Server 2005 Planning Guide.

Installing MSMQ

Before you install the Archiving Service, you must first install Microsoft Message Queuing (MSMQ) on each server that will have archiving enabled.

MSMQ is required because the archiving agent that is on the Live Communications Server uses MSMQ to receive notifications from the Archiving Service destination queue. It also uses MSMQ as a temporary queue if the Archiving Service is unavailable for any reason. Also note that MSMQ must be installed on all servers in a pool if you want to enable archiving for that pool.

If you have not already installed MSMQ, follow these steps on each server:

1. Select Control Panel ➤ Add and Remove Programs, and click Add/Remove Windows Components.

2. Highlight Application Server by selecting it, as shown in Figure 17-1, and then click Details.

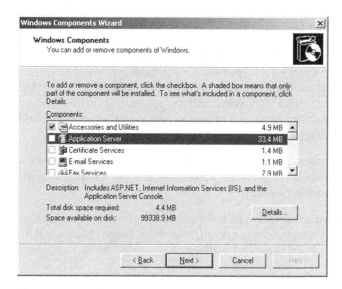

Figure 17-1. *Adding Windows components*

3. Check the Message Queuing box (as shown in Figure 17-2), click OK, and follow the steps to complete the MSMQ installation.

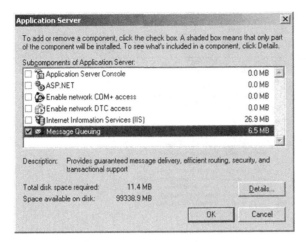

Figure 17-2. *Adding message queuing to the server*

Each computer that is running MSMQ must be a member of the Windows Authorization Access group so that it can authorize users.

Computer accounts for the following servers also need to be added to the Windows Authorization Access group:

- The server that hosts the SQL archiving database

- The server that is running the archiving service

- The Standard Edition server computer account if you want to archive any Standard Edition servers

- All Enterprise Edition servers in the pool you want to archive

- The server that has the back-end database on it

4. On a domain controller, open Active Directory Users and Computers, expand the Domain node, and click Builtin (as shown in Figure 17-3).

5. Double-click Windows Authorization Access Group, and click the Members tab (as shown in Figure 17-4).

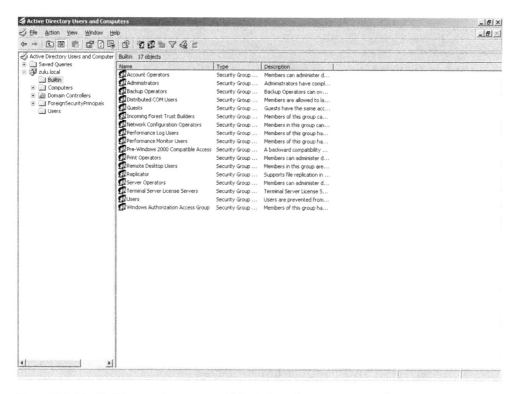

Figure 17-3. *The Builtin security groups within Active Directory Users and Computers*

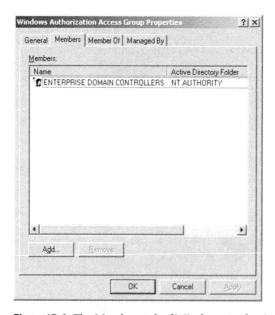

Figure 17-4. *The Members tab of Windows Authorization Access Group*

6. Click Add to open the Select Users, Contacts, Computers, or Groups dialog box (as shown in Figure 17-5).

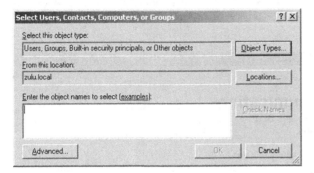

Figure 17-5. *The Select Users, Contacts, Computers, or Groups dialog box*

7. Click Object Types, ensure the Computers object type is checked (as shown in Figure 17-6), and then click OK.

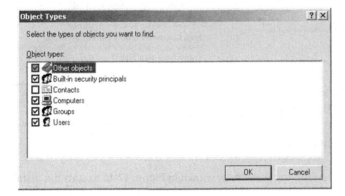

Figure 17-6. *Selecting the Computers object type*

8. Type the name of the computer that has MSMQ installed, and then click Check Names to ensure it is correct. If it is, click OK and then OK again to finish.

Installing the Archiving Service

As we already mentioned, you can install the Archiving Service on a dedicated server or on any Live Communications Server machine that already exists. You should be aware that MSMQ uses NetBIOS, which means the computer name that hosts the Archiving Service must be less than 15 characters; otherwise, it won't function correctly.

1. On the server you want to install the Archiving Service on, run Setup.exe from the Live Communications Server 2005 CD.

2. From the Live Communications Server deployment tool, click Archiving Service (as shown in Figure 17-7).

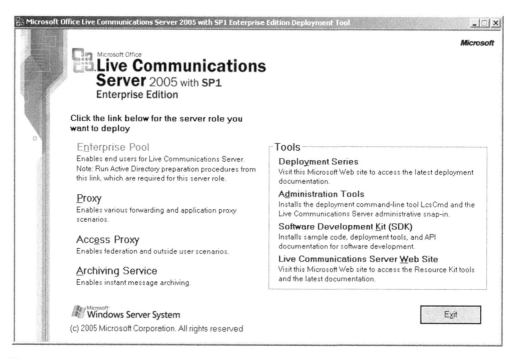

Figure 17-7. *Live Communications Server deployment tool*

3. Click Install Files for Archiving Service (as shown in Figure 17-8) to start the installation process.

4. Click Next, accept the terms in the license agreement, and then click Next again.

5. Enter your details, and click Next.

6. On the Live Communications IM Archiving Service Options page (as shown in Figure 17-9), click Next to accept the defaults. You can enter a different name for the message queue path if you want, along with a different location to which to install the files.

7. You will see a dialog box telling you that the message queue specified does not exist (as shown in Figure 17-10) and asking you whether you want to create it. Click Yes.

8. Click Install to continue, and then when the installation has completed, click Finish. You will then be asked whether you want to activate the service—if you click No, then you will have to complete the next few steps to activate it.

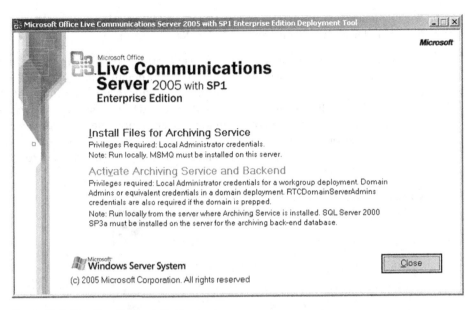

Figure 17-8. *Starting the installation process*

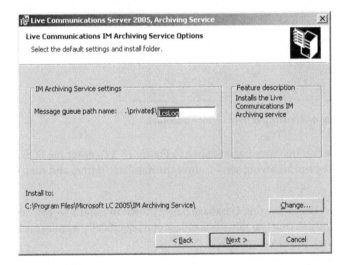

Figure 17-9. *The Live Communications IM Archiving Service Options page*

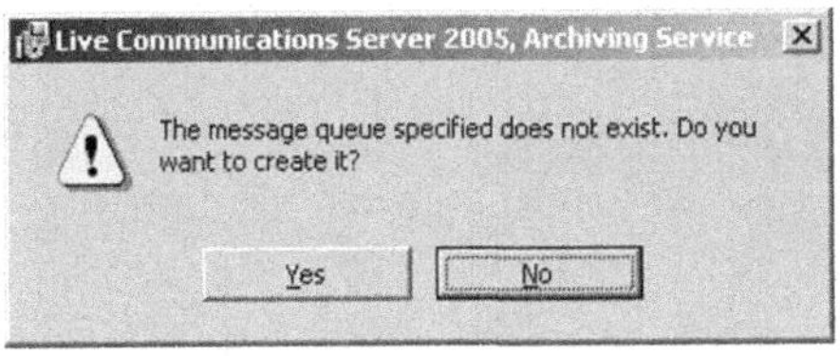

Figure 17-10. *The message queue specified does not exist.*

9. You might need to complete steps 1 and 2 again and then select Activate the Archiving Service and Backend. When prompted, click Next to continue.

10. On the Select Service Account page (as shown in Figure 17-11), you can choose to create a new service account or use an existing account. The default name for the new service account is LCArchivingService, but you can change this to anything you want. It is important to note that any new account that is created by the wizard has its password set to expire after 14 days. Ensure you modify the account to meet your organization's account policies once the installation is complete; otherwise, after 14 days, the Archiving Service will stop working. Enter a password, and then confirm it; click Next to continue.

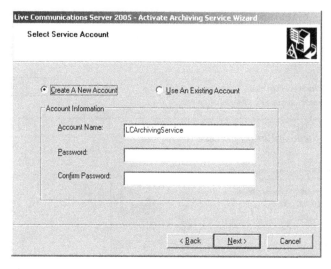

Figure 17-11. *Selecting or creating a new service account*

11. On the Select SQL Server Instance page (shown in Figure 17-12), enter the SQL Server instance to be used by the archiving server, enter the database name, and then click Next to continue.

12. On the Option for Re-Using Existing Database page (shown in Figure 17-13), do not check the Replace Any Existing Database box unless you specifically want to replace the existing database; click Next to continue.

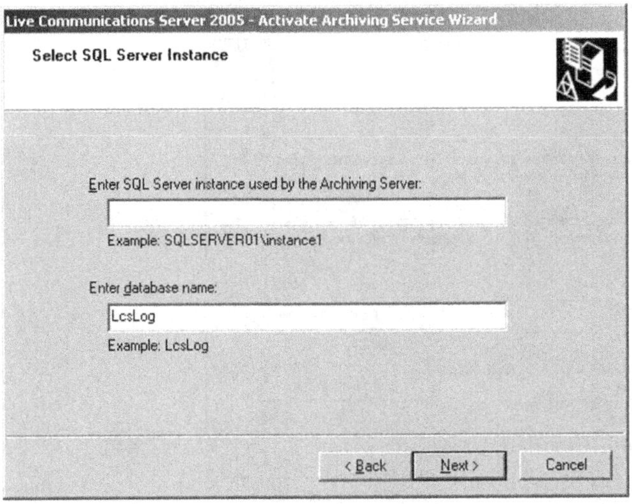

Figure 17-12. *Selecting a SQL Server instance*

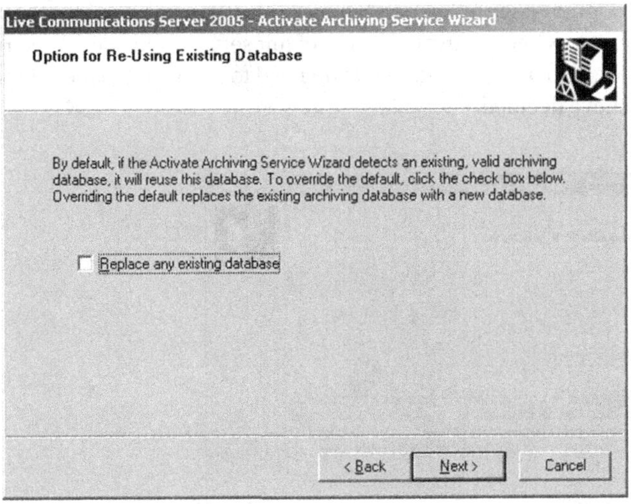

Figure 17-13. *Option for reusing the existing database*

13. On the Choose Destination Locations page (shown in Figure 17-14), you must specify the locations where to install the database and transaction logs. If you click the Local Server Directory button, you can browse the local directory. Don't forget that if you are using a clustered SQL back end, you must select a location for the database and transactions logs to which both nodes in the cluster have access.

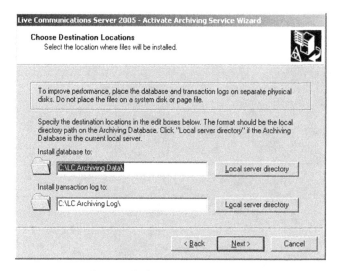

Figure 17-14. *Selecting the locations for the database and transaction logs*

14. On the Start Service Option page (shown in Figure 17-15), you can choose whether to start the service after it has been activated. The default setting is to start the service; however, you might want to uncheck the box if you need to do any further configuration. Click Next after you have decided.

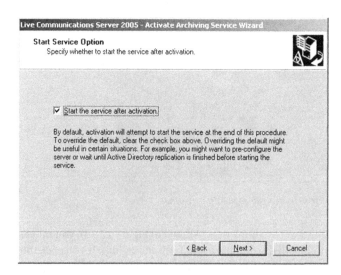

Figure 17-15. *Choosing to start the archiving service after activation*

15. Click Next to start the activation process.

16. When the activation process is complete, you should view the Deployment Log file that is created to check for any problems. It is a good idea to do this now before continuing so that you can correct any issues. Click View Log to view the log file (an example of which is shown in Figure 17-16). What you really want to see is the green "Success" statements in the Execution Result column.

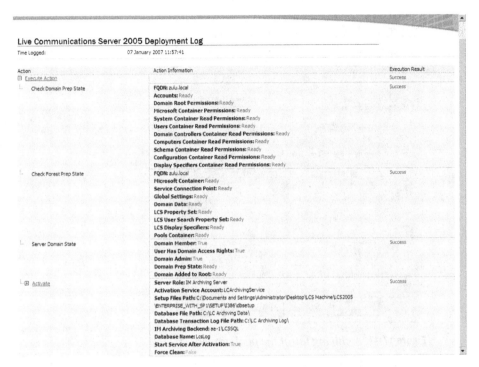

Figure 17-16. *Reviewing the archive service's Deployment Log file*

Enabling Archiving

Now that the Archiving Service has been activated, the next step is to actually enable archiving on each Live Communications Server machine on which you want to archive conversations.

You can perform the following steps on either a Live Communications Server Standard Edition server or an Enterprise Edition server:

1. If it's not open already, start the Live Communications Server administrative snap-in (click Start ➤ All Programs ➤ Administrative Tools, and then click Live Communications Server 2005).

2. Expand Microsoft Office Live Communications Server 2005.

3. Expand Forest.

4. Expand Domains, and then expand the domain you want to administer.

5. Expand everything underneath that domain until you have the pool displayed.

6. Right-click the pool, and select Properties.

7. Click the Archiving tab (as shown in Figure 17-17).

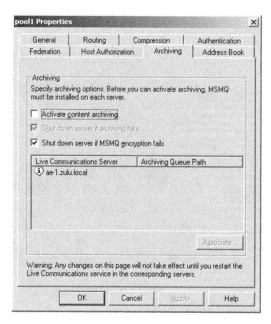

Figure 17-17. *Archiving tab of the pool properties*

8. Check the Activate Content Archiving box; a warning will appear saying that at least one Live Communications Server machine does not have an associated queue path (as shown in Figure 17-18). Just click OK for now.

Figure 17-18. *Associated queue path warning*

There are two additional check boxes, both of which are checked by default. The first is Shut Down Server If Archiving Fails; having this enabled is what you might have seen referred to as running archiving in critical mode. This means that if the archiving fails for any reason (such as lack of disk space), then the server will shut down, and the Live Communications Server service will become unavailable until the issue is resolved.

The other is Shut Down Server If MSMQ Encryption Fails. Both of these options are required if your organization must archive all messaging content for regulatory, legal, or policy compliance requirements.

9. Make changes to the two archiving shutdown options if required; otherwise, leave them enabled.

10. Select a Live Communications Server machine from the list (there might be only one as in the example), and click the Associate button.

11. Enter the name of the archiving server in the box on the left and the queue name in the box on the right (as shown in Figure 17-19). Remember that the queue name is the one you created earlier. Click OK when you have entered the names in both boxes.

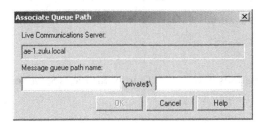

Figure 17-19. *Associating the queue path*

12. Repeat steps 10 and 11 for each Live Communications Server machine in the list.

13. Click OK to close the properties box.

14. Restart all the Live Communications Server services on all the Live Communications Server machines in the pool. For Live Communications Server Standard Edition servers, you need to restart the services only on that Standard Edition server. To do this, right-click the server name, and click Stop. Then right-click it again, and click Start.

If you now expand the Archiving Services node and select a server, you will see information about the Archiving Service such as the SQL instance, database name, and message queue name (as the example in Figure 17-20 shows). You can also deactivate the Archiving Service from here by clicking Deactivate.

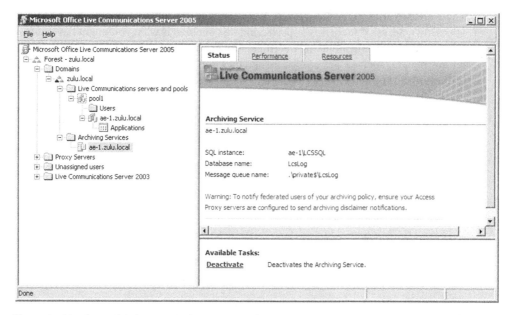

Figure 17-20. *The Archiving Service's status window*

Global Settings

If you want or need to archive all conversations in your Live Communications Server environment, you can do so by setting the global properties:

1. If it's not open already, start the Live Communications Server administrative snap-in (click Start ➤ All Programs ➤ Administrative Tools, and then click Live Communications Server 2005).

2. Expand Microsoft Office Live Communications Server 2005.

3. Right-click the Forest node, and select Properties.

4. Click the Archiving tab (as shown in Figure 17-21).

5. Check the Archive All Communications with Internal Users box if you want to archive all internal communications.

6. Check the Archive All Communications with Federated Partners box if you want to archive all communications with your federated partners (depending on your location, there may be a legal requirement to inform your federated partners that you are archiving messages).

7. Ensure that neither of the Do Not Archive Message Body boxes is checked.

8. Click Apply, and then click OK.

9. Restart all the Live Communications Server services on all the Live Communications Server machines. To do this, right-click the server name, and click Stop. Then right-click it again, and click Start.

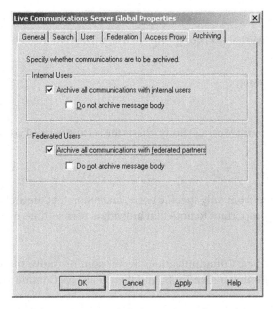

Figure 17-21. *Forest global properties for archiving*

If you now select the forest, you will see the status pane has been updated to include the new global archiving settings (as the example in Figure 17-22 shows).

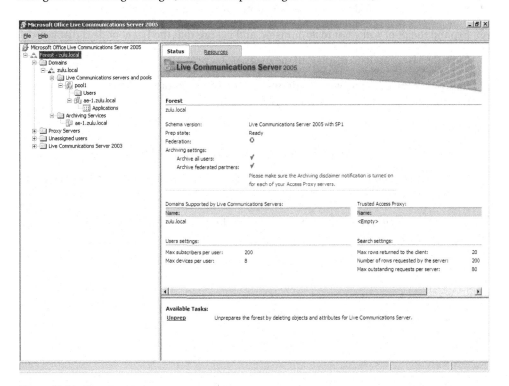

Figure 17-22. *Forest status pane*

User Settings

You can also configure settings for individual users or groups of users. The four available options are as follows:

- Use Global Default Archiving Setting

- Archive All Communications

- Archive All Communications Without Message Body (this is the setting to use if you want to archive only usage data)

- Do Not Archive Communications

If you want to archive conversations from only specific users, make sure that the archiving global settings are not configured. It is important to note that individual user settings override global settings.

1. If it's not open already, start the Live Communications Server administrative snap-in (click Start ➤ All Programs ➤ Administrative Tools, and then click Live Communications Server 2005).

2. Expand Microsoft Office Live Communications Server 2005.

3. Expand Forest.

4. Expand Domains, and then expand the domain you want to administer.

5. Expand the pool you want to administer, and ensure that the Users node is displayed.

6. Click the Users node to display all the users.

7. Right-click the user you want to administer, and select Properties. The User Properties window is displayed (as shown in Figure 17-23).

8. Click Advanced Settings.

9. Select the archiving setting you want to use for this user (as shown in Figure 17-24).

10. Click OK, click Apply, and then click OK again to close the User Advanced Settings dialog box.

11. Repeat steps 7 through 10 for each user you want to archive.

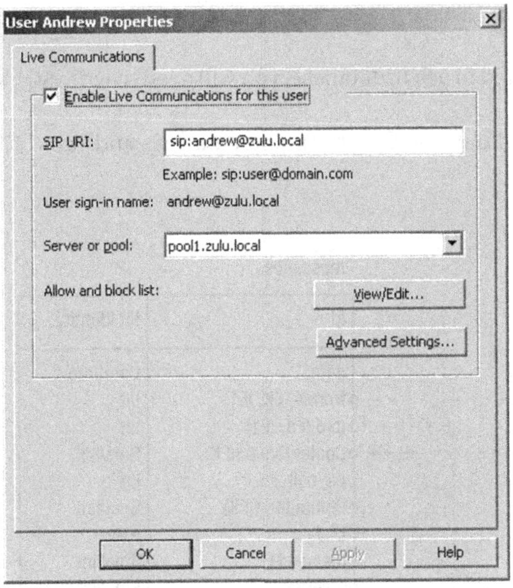

Figure 17-23. *User properties*

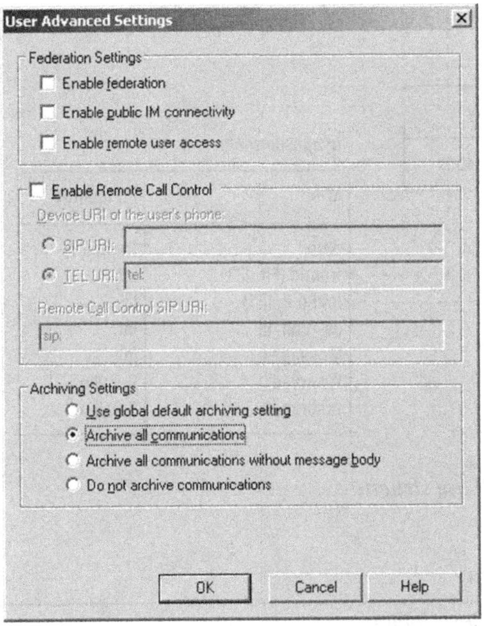

Figure 17-24. *User advanced settings*

Viewing the Archives

Because the archived messages are stored in a SQL database, you will need to write SQL queries in order to interrogate the database.

Figure 17-25 shows the structure of the archiving back-end database, and Table 17-1 describes the database schema.

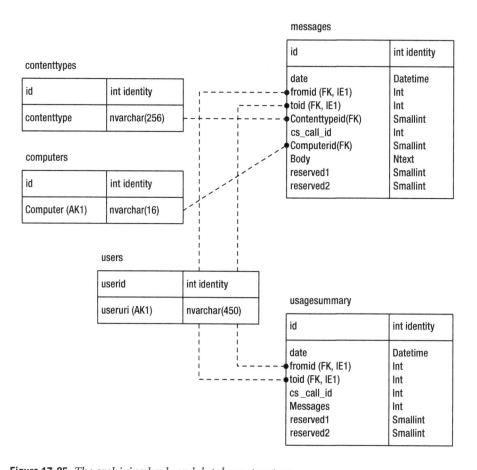

Figure 17-25. *The archiving back-end database structure*

Table 17-1. *The Archiving Database Schema*

Table Name	Column Name	Description
users	userid	Identity column
	useruri	URI of the user who sent or received the instant message
computers	id	Identity column
	computer	NetBIOS name of the home server that processed the instant message

Table 17-1. *The Archiving Database Schema*

Table Name	Column Name	Description
contenttypes	id	Identity column
	contenttype	MIME content type of the message
messages	id	Identity column
	date	Date and time at which the message was processed by a home server
	fromid	Identifies the sender of an instant message (corresponds with userid in users table)
	toid	Identifies the recipient of an instant message (corresponds with userid in users table)
	contenttypeid	Identifies what the content type of the message is
	cs_call_id	Unique identifier for the instant message session; checksum calculated from call_id
	computerid	Identifies the home server that processed an instant message (corresponds with id in computers table)
	body	Body of the instant message
	reserved1	Column reserved for future use
	reserved2	Column reserved for future use
usagesummary	id	Identity column
	date	Date and time at which the message was processed by a home server
	fromid	Identifies the sender of an instant message (corresponds with userid in users table)
	toid	Identifies the recipient of an instant message (corresponds with userid in users table)
	cs_call_id	Unique identifier for the IM session; checksum calculated from call_id
	messages	Number of messages sent
	reserved1	Column reserved for future use
	reserved2	Column reserved for future use

A quick and easy way to check that archiving is actually working is to check that the SQL database is being written to.

To do this, do the following:

1. Launch Enterprise Manager on the SQL Server machine.

2. Expand Microsoft SQL Servers, SQL Server Group, <servername>, Databases, and then LcsLog.

3. Click the Tables entry.

4. Select Messages from the Tables list (as shown in Figure 17-26).

5. Right-click Messages, highlight Open Table, and then click Return All Rows.

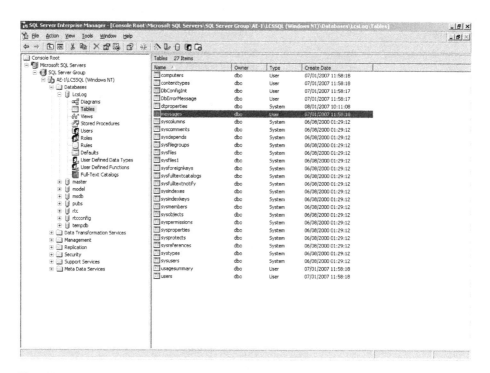

Figure 17-26. *SQL Server Enterprise Manager—Tables list*

You should then see a list of returned values (as shown in Figure 17-27). As you can see, under the Body column are the contents of the actual archived message. fromid and toid represent the users, and if you wanted to see what they were, you could run the same query from step 5 for the Users entry in the Tables list. It would show that 1 is rui@zulu.local and 2 is Andrew@zulu.local.

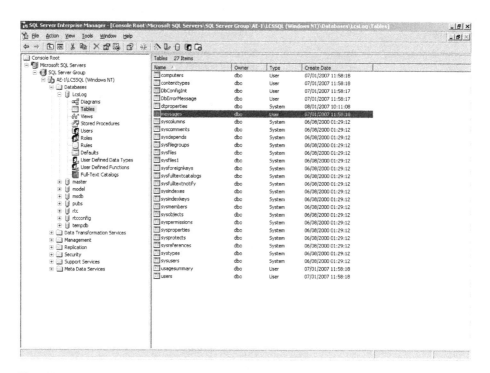

Figure 17-27. *Returned values for archived messages*

Several third-party products are available to help you view and interrogate the archive logs. If you are interested in what is currently available, refer to the Microsoft Office partner website (`http://directory.partners.extranet.microsoft.com/`), or do a search using your favorite search engine.

Summary

In this chapter, you learned about archiving and saw the difference between archiving and logging, which you learned about in the previous chapter. You learned about the requirements for the Archiving Service and how to install the requirement components prior to installing the Archiving Service. You then saw how to install and configure the Archiving Service and make changes to the global settings. Finally, you got a little insight into how SQL stores the archiving information and how you can perform simple queries against the SQL databases.

■ ■ ■

CHAPTER 18

Troubleshooting

Learning to effectively troubleshoot problems with Live Communications Server 2005 SP1 is important because problems may arise while setting up, configuring, or using the product. As is the case for most products, the large majority of problems often occur during setup and configuration. With a complex system such as Live Communications Server 2005 SP1, isolating the root cause of the problem is difficult and time-consuming without the right tools and expertise. This chapter aims to provide you with guidance on how to troubleshoot a problem with your Live Communications Server infrastructure, and we will point you to tools to assist you in the process.

Troubleshooting Deployment Issues

Often times, the first place where problems surface is right during the deployment phase. Problems often materialize after running one of the setup wizards. The majority of the problems are related to insufficient permissions. The best way to troubleshoot deployment problems is to view the log file generated after the setup wizard fails. These HTML log files are detailed and should provide you with sufficient information to pinpoint the failure point.

Troubleshooting User Issues

The most common problem users report to your help desk support is failure to sign in to Live Communications Server. Other possible problems are the inability to communicate with federated partners or PIC users (AOL, Yahoo!, or MSN contacts), issues with controlling their PBX phone from Office Communicator (RCC), or issues with communicating with other internal users homed on a different pool. This is by no means a comprehensive list.

Here are some recommendations:

- Check the user's Live Communications settings in Active Directory using DSA.MSC.

- Verify the user's OC configuration.

- If using manual configuration, verify the server FQDN is specified correctly.

- If using automatic configuration, verify the SIP SRV is resolvable using NsLookup.exe.

- Use LcsPing.exe to make sure the server or pool is listening on the appropriate TCP/TLS ports.

- Test connectivity with LcsDiag.exe.

- Test connectivity using TCP if TLS fails to determine whether it's a certificate issue:

  - Verify the server certificate is not expired.

  - Check that the server certificate is trusted by the client.

- Turn on WPP Tracing, and reproduce the problem.

The first step in troubleshooting client-side problems is to verify the configuration settings on the Communicator client. Once the configuration is confirmed to be correct, you should verify connectivity problems with the tools recommended in the previous list.

NsLookup

NsLookup.exe is a Windows system tool that you can use to verify whether you've configured your DNS SRV records for SIP correctly. The example in Figure 18-1 shows that the DNS SRV records _sipinternal._tcp.touareg.local and _sipinternaltls._tcp.touareg.local have been defined. Be sure to set the query type, q, to ANY ('set q=ANY'). This tool is helpful to make sure you've properly configured DNS SRV records for SIP, the FQDN of your Enterprise pool is resolvable, and your servers are reachable.

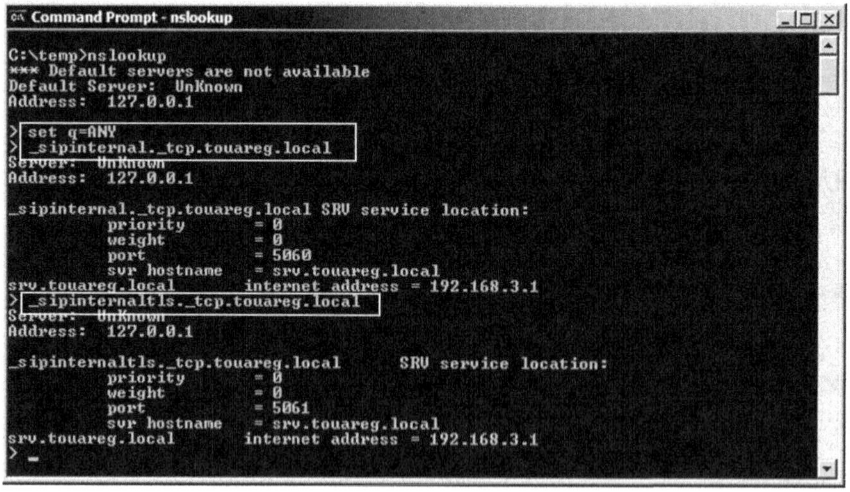

Figure 18-1. *Resolving SIP SRV using NsLookup.exe*

LcsPing

LcsPing.exe is a Live Communications Server Resource Kit command-line tool (see Figure 18-2). It's simple to use and provides help with the /? option, or you can read the HTML help file LcsPingReadme.htm. It checks connectivity to all the ports used by Live Communications Server.

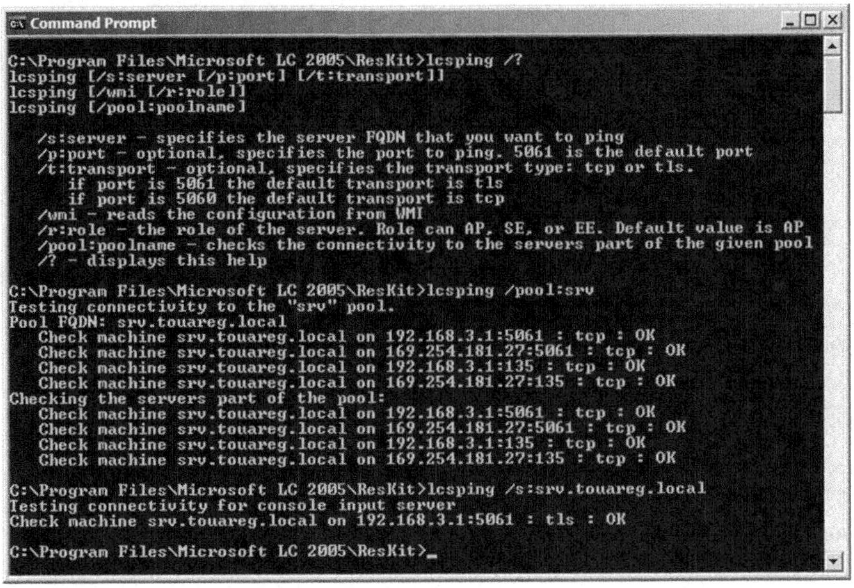

Figure 18-2. *LcsPing usage*

LcsDiag

Using the tool LcsDiag.exe is a quick and easy way for an administrator to troubleshoot client connections. We've illustrated the use of this tool in Chapter 13 to verify client connectivity without using Communicator. Select the option Diagnostic Client on the right menu, as shown in Figure 18-3. LcsDiag.exe provides a wizard-style GUI to check client connectivity to the user's home server and outputs a specific explanation of any failures. This tool is available in the Live Communications Server Resource Kit.

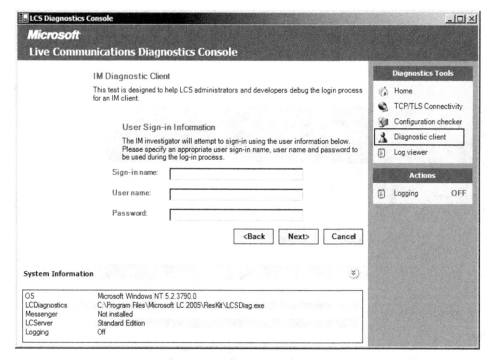

Figure 18-3. *Diagnosing the client using* `LcsDiag.exe`

WPP Tracing

To enable client-side tracing on Communicator 2005 to troubleshoot problems, you must set the following registry value on the user's computer. A log file will be generated in the directory `%userprofile%/Tracing`.

`HKEY_CURRENT_USER\Software\Microsoft\Tracing\communicator\EnableFileTracing = 1`

An alternative option to having users set this registry setting themselves, which could potentially put their computer at risk if misconfigured, is to use the free tool Communicator 2005 Trace Utility, available at `http://www.LcsSolutions.com` (see Figure 18-4). You could also create a REG file or script to set and unset this registry value.

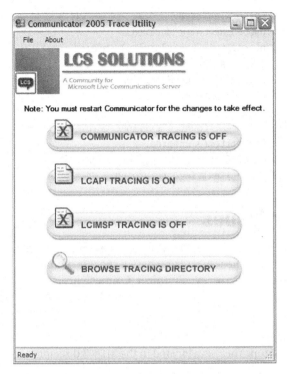

Figure 18-4. *Communicator Trace Utility*

The log file called CommunicatorX.log, where X is a monotonously increasing number, will trace all the calls Communicator 2005 makes. The following sample illustrates the format of the log file:

```
15:06:49.586 990:8DC TRACE :: GetServiceByName() entered.
15:06:49.586 990:8DC TRACE :: CBaseCollection::get_Count() entered.
15:06:49.586 990:8DC TRACE :: CBaseCollection::get_Count() exiting, returning S_OK.
15:06:49.586 990:8DC TRACE :: CBaseCollection::Item() entered.
15:06:49.586 990:8DC TRACE :: CBaseCollection::Item() exiting, returning S_OK.
15:06:49.586 990:8DC TRACE :: GetServiceByName() exiting, returning S_OK.
15:06:49.586 990:8DC TRACE :: CUIManager::LogonService() entered.
15:06:49.586 990:8DC TRACE :: CUIManager::LoadNameAndPassword() entered.
15:06:49.586 990:8DC TRACE :: CUIManager::LoadNameAndPassword() exiting,
        returning S_FALSE.
15:06:49.586 990:8DC TRACE :: In CUIManager::LogonService
        -- Logging on to Microsoft RTC Instant Messaging
        -- (annem@touareg.local touareg\annem, )
```

```
15:06:49.586 990:8DC TRACE :: CBLObject::Logon() entered.
15:06:49.636 990:8DC TRACE :: CBLObject::OnQueuedEvent() entered.
15:06:49.636 990:8DC TRACE :: CTaskbar::OnLocalStateChangeResult() entered.
15:06:49.636 990:8DC TRACE :: CBLObject::get_LocalState() entered.
15:06:49.636 990:8DC TRACE :: CPlatformUtil::GetServiceByName() entered.
15:06:49.636 990:8DC TRACE :: GetServiceByName() entered.
15:06:49.636 990:8DC TRACE :: CBaseCollection::get_Count() entered.
15:06:49.636 990:8DC TRACE :: CBaseCollection::get_Count() exiting, returning S_OK.
15:06:49.636 990:8DC TRACE :: CBaseCollection::Item() entered.
15:06:49.636 990:8DC TRACE :: CBaseCollection::Item() exiting, returning S_OK.
15:06:49.636 990:8DC TRACE :: GetServiceByName() exiting, returning S_OK.
```

Troubleshooting Server Issues

Server problems can arise from replication issues with Active Directory. For example, schema replication was not completed, or the schema cache was corrupted on a specific domain controller from which your Live Communications Server synchronizes. Connectivity issues can arise between pools, federation, and PIC links. This section provides guidance on what steps to take to debug such issues.

Here are some recommendations:

- Check the log files generated during Setup. These are located in the %TEMP% directory.

- Check the state of the pool/server by viewing the dashboard of the server status pane in the Admin Tools MMC.

- Check for server failures in the Application event log.

- Check the state of the server by running LcsCmd.exe in diagnostic mode. If the problem does not appear to be related to the server, you can verify the state of your Active Directory with LcsCmd.exe as well.

- Another great tool to get a detailed snapshot of your entire environment is Sasa Juratovic's Best Practice Analyzer (BPA).

- If the problem does not become apparent, then turn on flat-file logging on the server.

- Finally, often as a last resort, capture the SIP traffic on the wire using Ethereal, Microsoft Network Monitor, or any other network tracing tool of your choice.

Admin Tools MMC Status

When troubleshooting Live Communications Server problems, open the Admin Tools MMC, and examine the status of the server/pool. This console will give you a snapshot of the server state whether it is still running or stopped because of a failure (see Figure 18-5). If the server is stopped, try starting it. When restarting the server, if the failure persists, it will be logged in the Application event log. Check the Application event log to determine the nature of the failure.

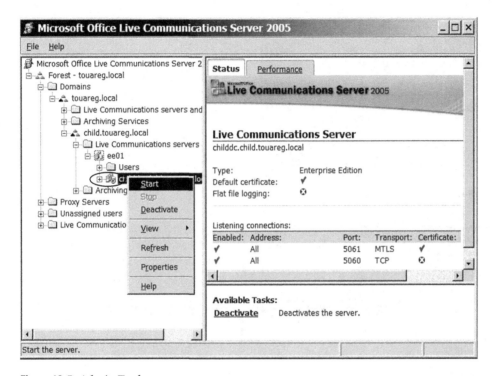

Figure 18-5. *Admin Tools*

Event Logs

Any time you suspect a server problem, your first reaction should be to check the Application and System event logs. Live Communications Server logs errors, warnings, and information in the Application event log; however, you should also check the System event log because the problem may be related to the server. Verify that the Live Communications Server service is started, as shown in Figure 18-6. There is a time lag before the Windows service control manager (SCM) indicates that the service is starting and indicates the time it actually starts. Figure 18-7 shows the Event Viewer.

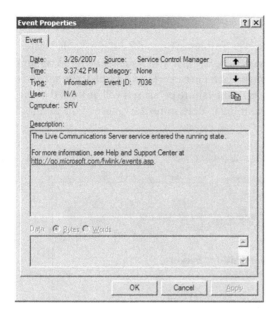

Figure 18-6. *Live Communications Server service started*

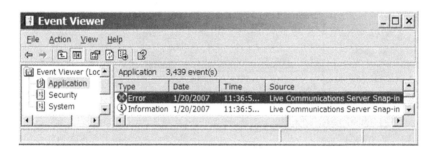

Figure 18-7. *Event Viewer*

In this example (Figure 18-8), the event indicates the failure is caused by the service account used to run the Live Communications Server service. Notice the HRESULT error code, 8007042d. The Live Communications Server Resource Kit tool, LcsError.exe, can help translate these cryptic error codes into a friendlier error message, as shown in Figure 18-9.

If you can't recall the exact account name used to run the Live Communications Server service, open the Services snap-in under the Administrative Tools folder (see Figure 18-10).

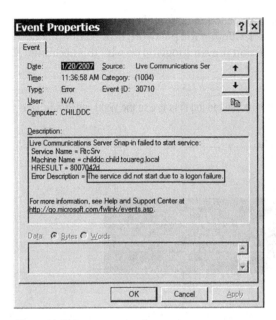

Figure 18-8. *Event properties*

Figure 18-9. *LcsError.exe*

Figure 18-10. *Live Communications Server service*

Now that you've determined the problem to be a logon failure of the service account, CHILD\LCService (in this example), you can check whether the password expired or is blank, the account is disabled, or a group policy restriction prevents logging on with this account.

■**Tip** A quick way to check whether the account can be used to log in is to use the Windows RunAs.exe utility, as shown in Figure 18-11.

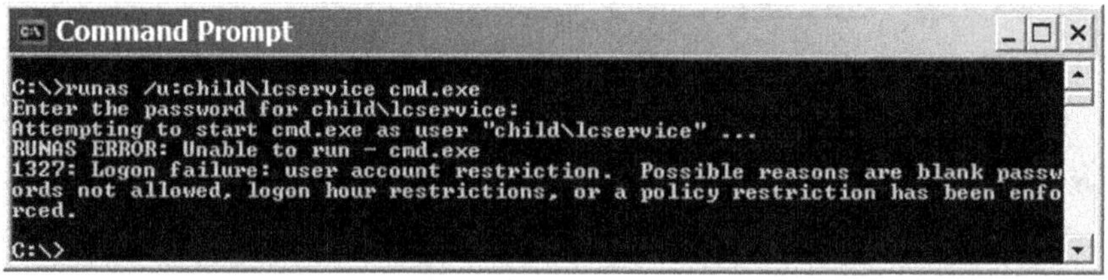

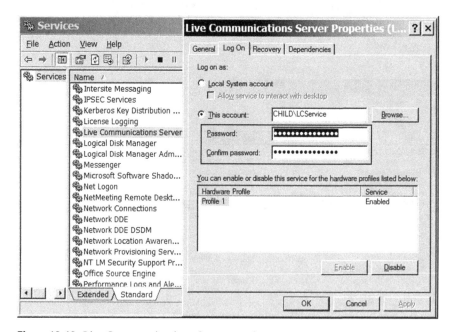

Figure 18-11. RunAs.exe

Often times, the issue is that the service account password has expired and needs to be changed even if you mark the service account's password to never expire. Once you've changed the password, make sure to update the password in the Services snap-in, as illustrated in Figure 18-12.

Figure 18-12. Live Communications Server service account

LcsCmd

The LcsCmd.exe tool is a command-line companion to the Setup program. Every operation/step available from the Setup program can be run from this tool and more. One of the many options available is the ability to verify the current state of Active Directory for Live Communications Server, the current state of one or all pools (Standard Edition Servers and Enterprise Edition pools), and the current state of individual servers. LcsCmd outputs the results to an HTML file by default. Alternatively, you can view the results in XML format by using the /XML parameter. Using this information can help you quickly hone in on the problem when you're trying to locate the root cause.

To check the state of your Active Directory, use the following commands.

- Use this to check the schema state:

  ```
  lcscmd /forest /action:CheckSchemaPrepState
  ```

- Use this to check the forest state:

  ```
  lcscmd /forest /action:CheckForestPrepState
  ```

- Use this to check all the domains' states:

  ```
  lcscmd /forest /action:CheckAllDomainsPrepState
  ```

- Use this to check the current domain state:

  ```
  lcscmd /domain /action:CheckDomainPrepState
  ```

- Use this to check the domain add state between the current domain and the reference domain:

  ```
  lcscmd /domain /action:CheckDomainAddState /refdomain:<domain FQDN> [/usersonly]
  ```

To check the state of your pools and servers, use the following commands.

- Use this to check the state of all the pools in your Active Directory forest:

  ```
  lcscmd /forest /action:CheckAllPoolsState
  ```

- Use this to check a specific pool state:

  ```
  lcscmd /domain /action:CheckPoolState /poolname:<pool FQDN>
  ```

- Use this to check a specific server state:

  ```
  lcscmd /server:<FQDN> /action:CheckLCServerState
  ```

One option that is not exposed in the Setup program is the ability to check whether permissions for the Live Communications Server administrative groups were set on a specific Active Directory organizational unit (OU).

To check permissions on an OU, use the following command:

```
lcscmd /domain /action:CheckLcsOUPermissions /ou:<DN-rootDN>
          /objectType:{user|contact|inetOrgPerson|computer}
      [/refdomain:<domain FQDN>]
```

Here are the options:

<DN-rootDN>: LcsCmd uses a truncated DN for the /OU parameter. This truncated DN is the full DN of the OU minus the DN of the root domain DN. It is easier to illustrate with examples. If the DN of the OU is "OU=Marketing,DC=touareg,DC=local," then the DN-rootDN is "OU=Marketing." If the DN of the OU is "OU=Engineering,DC=child,DC=touareg,DC=local," then the DN-rootDN is "OU=Engineering,DC=child."

/objectType: This specifies the type of objects to verify the LCS permissions on.

Flat-File Logging

Flat-file logging (FFL) allows you to generate log files to troubleshoot server problems. To turn on FFL, open the Live Communications Server MMC. Navigate to the target server, and right-click to modify its properties. Select the Logging tab. Figure 18-13 shows the Logging tab. By default, logging is disabled. You'll need to select the Enable Logging checkbox. FFL offers four different logging levels starting at level 1 with the least amount of logged data to the most comprehensive amount of data at level 4.

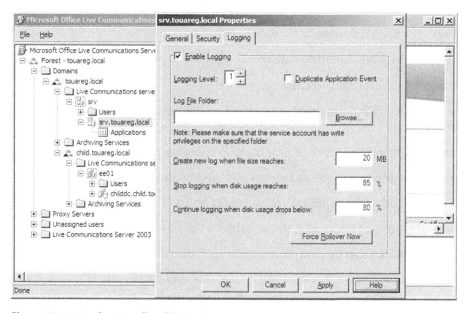

Figure 18-13. *Configuring flat-file logging*

■**Caution** You should be cautious setting the logging level to level 4 on a production Live Communications Server. We recommend you set this logging level only for a short period of time that is long enough to reproduce the problem and then disable FFL to minimize the performance impact on the server.

Each subsequent level incrementally increases the amount of data logged. Level 1 logging provides the minimum amount of information. It logs only diagnostic error events. Levels 2–4 log increasing information of SIP methods and SIP headers as well as warnings and information events.

The checkbox Duplicate Application Event logs the events the server sends to the Application event log in the log file as well. You'll need to specify a folder where the log files will be generated.

To limit the size of each log file to avoid viewing very large files, you can specify the maximum size of the log file. Once the log file reaches the file size specified in the field Create New Log When File Size Reaches, FFL closes the file and continues logging in a new file. To prevent FFL from tanking the performance of your server, the next two settings, Stop Logging When Disk Usage Reaches and Continue Logging When Disk Usage Drops Below, provide protective measures. If you need to view the latest log file that the server is logging to, click the Force Rollover Now button to force the server to commit the changes and close the file.

Microsoft's TechNet article provides additional detailed information at http://www.microsoft.com/technet/prodtechnol/office/livecomm/library/reference/lcsref_5.mspx.

To better view these log files, use the Live Communications Server 2005 Resource Kit tool called SipView.exe. SipView makes it more convenient to read the log file, as shown in Figure 18-14. You'll likely want to leave it to the Microsoft Product Support Service team to parse the file, because they will know what to look for. The effort is somewhat analogous to searching for a needle in a haystack.

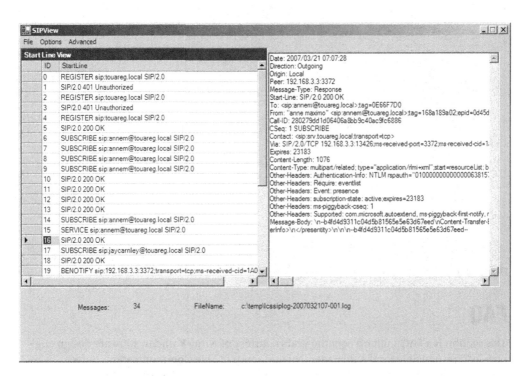

Figure 18-14. *Viewing FFL logs with SipView*

Network Capture

A network capture performs a sniff of the traffic on the wire. Such a capture provides all the details of the traffic and requires a great deal of expertise in SIP, SDP, and authentication protocols to understand. It is often best to start with the other suggested methods for trouble-shooting the problem. FFL logs and WPP tracing logs often provide enough detail that a network capture is not necessary. Since SIP is a text-based protocol similar to HTML and since SDP is XML based, it is easy to read SIP traffic because it doesn't require understanding binary-encoded data. Several network protocol analyzers are available that you can use to capture SIP traffic on the wire. Ethereal is an open source network analyzer that can dissect 759 protocols, including SIP and SDP, which makes it really easy to read SIP requests from the network capture. It is freely available at http://www.ethereal.com. Figure 18-15 provides an example of a SIP INVITE request from annem@touareg.local to jaycarnley@touareg.local with an SDP payload.

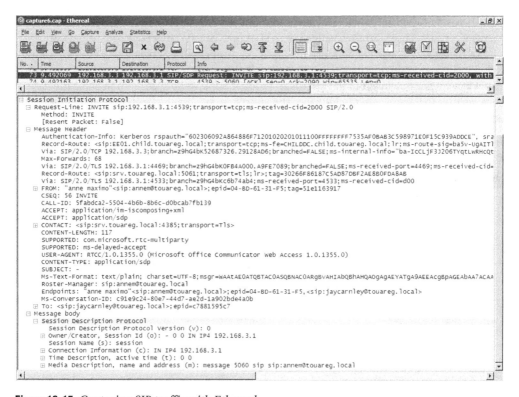

Figure 18-15. *Capturing SIP traffic with Ethereal*

FAQ

This section is a FAQ built up over the years courtesy of Nirav Kamdar, software design engineer lead responsible for the management and setup of Live Communications Server.
"I successfully completed the activation step, but the service isn't starting. What do I do?"

- Check the activation log file generated when you ran the Activate step, and verify activation was successful.

- Check the Application event log for errors.

- Wait until Active Directory replication completes. The domain controller closest to your Live Communications Server may not have obtained the updates made by the Activate step.

- Have you altered any permission manually? Try using LocalSystem to see whether service starts (use this only for debugging purposes).

- Make sure the Enterprise pool's back-end server is running and is the same version as the Enterprise pool's front-end server(s).

- Try connecting to both the Rtc and RtcConfig databases using service account credentials.

- Using the LocalSystem account to start the service is not a solution!

"I enabled federation/outside user, but it doesn't work. What do I do?"

- Make sure the global federation setting is configured.

- Make sure the default routes to the Director and Access Proxy servers are configured properly.

- Use `LcsPing.exe` to make sure the FQDNs of the Access Proxy server(s) and Director(s) are reachable.

- Make sure users are enabled for federation.

- Check the certificates on the Access Proxy and all Live Communications Servers in the SIP route.

- Make sure the Live Communications Server(s) is listening on MTLS.

"I enabled archiving, but messages don't seem to be getting archived. What do I do?"

- Check the Application and System event logs on both the Live Communications Servers configured to be archived and the Archiving Service server.

- Make sure MSMQ is installed and running.

- Make sure the Archiving Service is installed, activated, and running.

- Make sure the SQL Server service is running and the Archiving Service can connect to the database.

"I'm having database setup problems. What do I do?"

- Copy the command line from the setup logs/create pool logs, and run it on the command line with the /verbose option.

- Are you running the CreatePool setup step from a computer that doesn't have SQL Server tools installed?

- Are you running the CreatePool setup step on a Windows 2000 computer? If so, make sure you have WSH5.6 and reg.exe in the environment variable %PATH%.

- Make sure your old database files are not left behind in the LCS Data and LCS Log directories.

- Are you running on a 64-bit computer? The Enterprise pool's back-end server can be a 64-bit computer running SQL Server, but the setup step CreatePool must be executed from a 32-bit computer.

"Upgrade doesn't work for me. What do I do?"

- Are you trying to upgrade an MSDN version? If so, this is not supported.

- Check the setup logs in %temp% directory.

- Make sure you are using the correct package (use the upgrade version to upgrade the currently installed Live Communications Server running a previous version; use the setup version for new installation).

"Whenever I click Help in MMC, I get 'Page not found' in an IE window. What do I do?"

- If you don't have connectivity to the Internet, use the offline help settings.

"I get the following error: 'Action failed with error code 0xC3EC78C. Database needs major upgrade.' What do I do?"

- Use LcsCmd with CheckPoolState to make sure the version of the server you are using is what it is expected.

- Version 0.0 refers to Live Communications Server 2005.

- Version 2.0 refers to Live Communications Server 2005 SP1.

- There have been cases where customers landed in a mismatched situation where the back-end server database was on the SQL schema version for Live Communications Server 2005 and the front-end servers were upgraded to Live Communications Server 2005 SP1.

"I get the following error: 'Error 1722: There is a problem with this Windows Installer package . . .' What do I do?"

- Make sure you are not installing different versions of Live Communications Server on the same computer.

- If you have previously installed or uninstalled Live Communications Server, make sure the previous product is completely removed. Run cscript.exe LcsVerifyClean.vbs.

Summary

Troubleshooting Live Communications Server can be difficult and frustrating, but it doesn't have to be that way. With a good understanding of the tools available to you, you can quickly root out the cause of problems without much thrashing. We've covered a number of tools and when to use them more effectively depending on the nature of the problem. Based on our experience, it's more effective to start where the problem manifests itself (specific user or server) and work your way out to investigating the other elements of your environment (pool, interserver communication, Active Directory state, DNS, and so on). Happy troubleshooting!

CHAPTER 19

■■■

Live Communications Server Counters and Events

When it comes to monitoring Live Communications Servers, Live Communications Server 2005 SP1 provides performance counters and events that can alert the administrators to problems and give information about the health state of the service. Since Live Communications Server 2005 SP1 exposes more than 400 performance counters and more than 400 events, monitoring each of these is unpractical and leads to generating noise that administrators are unable to decipher. A lot of these counters and events were designed to aid programmers in developing the product and server applications. So, which performance counters and events should you monitor? Luckily, the product team at Microsoft has researched the most pertinent performance counters and events of interest to administrators to monitor their servers; we cover them in this chapter.

Using Microsoft Operations Manager

Microsoft Operations Manager (MOM) is an application and operations management tool used to monitor computers and applications within your organization. MOM does, however, require additional investment in hardware, software, and training but, if used correctly, can certainly be worth the investment.

The counters, the events, and the logic for interpreting these alerts are available in the Live Communications Server 2005 with SP1 Management Pack for MOM 2005 at http://www.microsoft.com/downloads/details.aspx?familyid=4C9837E1-1B92-4B98-A09C-BCD8F29B2831&displaylang=en.

If your organization is still using MOM 2000, there is also the Microsoft Office Live Communications Server 2005 with SP1 Management Pack for MOM 2000 SP1 available at http://www.microsoft.com/downloads/details.aspx?FamilyID=965d3467-7ef9-4e56-8e9f-a110bbe966cd&DisplayLang=en.

The MOM 2005 pack includes four files:

- LCS2005SP1-MOM2005MP-Readme.rtf

- Eula.rtf

- LCS2005MP.AKM

- LCS2005MP.html

The most important file is LCS2005MP.AKM, which needs to be imported into MOM 2005. It is also well worth reading through the LCS2005MP.html file because this includes a detailed breakdown of all the various counters, events, and logic that MOM will capture on your behalf. We won't reproduce the list here because it is 29 pages long, but it does include the following:

- Computer attributes

- Computer rules

- Views

- Tasks

- Notification groups

- Rule groups

Importing the Management Pack into MOM 2005

If you are familiar with importing and using management packs with MOM 2005, then you can skip this section. If you want some quick pointers, complete the following steps:

1. Download or copy the Live Communications Server 2005 with SP1 Management Pack for MOM 2005 to any computer in your network that has the MOM Administrator Console installed.

2. Install the management pack by double-clicking the downloaded file.

3. Confirm that you want to run the file (if prompted).

4. On the License Agreement page, click I Agree, and then click Next.

5. On the Select Installation Folder page (as shown in Figure 19-1), select the location where you want to install the management pack, and then click Next. Click the Disk Cost button to get a list of the available drives along with disk space information.

6. Click Next to confirm the installation, and then click Close when the installation has completed.

7. Launch the MOM Administrator Console.

8. Right-click the Management Pack tree, and select Import ➤ Export Management Pack.

9. On the Welcome to the Management Pack Import/Export Wizard page, click Next.

10. Select Import Management Packs and/or Reports (as shown in Figure 19-2), and then click Next.

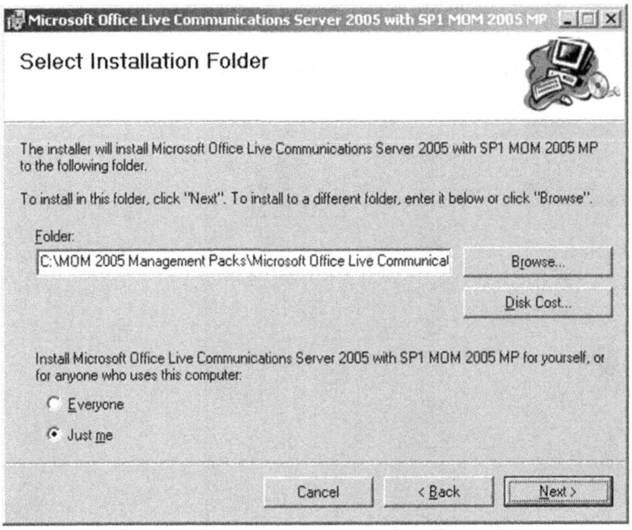

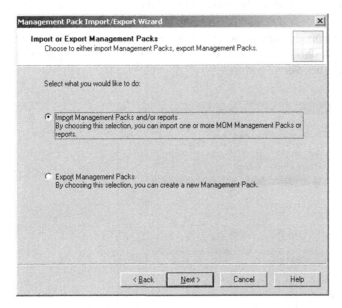

Figure 19-1. *Selecting the installation folder for the management pack*

Figure 19-2. *Selecting to import the management pack*

11. Select the location of the management pack you installed earlier (as shown in Figure 19-3), and click Next.

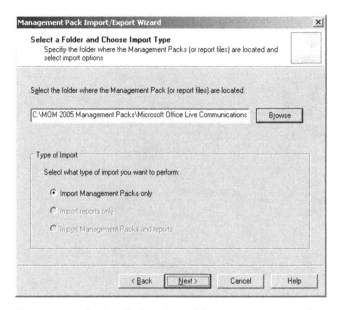

Figure 19-3. *Selecting the location of the management pack*

12. On the Select Management Packs page, click the LCS2005MP.AKM management pack, as shown in Figure 19-4. Choose the import options that you want to use (the default settings are likely to be OK). Click Next to continue.

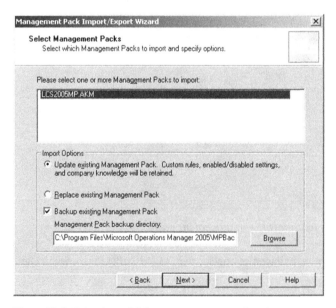

Figure 19-4. *Selecting which management pack to import*

13. Review your selection, and if it is correct, click Finish to commence the import process.

14. After the management pack has been imported, review the summary to confirm everything is in order, as shown in Figure 19-5.

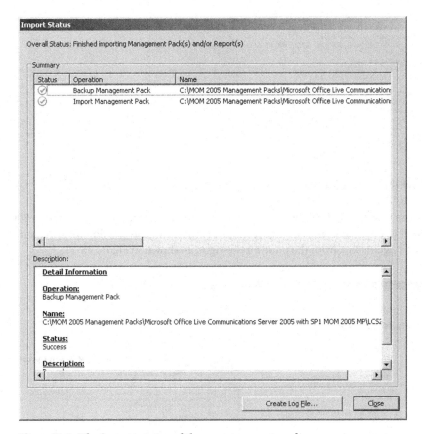

Figure 19-5. *The import status of the management packs*

15. You can also choose to create a log file and review it by clicking Create Log File. Figure 19-6 shows an example log file.

16. Click Close to complete the process.

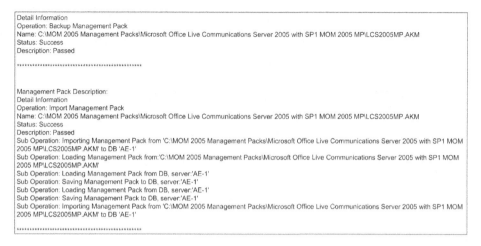

Figure 19-6. *An example log file after importing a management pack*

17. Ensure you have a MOM agent installed on each Live Communications Server 2005 SP1 server in your environment that you want to monitor. You can do this by selecting the Install Agents link from the pane on the right, as shown in Figure 19-7.

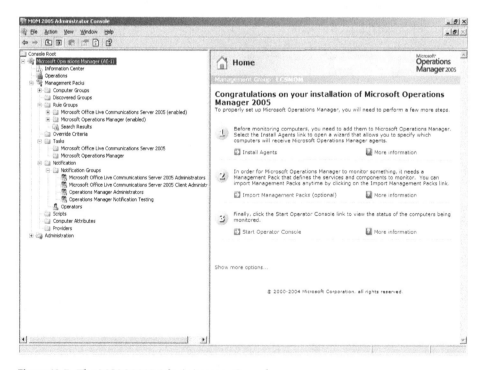

Figure 19-7. *The MOM 2005 Administrator Console*

Configuring MOM 2005

Now that the Live Communications Server 2005 with SP1 Management Pack for MOM 2005 has been installed, you still need to perform a couple of tasks before MOM can monitor your Live Communications Server environment:

1. Expand the Microsoft Operations Manager group.

2. Expand the Management Packs group.

3. Expand Computers Group.

4. Select the type of group you want to configure, such as Microsoft Office Live Communications Server 2005 Enterprise Edition (as shown in Figure 19-8), and then right-click.

Figure 19-8. *Configuring a group in the MOM Administrator Console*

5. Select Manage Subgroups from the menu.

6. From the property page, click the Included Computers tab, as shown in Figure 19-9.

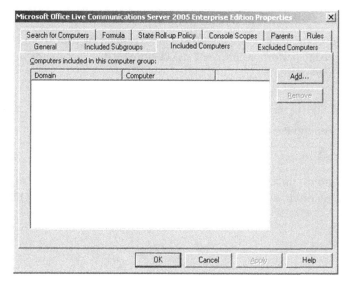

Figure 19-9. *The Included Computers tab in the server property page*

7. Click the Add button.

8. Expand your domain, and select each server that you want to add, as shown in Figure 19-10. Click OK when you have selected all the servers and then OK again to finish.

Figure 19-10. *Adding computers*

9. Repeat steps 4 through 8 for each Live Communications Server 2005 SP1 server you want to add.

By default, many events and rules are enabled to make life easier for you. You can of course add more or even remove some if they are of little or no use to you. Take a look at the various rules and events that are available in order to get a feel for what is being monitored for you. Figure 19-11 shows the Live Communications Server 2005 Enterprise Edition rule group, along with a list of event and alert rules for that group.

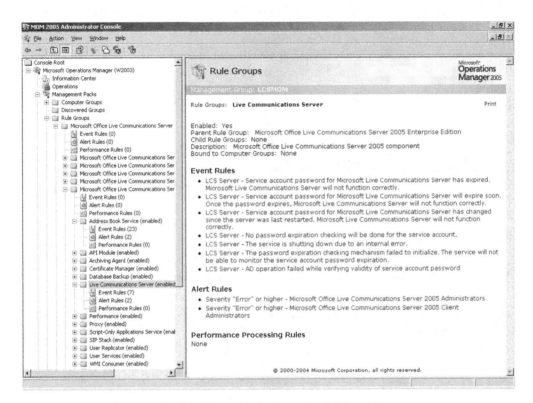

Figure 19-11. *Live Communications Server 2005 Enterprise Edition rule group*

You can examine any event or rule to see what it is doing, its resulting action, suggestions from the Microsoft Knowledge Base for resolution, and more, as shown in Figure 19-12.

You can then use the MOM Operator Console to view and monitor your servers. Figure 19-13 shows an example Operator Console view.

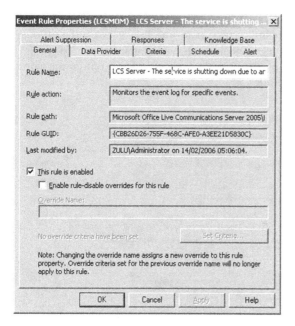

Figure 19-12. *Examining the properties of an event rule*

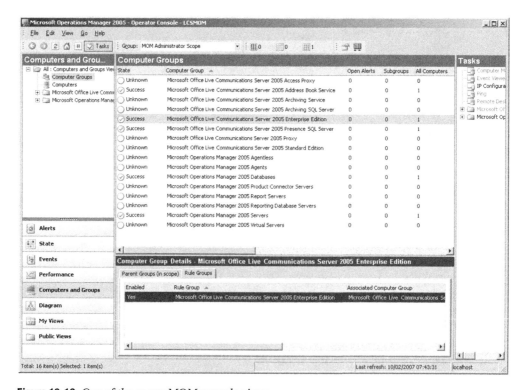

Figure 19-13. *One of the many MOM console views*

You can add, remove, and configure rules and alerts using the MOM Administrator Console as you need. If you are going to use MOM, it is important that you get to know the product and how to use it; otherwise, you could be missing important events, and you really don't want that.

Using the Live Communications Server Administration Console MMC Snap-In

The Live Communications Server administration console MMC snap-in can provide a quick and simple view into the status of your Live Communications Server environment.

The various status views display what is installed and configured and also the status of that component. You can also select available tasks in each view if required. The following examples will demonstrate these status views.

Forest Status

Information available from the Forest status view includes whether federation is enabled, whether archiving is enabled for users and federated partners, and other useful information, as shown in Figure 19-14.

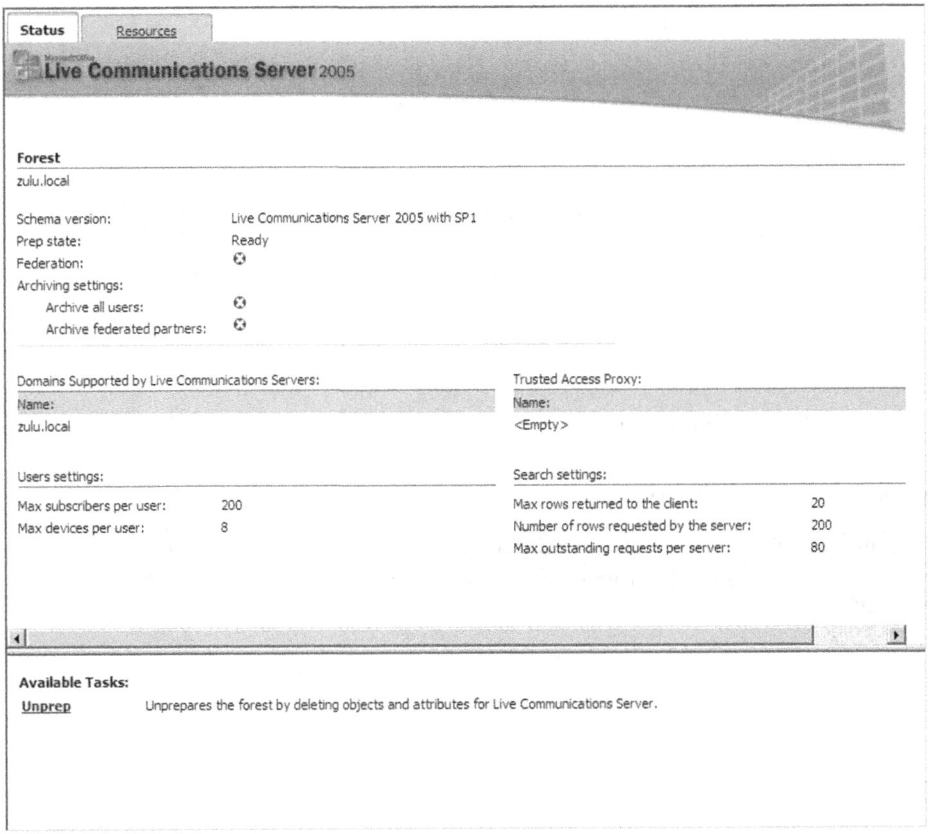

Figure 19-14. *The Forest status view*

Domain Status

Information available from the Domain status view includes archiving and default certificate settings, as shown in Figure 19-15.

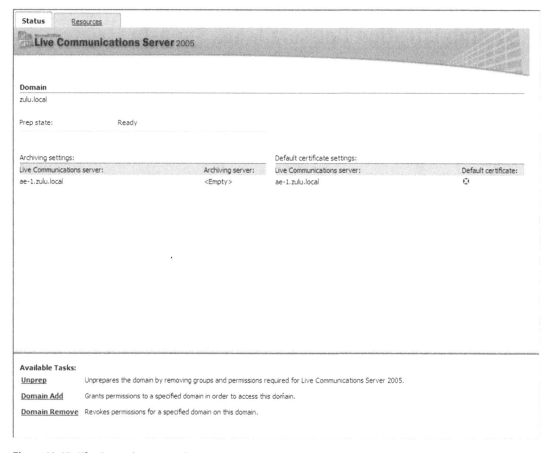

Figure 19-15. *The Domain status view*

Enterprise Pool Status

Information available from the Enterprise Pool status view includes the number of servers, authentication information, client-to-server compression settings, and more, as shown in Figure 19-16.

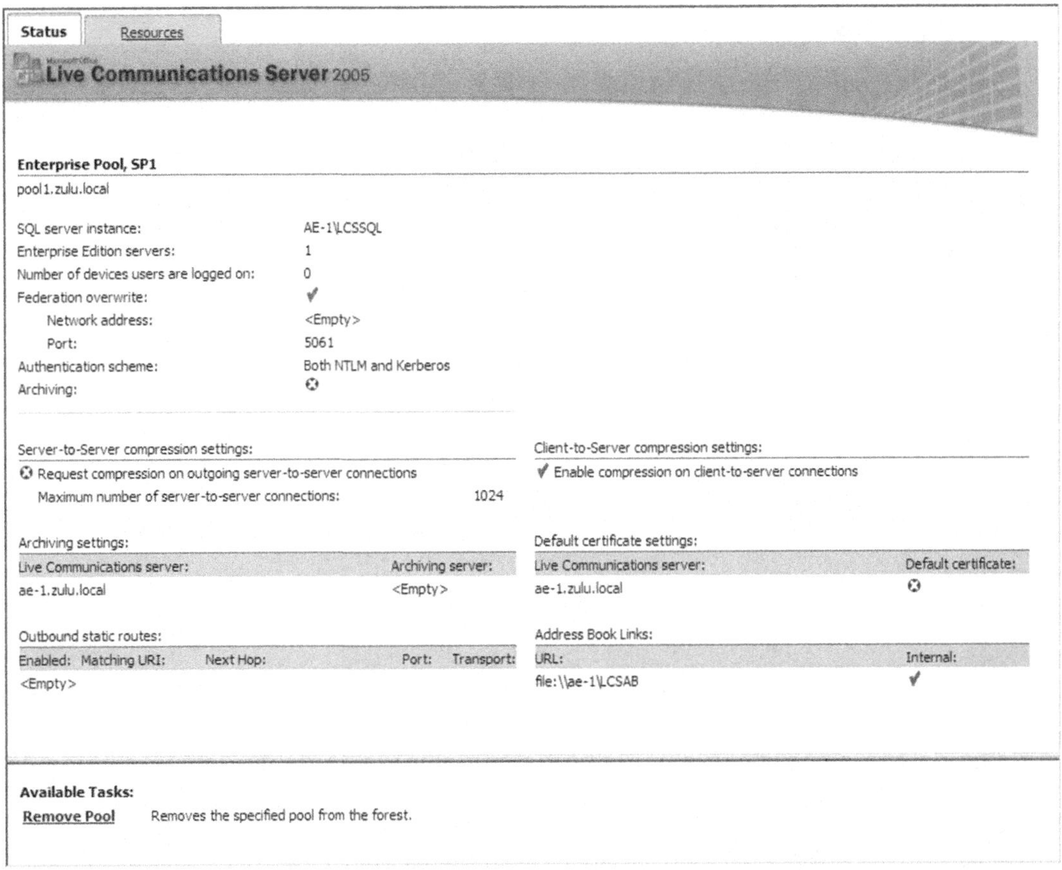

| Status | Resources |

Live Communications Server 2005

Enterprise Pool, SP1

pool1.zulu.local

SQL server instance:	AE-1\LCSSQL
Enterprise Edition servers:	1
Number of devices users are logged on:	0
Federation overwrite:	✔
Network address:	\<Empty\>
Port:	5061
Authentication scheme:	Both NTLM and Kerberos
Archiving:	✪

Server-to-Server compression settings:

✪ Request compression on outgoing server-to-server connections

    Maximum number of server-to-server connections: 1024

Client-to-Server compression settings:

✔ Enable compression on client-to-server connections

Archiving settings:

Live Communications server:	Archiving server:
ae-1.zulu.local	\<Empty\>

Default certificate settings:

Live Communications server:	Default certificate:
ae-1.zulu.local	✪

Outbound static routes:

Enabled:	Matching URI:	Next Hop:	Port:	Transport:
\<Empty\>				

Address Book Links:

URL:	Internal:
file:\\ae-1\LCSAB	✔

Available Tasks:

Remove Pool   Removes the specified pool from the forest.

Figure 19-16. *The Enterprise Pool status view*

Server Status

Information available from the Server status view includes the server type, whether flat-file logging is enabled, and information about connections, as shown in Figure 19-17.

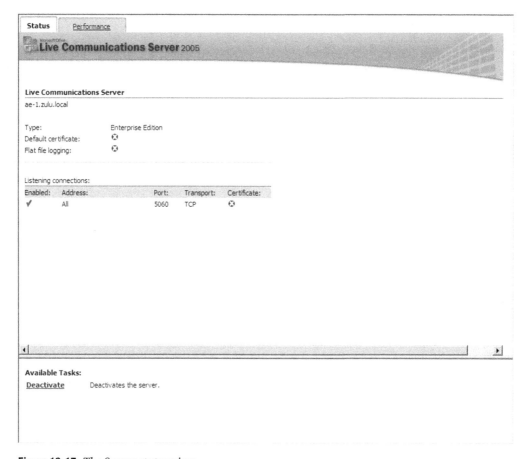

Figure 19-17. *The Server status view*

You will also notice a tab called Performance in this view. This is a snapshot of events viewed through the Performance Monitor application but placed here for your convenience, as shown in Figure 19-18.

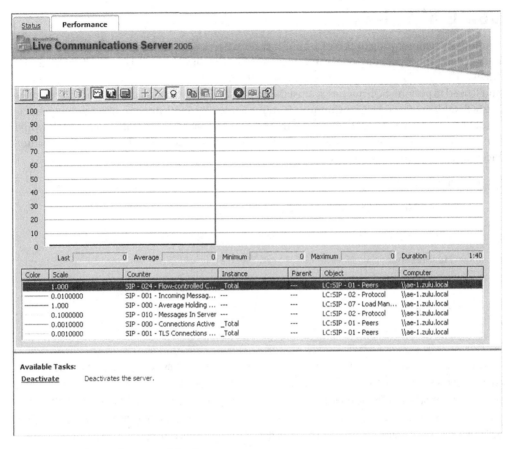

Figure 19-18. *The Performance Monitor screen*

Applications Status

Information available from the Applications status view includes what applications are enabled and running, as shown in Figure 19-19.

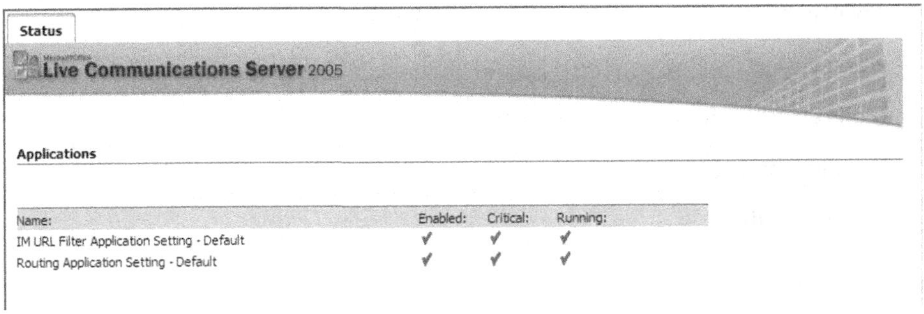

Figure 19-19. *The Applications status view*

Using SQL Queries

In addition to monitoring the Live Communications Servers, organizations often require usage data to determine ROI metrics. You can glean the metrics, often referred to as *call detail records* (CDRs), directly from the back-end database or the Archiving Service. To obtain these metrics, you'll need to perform SQL queries against the database. Since Microsoft does not advise querying the SQL tables defined by Live Communications Server 2005 SP1 directly (the product team is most likely to change the SQL schema with updates or service pack installations, which would break your queries), it provides public interfaces that you can use to build queries. These interfaces and associated attributes are as follows:

- EndPointView1

  - UserAtHost

  - Epid

  - HasPresence

  - Activity

  - Availability

■Note Epid specifies an endpoint identifier (EPID) that uniquely identifies each client (that is, endpoint) when a user is signed in to Live Communications Server. Activity specifies an aggregate value that indicates the current level of activity for the user. This value is used, along with availability level, in determining presence ranking of the user by the Live Communications Server. The activity numbers correspond to Table 19-1. Availability defines the availability of the user on this endpoint. The numbers correspond to Table 19-2.

  - AgeOfPresence

  - StdMethods

  - ExtraMethods

  - SipQValue

  - PresenceDoc

- EndPointView2 = EndPointView1 + 2 attributes

  - SupportsForking

  - FrontEndFqdn

- MonthlyRegisterUsageView

  - Year

  - Month

  - Count

  - IsPartialCount

Table 19-1. *Activity Numbers*

Activity	Description
800–999	Active (online)
700–799	Away
600–699	Busy
500–599	On the phone
400–499	Active (online)
300–399	Be right back
200–299	Idle
150–199	Out to lunch
100–149	Away
0–99	Offline (no activity)

Table 19-2. *Availability Numbers*

Availability	Description
300–999	The user is online and active.
200–299	The user is connected, but client activity is low.
100–199	The user's availability cannot be determined.
0–99	The user is considered offline.

Using Other Tools

To monitor your Live Communications Servers, the simplest solution is to install MOM 2005 and the Live Communications Server 2005 with SP1 Management Pack for MOM 2005. However, not every organization uses MOM. For such situations, knowing what performance counters and events to monitor so that you can incorporate this logic into your existing monitoring systems is necessary. Even if you don't have MOM, you can learn a lot about what to monitor by reading the LCS2005MP.html file.

A tool that is provided as part of the Live Communications Server 2005 Resource Kit is LCS Monitor. This is a command-line tool that is designed to enable the logging of Live Communications Server–specific application Event Log entries and tracing information. To find out more about this useful tool, take a look at the `LCSMonitorReadme.html` file that is located in the `LCSMonitor` directory within the resource kit.

Finally, a little-known Microsoft tool is the Windows Server 2003 Performance Advisor Management Pack for Microsoft Operations Manager 2005, freely downloadable from `http://www.microsoft.com/downloads/details.aspx?FamilyID=82632729-3263-4254-9332-1F51815C55FB&displaylang=en`. This tool can help you diagnose performance-related problems that might affect your Windows 2003 environment. If you are not using it, or something like it, to monitor your environment, you should consider adding it now. You can never have too much information when it comes to monitoring your environment.

Summary

This chapter covered some of the tools you can use to monitor your Live Communications Server 2005 environment, ranging from using the Live Communications Server Administration Console all the way to using a product such as Microsoft Operations Manager, which you can also use to monitor other servers and components within your environment. Monitoring your environment is important to ensure that your systems run smoothly and also to quickly pinpoint and diagnose any problems that might occur. The faster you can do this, the less time parts of your environment are unavailable. And as the old saying goes, time is money.

CHAPTER 20

■■■

The SDK

Developers can use the software development kit (SDK) to create applications and add-ins for Live Communications Server 2005. Specifically, the Live Communications Server 2005 API suite enables developers to create custom SIP applications.

The chapter takes a brief look at the SDK, explains how to install it, describes what it contains, and shows how to compile and install one of the sample applications.

The SDK contains a number of code samples that you can use, along with the relevant development tools and the API documentation used for software development.

Installing the SDK

Installing the SDK is simple. All you need to do is insert either the Live Communications Server 2005 with SP1 Standard Edition CD or the Enterprise Edition CD to launch the setup menu, as shown in Figure 20-1.

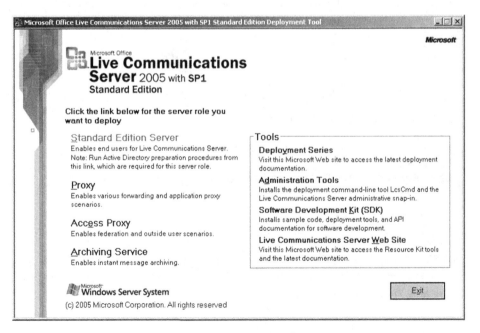

Figure 20-1. *The Live Communications Server 2005 with SP1 setup menu*

Then follow these steps:

1. Click the Software Development Kit (SDK) menu item in the Tools box to start the installation process.

2. Click Next to continue past the welcome screen (as shown in Figure 20-2).

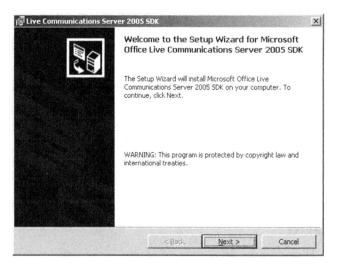

Figure 20-2. *The Live Communications Server 2005 SDK welcome screen*

3. Accept the terms in the license agreement, and click Next (as shown in Figure 20-3).

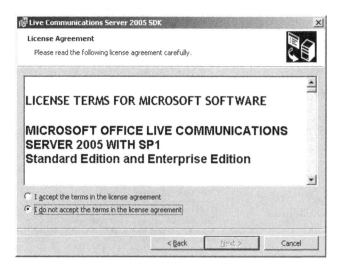

Figure 20-3. *The license agreement*

4. Enter your username and organization, and then click Next (as shown in Figure 20-4).

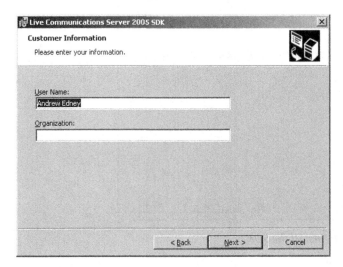

Figure 20-4. *Customer Information screen*

5. Choose the location where you want to install the SDK; the default location is
`C:\Program Files\Microsoft LC 2005\SDK\`. Then click Next (as shown in Figure 20-5).

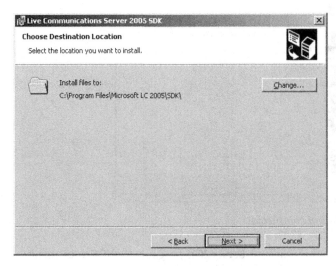

Figure 20-5. *Choose Destination Location screen*

6. Finally, click Install to begin the actual installation process (as shown in Figure 20-6).

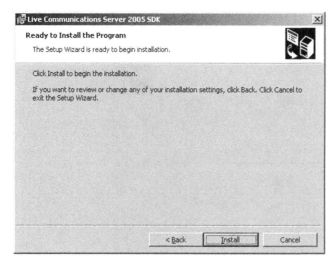

Figure 20-6. *Ready to install the SDK*

7. At the end of the installation process, click Finish (as shown in Figure 20-7).

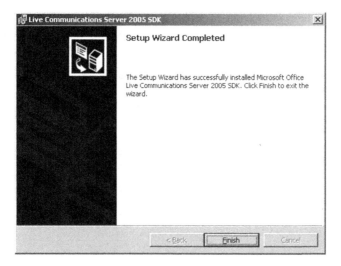

Figure 20-7. *Installation completed*

Unlike the main Live Communication Server 2005 program, the SDK does not have its own program icon.

To access the files installed as part of the SDK installation process, browse to the location you specified during the installation, remembering that the default location is `C:\Program Files\Microsoft LC 2005\SDK\`.

Here you will see four folders (as shown in Figure 20-8):

- Bin (contains the file ServerAgent.dll)

- Docs (contains a readme.htm file that links to the Live Communications Server 2005 SDK documentation at http://r.office.microsoft.com/r/rlidLCS?clid=1033&p1=2&p2=library&p3=serverSDK)

- Samples (see the "SDK Samples" section)

- Tools (contains the files ApiLogger.exe, CompileSPL.exe, and RegApp.exe)

Figure 20-8. *The contents of the SDK installation*

Using the SDK Samples

The Samples directory contains a number of useful code examples that demonstrate the various features that are exposed by the Live Communications Server 2005 API. These samples include the following:

- Application Stamping (demonstrates using the Message.Stamp property to mark messages as having been seen by the same application on a different server)

- Archiver (demonstrates an example C# logging application)

- Client Version Filter (demonstrates inspecting headers in SIP traffic)

- ContentModification (demonstrates modifying a message content body)

- Federation Edge (demonstrates using the MessageOrigin property to determine from where in the topology a message was received)

- FilteringApp (demonstrates using the flat-file access feature to demonstrate a message filter based on a simple rule set)

- LoggingNotice (demonstrates adding a warning notice to the first IM in each session for all participants)

- MPOP (a script that demonstrates presence-based routing)

- SipSnoop (a C# application that demonstrates logging all messages to a window)

- Phone2PC (a C# application that demonstrates routing messages between a telephony gateway and users)

Each sample is located within its own directory, which also includes a readme.txt file with more information about each, including how to build and install each application.

Compiling and Installing a Sample

In this section, we will walk you through compiling and installing the SipSnoop sample application:

1. The first step is to make sure you have the .NET Framework 1.1.4322 installed. If you don't have it installed, you can download it from http://www.microsoft.com/downloads/details.aspx?FamilyID=262d25e3-f589-4842-8157-034d1e7cf3a3&DisplayLang=en.

2. After you have installed it and rebooted your computer, you need to add the folder to the system path. The addition should be %WINDIR%\Microsoft.NET\Framework\v1.1.4322.

3. Next, copy the file serveragent.dll from the Bin directory into the \Samples\SipSnoop directory.

4. After that, copy the file RegApp.exe from the Tools directory into the \Samples\SipSnoop directory.

5. You need to perform the next few steps from a command prompt, so launch a command prompt by clicking Start ➤ Run and typing **CMD**.

6. Change the directory to c:\Program Files\Microsoft LC 2005\SDK\Samples\SipSnoop.

7. Type **RegApp.exe /i sipsnoop.am**, and press Enter. This will compile the SipSnoop sample, as shown in Figure 20-9.

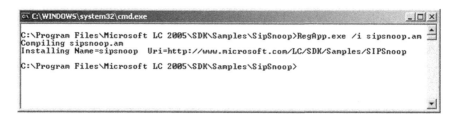

Figure 20-9. *Compiling SipSnoop.am*

8. For each server you want to install SipSnoop on, you must compile it on that server.

9. In the SipSnoop directory you'll find a file called SipSnoop.exe. To launch SipSnoop, just double-click the SipSnoop.exe file. When launched, you will see the screen shown in Figure 20-10.

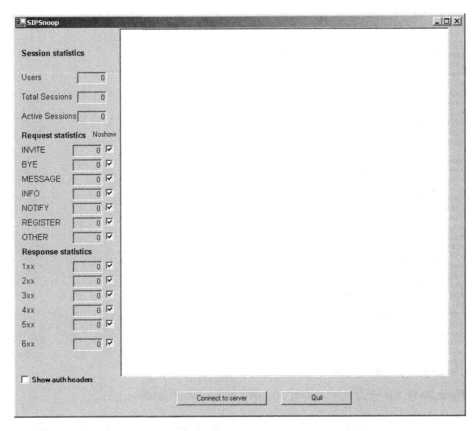

Figure 20-10. *SipSnoop*

10. Click the Connect to Server button, and if all is well, you should see a message that says "---Connect success . . .."

11. To see specific statistics, make sure you uncheck the relevant boxes (the checked boxes are those you *don't* want to show).

Now all messages that pass through Live Communications Server 2005 will be displayed in the status window. Figure 20-11 shows an example of the type of information captured when a user logs in to Microsoft Office Communication.

```
----- Connect success at 19:26:47 -----

----- Request (19:27:04) -----
BENOTIFY sip:192.168.1.73:1034;transport=tcp;ms-received-cid=500 SIP/2.0
content-length: 1129
from: <sip:andrew@zulu.local>;tag=E7D8F339
to: <sip:andrew@zulu.local>;tag=571bfa1cd3;epid=a0c8c752ad
call-id: e7e851bd9e22466083e51418c691b895
cseq: 2 BENOTIFY
require: eventlist
content-type: text/xml+msrtc.pidf
event: presence
subscription-state: active;expires=29951

<presentity uri="andrew@zulu.local"
xmlns="http://schemas.microsoft.com/2002/09/sip/presence"
xmlns:xsi="http://www.w3.org/2001/XMLSchema-instance" >
<availability aggregate="300" description="" epid="a0c8c752ad" />
<activity aggregate="400" description="" epid="a0c8c752ad" />
<displayName displayName="Andrew Edney" />
<userInfo > <contact> </contact>
</userInfo>
<devices>
<devicePresence epid="a0c8c752ad" ageOfPresence="0" >
<availability aggregate="300" description="online" />
<activity aggregate="400" description="Active" />
<deviceName name="XP" > </deviceName>
<rtc:devicedata namespace="rtcService"
xmlns:rtc="http://schemas.microsoft.com/winrtc/2002/11/sip" > <![CDATA
[<caps> <renders_gif/> <renders_isf/> </caps> ]]> </rtc:devicedata>
<device deviceId="a0c8c752ad" since="2006-12-04T19:27:05Z" > <prescaps>
<audio> <render> </render>
<capture> </capture>
</audio>
<video> <render> </render>
</video>
<text> <ink> <renderGif> </renderGif>
```

Figure 20-11. *Example information captured in the status window*

This particular application is great for troubleshooting problems, so you might want to compile it and have it ready to use in your environment just in case.

When you have finished using it, just click the Disconnect from Server button to end the session.

If you decide to unregister SipSnoop, type the following from the command prompt: **RegApp.exe /u SipSnoop.am**.

Further Reading

Obviously, we could have written an entire book about the SDK and developing applications for Live Communications Server, so if you are a developer reading this, you will probably find it beneficial to read through the published API specs at http://msdn.microsoft.com/library/ default.asp?url=/library/en-us/lcs2005/rtc/about_the_rtc_server_application_api.asp.

Other useful links for further reading include the following:

- http://msdn.microsoft.com/library/default.asp?url=/library/en-us/lcs2005/rtc/ rtc_server_application_api_reference.asp

- http://msdn.microsoft.com/library/default.asp?url=/library/en-us/lcs2005/rtc/ using_the_rtc_server_application_api.asp

Summary

This very brief look at the SDK should have given you an idea of how extensible Live Communications Server 2005 actually is. Although you don't actually need to be a developer to use some of the sample applications that come with the SDK, if you want to develop your own applications, you will need development knowledge. As you have seen, some of the applications can be useful in helping to examine and even troubleshoot your Live Communications Server environment. Additional materials are available that you should certainly download and read if you are considering writing your own applications.

CHAPTER 21

■ ■ ■

Telephony Integration

One important topic that is garnering more and more interest is VoIP. VoIP, however, entails a host of scenarios and can often be a term that is overused. It's important to clarify what we mean by VoIP. As the term indicates, Voice over IP (VoIP) refers to transporting voice over an IP network. Communicator 2005 offers peer-to-peer VoIP calls between internal users enabled for Live Communications where the media (that is, voice) traverses the IP network uniquely without bridging to the PSTN network. Calling is based on the user's identity (that is, the SIP URI).

Ninety-nine percent of today's voice traffic traverses the PSTN network, which is managed by telecom providers such as AT&T, Qwest, and so on. It's therefore unreasonable to expect that all of your organization's calls can remain on the IP network without needing to bridge to the PSTN network for external calls. A media gateway is needed to bridge the call between the IP network and the PSTN network.

Many medium-to-large companies host their own private branch exchange (PBX) systems. The PBX system is a network of its own, independent from the IP network that connects all the phones in your organization, and it supports a high degree of reliability over the IP network because of business and safety (911) requirements for voice. Organizations are not about to rip out and replace their PBX systems just to have access to the benefits that VoIP promises. Most likely, such organizations will take a progressive approach by introducing VoIP aspects into their existing infrastructure such as by controlling their phones from desktop applications such as Office Communicator 2005.

Integrating the PBX system with the convenience and presence integration that Live Communications Server 2005 SP1 provides is referred to as *telephony integration*. Telephony integration—or more precisely Remote Call Control integration (also called Third-Party Call Control [3PCC])—with Communicator 2005 is a great way to harness the functionality we've all grown accustomed to on traditional phones from our desktop computers by leveraging the existing PBX infrastructure. Not to be confused with VoIP where the audio (that is, media) travels over the IP network, Remote Call Control enables users to control their PBX desk phones via Communicator 2005. The actual call still terminates on the phone.

Communicator 2005 can expose in a simpler and more intuitive way the richer capabilities of the phone that are largely hidden to most people because of the difficulty in remembering complex codes that include special keys such as # and *. Tasks such as setting up a conference bridge between multiple users, setting up call-forwarding rules, and even calling a user become simple steps to perform through a few clicks. It goes even further by integrating presence information such as automatically changing the user's presence to indicate the user is on the phone and should not be disturbed. Communicator 2005 brings a new-user experience to calling while further extending the value of your PBX investments.

To enable PBX integration with Live Communications Server, Microsoft leveraged the European Computer Manufacturers Association (ECMA) standard, ECMA 323 III. This is often referred to as Computer Supported Telephony Application (CSTA), and it defines an XML protocol for interfacing with telephone switches (PBX) as described in ECMA 269. You can find details of the ECMA 323 standard at `http://www.ecma-international.org/publications/standards/Ecma-323.htm`. Many PBX manufacturers support the CSTA standard, and it works with either IP or TDM PBXs. However, legacy PBXs that do not support this standard will require a SIP/CSTA gateway to interface with Live Communications Server. CSTA is the only standard supported by Communicator for Remote Call Control.

RCC integration of your PBX phone with Communicator 2005 relies on a SIP/CSTA gateway that bridges the SIP network and the PBX network using the SIP/CSTA specification created by Microsoft. Communicator 2005 encodes the CSTA commands into the XML format. The XML document, also referred to as the *payload*, is then encapsulated within a SIP INFO request, which Live Communications Server can then route to the SIP/CSTA gateway. The SIP/CSTA gateway retrieves the CSTA commands. It performs authorization by verifying that the user's request to control a device and perform operations is allowed before forwarding the commands to the PBX in its proprietary format understood by the PBX. The PBX performs the call control commands such as initiating a call, and so on.

Enabling RCC requires five steps. The first is to configure the SIP/CSTA gateway to talk to your PBX. The second is to configure your Live Communications Servers to route CSTA requests to the SIP/CSTA gateway. The third is to configure users for RCC. The fourth step is to configure Communicator. The fifth is to configure the phone number normalization rules.

Configuring the SIP/CSTA Gateway

To perform the first step, you'll need to select a SIP/CSTA gateway compatible with Live Communications Server 2005 SP1 that supports your particular brand of PBX system. Microsoft has partnered with a number of partners including Genesys, Mitel, Siemens, Nortel, NEC, BroadSoft, iQ NetSolutions, and so on. This book won't cover the steps required to configure your CSTA gateway with your PBX since this configuration is specific to the CSTA gateway you select. Please refer to your vendor's documentation.

We recommend you use a CSTA gateway that supports TLS. If your SIP/CSTA gateway supports TLS, we recommend enabling this feature and configuring your SIP/CSTA gateway with a certificate from a CA trusted by your Live Communications Servers. This certificate must be requested with both server and client authentication–enhanced key usage (EKU). This will ensure that all traffic to the SIP/CSTA gateway is secured. This will prevent rogue users from hijacking by controlling your PBX phone. If your SIP/CSTA gateway does not support TLS, we recommend configuring a secure VLAN between the Live Communications Servers and SIP/CSTA gateway. Alternatively, you can dedicate a Director to interface with the SIP/CSTA gateway while all the other Live Communications Servers route to the Director. The CSTA traffic from the Communicator clients to the Live Communications Servers to the Director can be secured via TLS, while the unsecured traffic from the Director to the SIP/CSTA gateway can be isolated to a private network to avoid hijacking. This architecture helps secure the communication from Live Communications Servers to the SIP/CSTA gateway that doesn't support TLS; however, it incurs the cost of an additional server dedicated as a Director.

Configuring Live Communications Servers

The second step involves making sure your Live Communications Servers will route RCC requests correctly to your SIP/CSTA gateway. You'll need to configure static routes and the host authorization lists on all your Live Communications Servers to route RCC commands to the SIP/CSTA gateway. The static route tells your Live Communications Server where to route RCC requests. In this case, you want these requests to be routed to your SIP/CSTA gateway. Configuring the host authorization list with the address of your SIP/CSTA gateway tells your Live Communications Server to trust incoming messages from your SIP/CSTA gateway. This is required as a built-in measure of precaution in Live Communications Server 2005 SP1 because the SIP/CSTA gateways do not publish their identity (that is, FQDN) in the Trusted Server list in Active Directory used by Live Communications Server 2005 SP1.

To configure the static route, open the Admin Tools MMC, right-click each Standard Edition Server and Enterprise pool, and select Properties. Navigate to the Routing tab, as shown in Figure 21-1. Click the Add button. Specify (*) in the User field to allow all SIP URIs with the SIP domain name as specified in the Domain field to match this static route criteria. Specify a SIP domain name portion you'll reserve for RCC. This SIP domain name is a virtual namespace reserved for your RCC integration with your PBX. This SIP domain name can be any name of your choice, as long as it doesn't already exist, creating potential DNS resolution conflicts that are difficult to troubleshoot. You'll use this SIP domain name when defining the SIP URI of your SIP/CSTA gateway in the field, called Remote Call Control SIP URI. We refer to this SIP namespace as the PBX domain name. In fact, it should not match any of the SIP domain names that your Live Communications Server infrastructure is authoritative for or existing SIP domains that you federate with. This should be of the form *.<domain>. In the Next Hop Group box, specify the SIP/CSTA gateway as either its FQDN or an IP address. If using TLS, the SIP/CSTA gateway must be specified as an FQDN. The Transport field should be set to TLS, and the Port field should be set to 5061 or whatever port number you configured the SIP/CSTA gateway to listen on for incoming connections from your Live Communications Server. The checkbox Replace Host in Request URI should usually be checked; however, please refer to your specific SIP/CSTA gateway documentation. Make sure your Live Communications Server is configured with a certificate if using TLS.

To configure the SIP/CSTA gateway as an authorized host to each Standard Edition Server and Enterprise pool, select the properties of each server/pool, and navigate to the Host Authorization tab, as shown in Figure 21-2. Click the Add button. In the Add Authorized Host dialog box, specify the FQDN of the SIP/CSTA gateway. This is the same FQDN you specified in the Static Route area created earlier. This dialog box offers the option to specify the IP address; however, if using TLS, you must specify the FQDN. Select the checkboxes Throttle As Server and Treat As Authenticated. The setting Treat As Authenticated will make sure that the Standard Edition Server or Enterprise pool will trust the SIP/CSTA gateway without challenging it. The setting Throttle As Server will make sure that the Standard Edition Server or Enterprise pool won't perform any throttling of traffic coming from the SIP/CSTA gateway. Live Communications Server, by default, throttles connections from clients by dropping requests when they come too fast in a short period of time from the same client. This setting will prevent the server from throttling requests from the SIP/CSTA gateway.

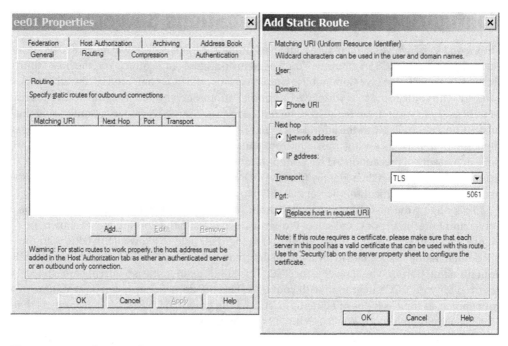

Figure 21-1. *Configuring the static route to CSTA gateway*

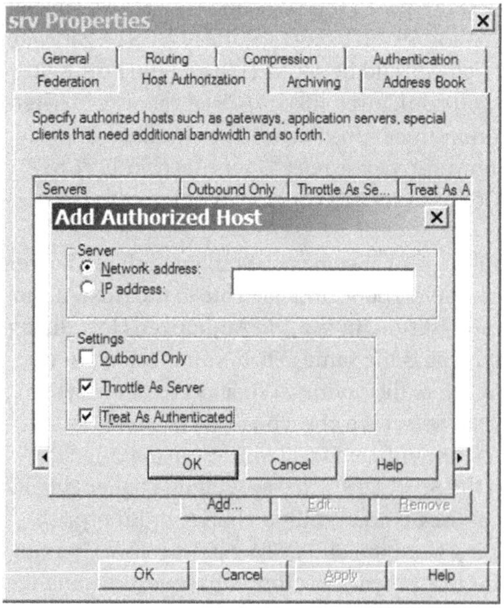

Figure 21-2. *Configuring CSTA gateway as authorized host*

Configuring these settings on every Standard Edition Server and Enterprise pool is tedious and error prone. A better way to configure these RCC settings is to use the tool LcsRcc.exe, which is available on the book's page at http://www.apress.com. It queries all the Standard Edition Servers and Enterprise pools in your Active Directory forest, connects to each, and configures the static routes and host authorization list based on the input XML file provided on the command line.

Since these settings, the static route and the host authorization list, are not configurations stored in Active Directory but are local, it's a good idea to preserve the configuration for your Standard Edition Servers and Enterprise pools in your organization. In the unfortunate case of a server failure, such as a disk failure where you have to completely rebuild your server, you'll likely forget to reconfigure these settings. We recommend you store a copy of the server/pool configuration as a backup by using the import/export functionality available on Live Communications Server. You can use the export option of LcsCmd.exe to generate an XML file with the entire configuration of your server. Then, when needed, use the XML file to import the configuration to your new Live Communications Server. The tool LcsCmd.exe is part of your Live Communications Server installation and is in the directory %CommonProgramFiles%\Microsoft LC 2005\ LcsCmd.exe.

The command-line arguments for the export operation are different for a Standard Edition Server versus an Enterprise pool.

Use the following command-line options when exporting from a Standard Edition Server:

```
LcsCmd.exe  /server /action:ExportServerConfig /role:SE
            /configFile:c:\HSConfig.xml
```

Use the following command-line options when exporting from an Enterprise pool:

```
LcsCmd.exe  /forest /action:ExportPoolConfig
            /poolName:MyExportPool /configFile:c:\MyExportPoolConfig.xml
```

To locate the section containing the configuration for the static route in the XML file generated by the export operation, search for the class name MSFT_SIPRemoteAddressData:

```
<class name="MSFT_SIPRemoteAddressData">
    <instances>
        <instance>
            <property name="Backend">
<![CDATA[(local)\rtc]]>
</property>
            <property name="InstanceID">
<![CDATA[{A46324CB-2136-43AB-8416-9ED70669A340}]]>
</property>
            <property name="OutboundOnly">
<![CDATA[false]]>
</property>
            <property name="Server">
<![CDATA[rcc_gateway.touareg.local]]>
</property>
            <property name="ThrottleAsServer">
<![CDATA[true]]>
</property>
            <property name="TreatAsAuthenticated">
```

```
<![CDATA[true]]>
</property>
        </instance>
    </instances>
</class>
```

To locate the section containing the configuration for the host authorization list in the XML file generated by the export operation, search for the class name MSFT_SIPRoutingTableData:

```
<class name="MSFT_SIPRoutingTableData">
    <instances>
        <instance>
            <property name="Backend">
<![CDATA[(local)\rtc]]>
</property>
            <property name="InstanceID">
<![CDATA[{A46324CB-2136-43AB-8416-9ED70669A340}]]>
</property>
            <property name="DropRouteHeaders">
<![CDATA[false]]>
</property>
            <property name="Enabled">
<![CDATA[true]]>
</property>
            <property name="MatchURI">
<![CDATA[SIP:*@*.rcc_contoso.com;USER=PHONE]]>
</property>
            <property name="NextHop">
<![CDATA[rcc_gateway.touareg.local]]>
</property>
            <property name="NextHopPort">
<![CDATA[5061]]>
</property>
            <property name="NextHopTransport">
<![CDATA[TLS]]>
</property>
            <property name="ReplaceHostInRequestURI">
<![CDATA[true]]>
</property>
            <property name="TLSCertIssuer" isNull="true"/>
            <property name="TLSCertSN" isNull="true"/>
            <property name="TreatAllConnectionsAsServer">
<![CDATA[false]]>
</property>
            <property name="TreatAllConnectionsAsTrusted">
<![CDATA[false]]>
```

```
</property>
        </instance>
    </instances>
</class>
</classes></configData>
```

Configuring Users

The third step requires configuring users for RCC, as shown in Figure 21-3. First, you must enable the user for RCC by selecting the checkbox Enable Remote Call Control. The grayed-out settings within the group box then become active. The user's phone number must be associated with the user's account to avoid other users from controlling it. This phone number is identified by a unique SIP URI or a TEL URI. The SIP/CSTA gateway solution from Genesys, GETS, uses the TEL URI and must be of the form `tel:+12345678900;ext=8900` (note that the portion of the TEL URI, +12345629734, is normalized in the global E.164 format) or `tel:29734;phone-context=dialstring`. This URI must be specified in the Device URI of the User's Phone field. You must configure your SIP/CSTA gateway to map this SIP/TEL URI to the user's PBX directory number (DN) (that is, the corresponding phone line that connects to the telephony device that sits on the user's desk).

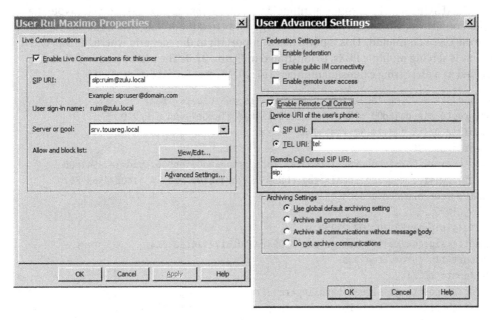

Figure 21-3. *RCC user settings*

The SIP/CSTA gateway must be addressable via a SIP URI. Just as a user has a SIP URI to uniquely identify it, the SIP/CSTA gateway is uniquely identified by its SIP URI, which you must specify in the Remote Call Control SIP URI field prefixed by the tag "sip:". The domain name portion of this SIP URI is the value as defined in the Domain field shown in Figure 21-1. The name portion before the @ can be any value you want. The SIP URI would be of the form sip:<anything>@<Domain: field value>, where the domain portion is the same domain name specified in the static route.

These three settings are represented in Active Directory in the User class as the following attributes:

msRTCSIP-OptionFlags: This attribute is used as a bit array controlling multiple options (PIC, federation, remote access, and so on). Bit 16 represents the option to enable/disable the user for RCC.

msRTCSIP-Line: This attribute stores the SIP/TEL URI of the phone line (that is, the device) representing the user's phone. This setting is enforced only when bit 16 of msRTCSIP-OptionsFlags is set.

msRTCSIP-LineServer: This attribute stores the SIP URI of the SIP/CSTA gateway. All RCC requests (that is, the SIP requests with a CSTA payload) are routed to the SIP/CSTA gateway addressable by the SIP URI defined in this attribute.

An example of an RCC SIP request is illustrated next. This CSTA payload requests to make a call by the user chermali. The SIP request is routed to the SIP/CSTA gateway gw1@mycsta. touareg.local, as specified in the msRTCSIP-LineServer attribute, where rcc.touareg.local is the domain name that is specified in the Domain field of the static route. Chermali's TEL URI, as specified in the msRTCSIP-Line attribute, is tel:29769;phone-context=intecom. Note the phone-context value is used by the SIP/CSTA gateway to differentiate which PBX server to route the CSTA command. This is particularly important in the scenario where the SIP/CSTA gateway is serving multiple PBXs, as illustrated in Figure 21-4. The phone number dialed is specified as a dial-string extension number, tel:29734;phone-context=dialstring.

```
INFO sip:srv.touareg.local:5061;transport=tls;ms-role-rs-from;
lr;ms-route-sig=da3zdQD_o7kga5vWrKwEvrSWilBE3dQjTwxGcY9wAA SIP/2.0
Via: SIP/2.0/TLS 172.24.32.214:3098
Max-Forwards: 70
From: "chermali" <sip:chermali@touareg.local>;tag=ad0efdbb06;epid=3a73541b06
To: <sip:gw1@rcc.touareg.local>;tag=FDDB95D5-3DF4-4101-9B63-A54140B3A563-867
Call-ID: 7e082b2e9aba4ae4aeacc526816eb359
CSeq: 5 INFO
Route: <sip:gw1@172.29.107.232>
Contact: <sip:chermali@touareg.local:3098;maddr=172.24.32.214;
transport=tls>;proxy=replace
User-Agent: LCC/1.3
Content-Disposition: signal;handling=required
Proxy-Authorization: Kerberos qop="auth", realm="SIP Communications Service",
opaque="C5C9B6B4", crand="215e744b", cnum="13",
```

```
targetname="sip/srv.touareg.local",response=
"602306092a864886f71201020201011100ffffffff8d2ddf06a8fef0a97b073b0d6d42c84d"
Content-Type: application/csta+xml
Content-Length: 301
<?xml version="1.0"?>
<MakeCall xmlns="http://www.ecma-international.org/standards/ecma-323/csta/ed3">
 <callingDevice>tel:29769;phone-context=intecom</callingDevice>
 <calledDirectoryNumber>tel:29734;phone-context=dialstring</calledDirectoryNumber>
 <autoOriginate>doNotPrompt</autoOriginate>
</MakeCall>
```

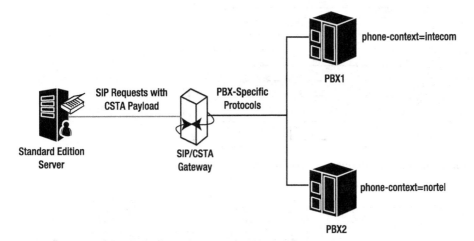

Figure 21-4. *Using the phone-context value to differentiate multiple PBXs connected to the same SIP/CSTA gateway*

Configuring Communicator

The fourth step is enabling Communicator for phone integration. You'll notice by default that the phone integration option is grayed out, as shown in Figure 21-5.

Figuring out how to enable the phone integration option can become an exercise in frustration if you're not aware that you must first enable the correct group policy setting before the options become available in Communicator. Figure 21-6 shows the correct policy setting to enable in the Communicator.adm policy file. Please refer to Chapter 5 for more information about the Communicator.adm policy file.

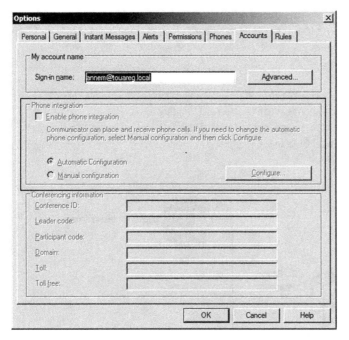

Figure 21-5. *Communicator phone integration options*

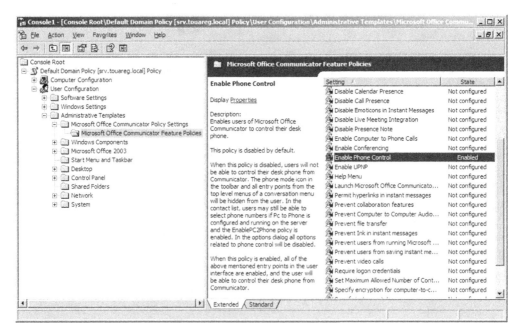

Figure 21-6. *Enabling the phone control policy setting*

This policy setting corresponds to the following registry key:

```
[<HIVE>\SOFTWARE\Policies\Microsoft\Communicator]
```

```
"EnablePC2Phone"=dword:00000001
```

where <HIVE> can be either set to HKEY_CURRENT_USER or set to HKEY_LOCAL_MACHINE.

Once enabled, you'll notice that users have the option of setting the phone integration to automatic configuration or manual configuration, as illustrated in Figure 21-7. With the automatic configuration, Communicator will query Active Directory for the user's RCC settings, as defined in the "Configuring Users" section. If set to manual configuration, the user must set this information manually by specifying the SIP/CSTA gateway's SIP URI and the user's TEL URI.

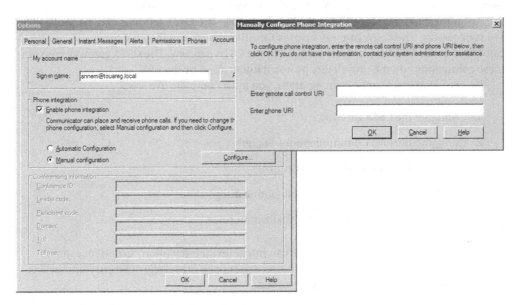

Figure 21-7. *Phone integration configuration*

Configuring Phone Number Normalization

The fifth step involves configuring phone number translation rules, also referred to as *phone number normalization rules*. Phone number normalization is required for inbound (incoming) and outbound (outgoing) calls. Live Communications Server understands phone numbers only in TEL URI format. Therefore, the SIP/CSTA gateway must translate the caller's phone number for inbound calls into a TEL URI so Communicator can correctly interpret it. If the caller is an internal user, then Communicator can resolve the TEL URI to the caller's display name, providing the caller ID feature in the pop-up toast when the call comes in. For outbound calls, the SIP/CSTA gateway must translate the phone number called from its TEL URI format sent by Live Communications Server into the proprietary format understood by the PBX.

The SIP/CSTA gateway is responsible for normalizing phone numbers for inbound calls. Please refer to your SIP/CSTA gateway product documentation for configuring these normalization rules into TEL URIs. For outbound calls, the regular expression (regex) rules defined in the Address Book Service is responsible for normalizing phone numbers for outbound calls. Chapter 12 covers the Address Book Service in more detail. Dial plans must be configured on the SIP/CSTA gateway so it knows how best to route outbound calls to the preferred PBX.

Summary

Users enabled for Live Communications can use Communicator 2005 to control their desktop PBX phones. This feature, referred to as Remote Call Control, enhances the user experience of answering calls by automatically placing the phone in speaker mode, placing calls (that is, clicking to call) based on the user's identify without needing to dial a phone number, deflecting calls to a cell phone (for example), holding and retrieving a call, forwarding a call, and quickly escalating a two-party call into a multiparty conference call very easily.

To enable this feature, a CSTA gateway compatible with Live Communications Server 2005 SP1 is necessary. The CSTA gateway bridges the SIP network and the PBX network. Communicator 2005 sends CSTA commands over SIP to the CSTA gateway. The CSTA gateway converts these commands into the proprietary protocol understood by the PBX.

To configure this telephony integration, you must complete five steps:

1. Configure the CSTA gateway.

2. Configure the Live Communications Servers.

3. Configure users for Remote Call Control.

4. Configure Communicator to enable phone integration.

5. Configure the phone number normalization rules.

Once these steps are complete, users can integrate their telephony experience into Communicator 2005 and get a convenient user experience drastically different from the 3×4 dial pad to which we've all become accustomed.

CHAPTER 22

■■■

Additional Resources

Because this is the last chapter in the book, we thought we would take a couple of pages to tell you about some of the resources that will not only help you learn even more about Live Communications Server 2005 but could also help you troubleshoot problems, answer questions, and more.

Online Help

One of the first places you can try to find an answer or some other kind of help is from within the Live Communications Server 2005 MMC snap-in. A number of the objects, when selected, have a Resources tab associated with them. For example, when you click the server name and then click the Resources tab, you will be presented with the screen displayed in Figure 22-1.

From here you can search Office Online, view available technical documentation, and connect to various Live Communications Server resources hosted at Microsoft.com.

Obviously, to view the online help, the server will need Internet access. If your organization's security policy prohibits servers from connecting to the Internet or blocks certain online content, you can always access the same content from a regular workstation by browsing to the Microsoft website.

You can also access the same content from a regular workstation by going to the Microsoft website and browsing the content there. A good site is the Live Communications Server Technical Library, which you can find at `http://www.microsoft.com/technet/prodtechnol/office/livecomm/library/default.mspx`. This website contains all the Live Communications Server documents, and it links to other useful sites.

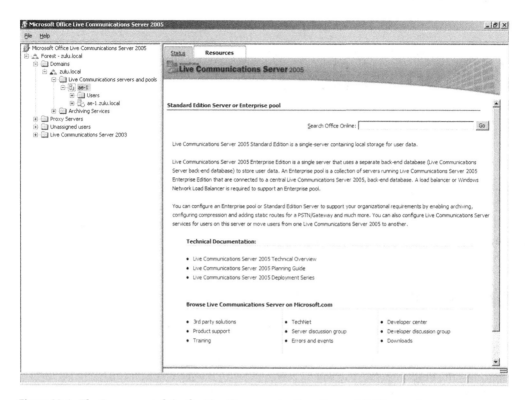

Figure 22-1. *The Resources tab in the Live Communications Server MMC snap-in*

Newsgroups

One of the best places to find answers to questions you might have (and to even actually ask some questions yourself, if you feel brave enough) is a newsgroup.

People from all around the world view and post to newsgroups, and in a lot of cases some of these people are Microsoft personnel who want to help people like you with any questions, problems, or comments.

Two Live Communications Server newsgroups are available in the English language:

- Live Communications Server (*microsoft.public.livecomm.general*)

- Live Communications Server Dev (*microsoft.public.livecomm.developer*)

This newsgroup is dedicated to Office Communicator:

Office Communicator (*microsoft.public.office.communicator*)

Note Unless your question or problem is developer related (which it very well could be), the place you want to go is the Live Communications Server "general" newsgroup at *microsoft.public.livecomm.general.*

You can view and post to newsgroups using an NNTP-based newsreader, such as Microsoft Outlook Express, or you can use a web-based newsreader. Both have their advantages; for example, if you use Outlook Express, you can keep all the messages that are posted and view them at any time, regardless of whether you are connected to the Internet or whether the message might have expired or been deleted. Keeping a historical record can be useful because you never know when you might need that answer to the obscure question someone posted three weeks ago that at the time you thought, "I'll never need to know that . . .." Also, you can subscribe to a number of different newsgroups at the same time using Outlook Express, whereas with the web-based newsreader, you can look at only one newsgroup at a time (although you could obviously have multiple windows open, but that might get a little confusing). At the end of the day, it mainly comes down to personal preference, so you can decide which of the two suits you the best. Maybe it's even both depending on where you are at the time!

Setting Up Outlook Express

Setting up Outlook Express to use is simple. Follow these steps, and you will be ready to browse the newsgroups in no time at all:

1. Launch Outlook Express on the computer you want to use. It is a good idea not to use the Live Communications Server for this. If this is the first time you have used Outlook Express, you might want to complete all your details. For now, though, just click Cancel.

2. From the Tools menu, click Accounts, and select News to open the Internet accounts list (which should be empty, as shown in Figure 22-2). Click the Add button, and select News.

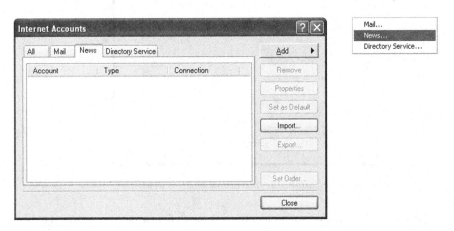

Figure 22-2. *Outlook Express Internet accounts list*

3. When prompted, enter your name and your email address, and then click Next after each step (as shown in Figure 22-3).

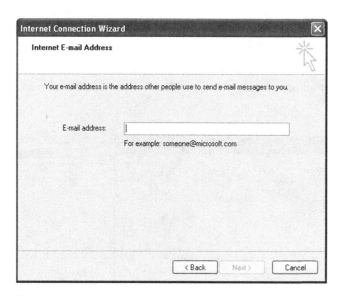

Figure 22-3. *Entering your name and email address details*

Be aware, though, that spammers trawl through the various newsgroups to obtain email addresses. It is a good idea either to have a special email address that you use only for newsgroups or to be a little creative with your address, such as andrewATzuludotcom. Most people when they respond to newsgroups posts will respond to the whole group so that everyone can benefit from the answer. If someone wants to respond directly to you, they can just change the address to be andrew@zulu.com, for example, and send you the email. However, if you are only reading messages, this is not an issue because no one will ever see your email address.

4. You will then be asked for the Internet news server name. You can either use the NNTP server of your ISP (if it has one), or you can use the free one that Microsoft provides.

5. Enter **msnews.microsoft.com** as the NNTP server, and click Next to continue, as shown in Figure 22-4.

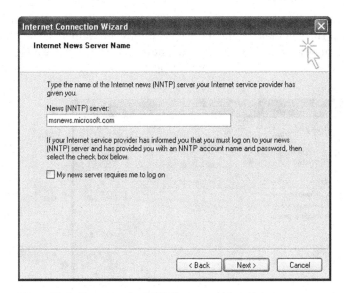

Figure 22-4. *Entering the NNTP server address*

6. And that's pretty much it for configuring Outlook Express to connect to the Microsoft news server. Click Finish to take you back to the Internet accounts list.

7. Then click Close; you might be asked whether you want to download newsgroups for the account you just added—click Yes. Figure 22-5 shows the progress of the download (in this example, 324 have already been received).

Figure 22-5. *Downloading the list of available newsgroups*

When the list of available newsgroups from the server has downloaded, you can subscribe to any you want (not just Live Communications Server newsgroups). For now, though, let's just stick to Live Communications Server.

Subscribing to Newsgroups

The easiest way of finding those newsgroups is to enter **livecomm** in the Display Newsgroups Which Contain search box. You can then highlight the newsgroups you want to add and click the Subscribe button. An icon of a folder with a pin in it will be displayed next to the newsgroup name to show that you have subscribed to it, as shown in Figure 22-6.

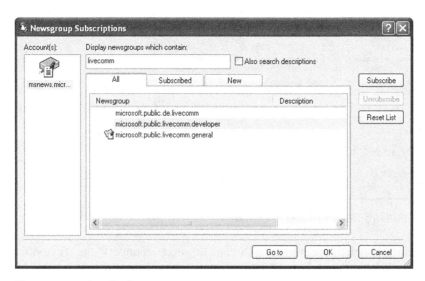

Figure 22-6. *Subscribed to a newsgroup*

When you have subscribed to all the newsgroups you want, click the OK button to return to the main Outlook Express screen. As you can see from Figure 22-7, any newsgroups you subscribed to will be shown along with the headers for any articles within those newsgroups. In the figure, there are 1,381 unread articles.

If you want to read a post, just double-click it to download it and open it. You can then reply to a post or close it.

To reply to a post or submit a new one, you must ensure the details of your mail server are entered into Outlook Express. You enter those details by going to the Internet accounts list, clicking Add, choosing Mail, and working through the wizard.

If you want to submit something, click the New Post icon near the top of the screen. This will open the new posting window, and from here you can enter the subject and a message, just like the example shown in Figure 22-8.

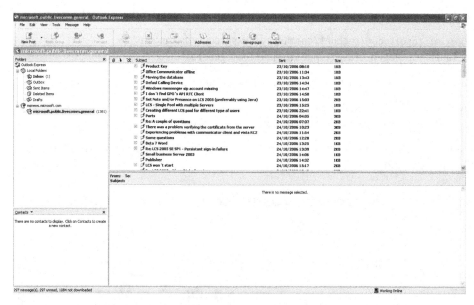

Figure 22-7. *Available articles for the* livecomm.general *newsgroup*

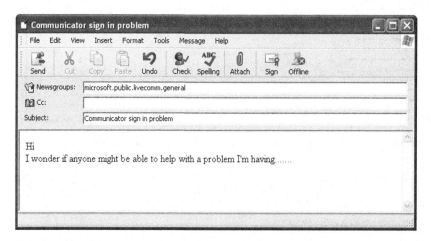

Figure 22-8. *Posting a new question*

You can set up a number of options within Outlook Express, including automatically downloading the headers plus the actual messages, and more. Play with Outlook Express, and configure it to suit your needs.

Setting Up a Web-Based Newsreader

If you want to access the web-based newsreader for these two newsgroups, here are the URLs you will need to enter in Internet Explorer or any other browser of your choice.

For the Live Communications Server general group, enter this (without line breaks):

```
http://www.microsoft.com/technet/community/newsgroups/dgbrowser/ ➥
en-us/default.mspx?dg=microsoft.public.livecomm.general&lang=en&cr=US
```

For the Live Communications Server Dev group, enter this (without line breaks):

```
http://www.microsoft.com/technet/community/newsgroups/dgbrowser/➥
en-us/default.mspx?dg=microsoft.public.livecomm.developer&lang=en&cr=US
```

As you can see from Figure 22-9, you get all the same functionality as you would with an NNTP-based newsreader.

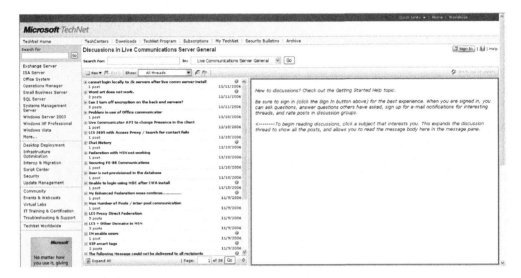

Figure 22-9. *Viewing the Live Communications Server general newsgroup in Internet Explorer*

NEWSGROUP ETIQUETTE

Remember these tips while working with newsgroups:

- The messages don't always appear straightaway; therefore, don't keep posting the same question if it has not appeared after several minutes—give it some time.

- Be polite. If no one responds to your post, don't post something else complaining about a lack of response. That will get you a response, just not the one you want.

- If you happen to know the answer to a question someone is asking, respond with the answer to the group. Not only does it help the community, but one day someone else might return the favor!

Live Communications Server Tools

Several tools are available to help you with your Live Communications Server deployment. Some the best tools come as part of the Live Communications Server 2005 with Service Pack 1 Resource Kit.

The resource kit, if you have not already downloaded and installed it, is a fantastic collection of tools, utilities, documentation, templates, and more, and I highly recommend you get it now. You can find the resource kit at http://www.microsoft.com/downloads/details.aspx? FamilyID=d21c38e5-5d8f-44c7-ba17-2cc4f85d8b51&DisplayLang=en.

As you already saw in Chapter 23, you can use several resource kit tools to troubleshoot your environment, but that is not all they do. We won't cover each of the tools here, but have a look at them; there is bound to be something of use to you in the kit. Take a look at the RKReadme.htm file that is in the ResKit directory once you have installed it for more information about what is included.

Another really useful tool is the Live Communications Server 2005 with Service Pack 1 Capacity Planning Toolkit. This provides you with a set of tools that can help you plan your Live Communications Server environment. You can download the toolkit from http://www. microsoft.com/downloads/details.aspx?FamilyId=F249A48A-FC42-4D30-B60B-CB91BF8F2191& displaylang=en.

Before you install it, though, you should be aware that it should only ever be installed in a preproduction test environment and never in your live environment. This is because the tool modifies Active Directory, and besides, it's always good practice to use a test environment for anything you want to try.

The tools provided in the Capacity Planning Toolkit include the following:

The Live Communications Server system model: This is a Microsoft Excel spreadsheet that enables you to model the network traffic by entering a number of parameters.

LcsLoadSim: This tool is used to test your back-end database by simulating database traffic.

Stress Setup: This tool is used to prepare your preproduction test environment.

LcsUserStress: This tool simulates users connecting to LCS.

To gain the most benefit from running this tool, your preproduction test environment should, in hardware terms, match your production environment—or at least what you think your production environment will look like. You don't need any additional software installed on the servers other than what you would install for your production Live Communications Server 2005 environment and the Capacity Planning Toolkit. To make changes to the system model, you will need Microsoft Excel installed.

You will need to run the LcsLoadSim and LcsUserStress tools on a separate machine to get accurate test results. Microsoft provides a hardware recommendation for this machine, which will then simulate the network traffic of 10,000 active concurrent clients:

- Dual Intel Xeon 3.06GHz, 1MB cache, 533MHz FSB (a dual processor with hyperthreading is recommended)

- 2GB DDR, 266MHz RAM

- 100Mb network adaptor (if you are going to simulate more than 50,000 users, a Gb network adaptor is required)

After you have downloaded and installed the toolkit, the first step is to run the Live Communications Server 2005 system model, which you can find in the Live Communications Server 2005 Capacity Planning Tools program folder, which now appears in the All Programs group on the Start menu.

The system model creates an XML file, which will be used by the LcsLoadSim tool to stress test your environment. You can set a number of parameters on the model, as shown in Figure 22-10.

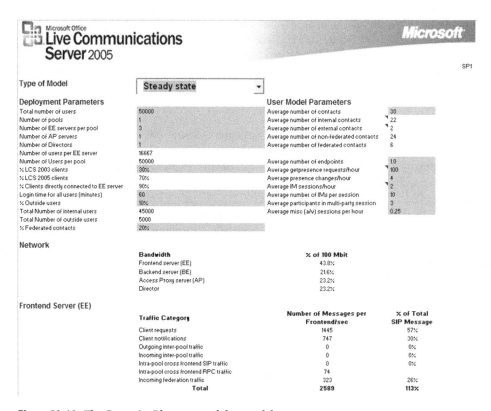

Figure 22-10. *The Capacity Planner model spreadsheet*

You can select which type of model you want to use; Steady State simulates the environment when all the users have logged in, and Login Ramp Up simulates the users logging in (which is the sort of behavior you would expect to see first thing in the morning).

You then set the various parameters as to how you want to stress test your environment. You can find more details about the different parameters in the Capacity Planning Guide, which is in the same program folder as the system model.

Once you have made all your configuration changes, click the Back End tab in the spreadsheet. Figure 22-11 shows you a summary of your settings in preparation of creating the XML file.

Click the Generate XML button, and when prompted, enter a name for the file, ensure you change the default extension from .xls to .xml, and choose a location to save it.

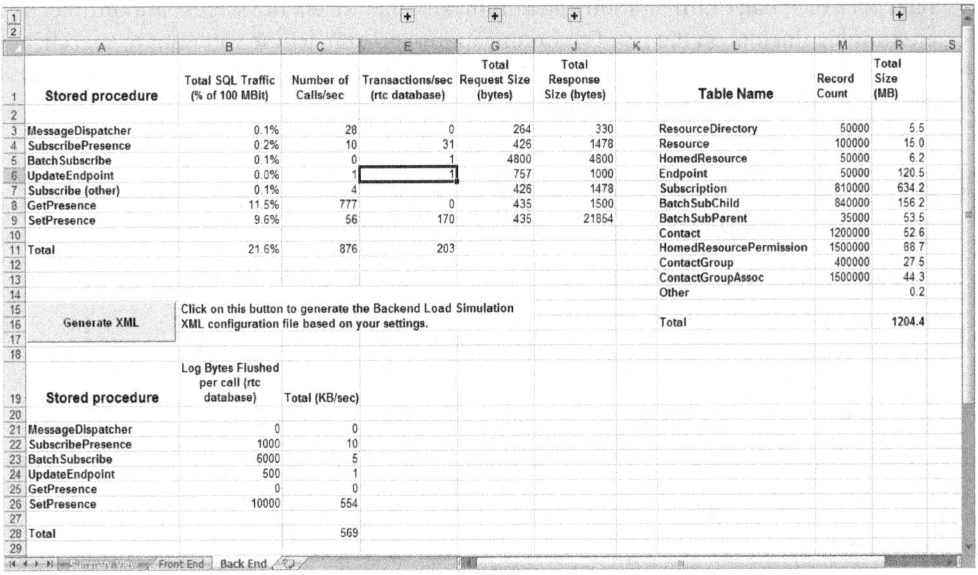

Stored procedure	Total SQL Traffic (% of 100 MBit)	Number of Calls/sec	Transactions/sec (rtc database)	Total Request Size (bytes)	Total Response Size (bytes)
MessageDispatcher	0.1%	28	0	264	330
SubscribePresence	0.2%	10	31	426	1478
BatchSubscribe	0.1%	0	1	4800	4800
UpdateEndpoint	0.0%	1	1	757	1000
Subscribe (other)	0.1%	4		426	1478
GetPresence	11.5%	777	0	435	1500
SetPresence	9.6%	56	170	435	21854
Total	21.6%	876	203		

Table Name	Record Count	Total Size (MB)
ResourceDirectory	50000	5.5
Resource	100000	15.0
HomedResource	50000	6.2
Endpoint	50000	120.5
Subscription	810000	634.2
BatchSubChild	840000	156.2
BatchSubParent	35000	53.5
Contact	1200000	52.6
HomedResourcePermission	1500000	88.7
ContactGroup	400000	27.5
ContactGroupAssoc	1500000	44.3
Other		0.2
Total		1204.4

Generate XML

Click on this button to generate the Backend Load Simulation XML configuration file based on your settings.

Stored procedure	Log Bytes Flushed per call (rtc database)	Total (KB/sec)
MessageDispatcher	0	0
SubscribePresence	1000	10
BatchSubscribe	6000	5
UpdateEndpoint	500	1
GetPresence	0	0
SetPresence	10000	554
Total		569

Summary View | Front End | Back End

Figure 22-11. *The Back End tab of the system model*

If you are curious as to what the XML file contains, here it is:

```
  <?xml version="1.0" encoding="UTF-8" standalone="yes" ?>
- <Config>
  <NumberOfUsers>50000</NumberOfUsers>
  <NumberOfContacts>30</NumberOfContacts>
  <LoginPeriod>60</LoginPeriod>
  <OldClientRatio>0.3</OldClientRatio>
- <StoredProcedures>
  <MessageDispatcher>28</MessageDispatcher>
  <UpdateEndpoint>1</UpdateEndpoint>
  <GetPresence>777</GetPresence>
  <SetPresence>56</SetPresence>
  </StoredProcedures>
  </Config>
```

You need this XML file only if you plan on testing simulated traffic to a back-end SQL database. If you want to test only a Standard Edition Server, you can skip this completely.

Because of the complexities of SQL Server, follow the detailed steps in the guide if you want to perform SQL back-end testing using the XML file you just created.

The next step in the testing process is to launch Stress Setup from the same `Program Files` group.

First click the Load Configuration File button, and then select the SampleData.ini file. If you are running the tool on the Live Communications Server machine you want to use, click the button next to the Server or Pool FQDN box to use the machine name, or enter the details manually. You will then see a screen similar to Figure 22-12.

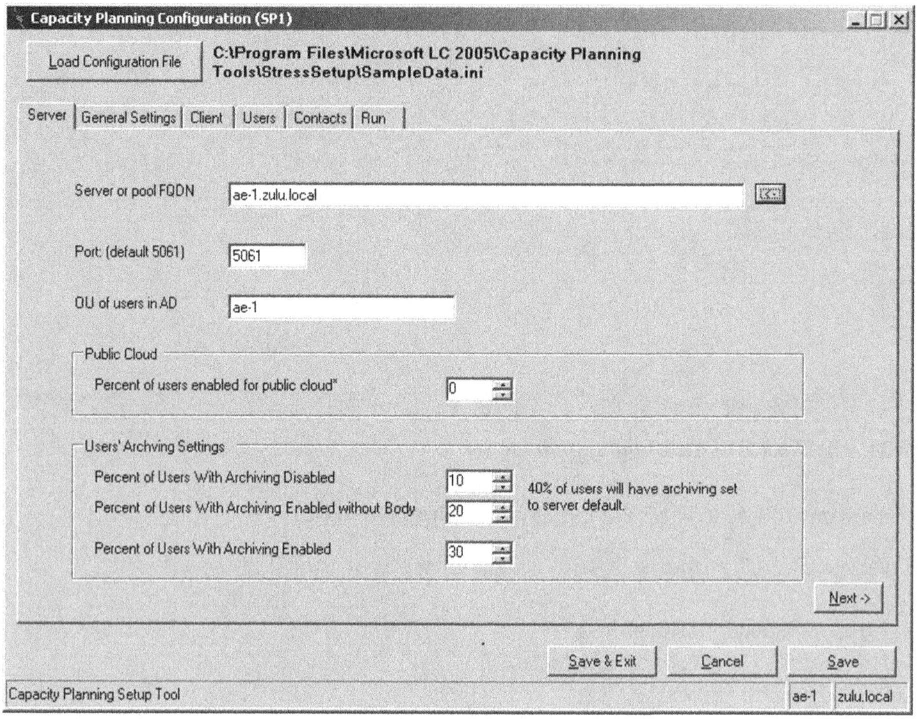

Figure 22-12. *The Stress Setup program*

You can change any of the settings on the screen and then click Next to continue to the General Settings tab. From here you can set the prefix for the usernames, enter a password that will used for all those test accounts, set the number of users, and do much more, as shown in Figure 22-13.

Click Next to go to the Client tab, as shown in Figure 22-14.

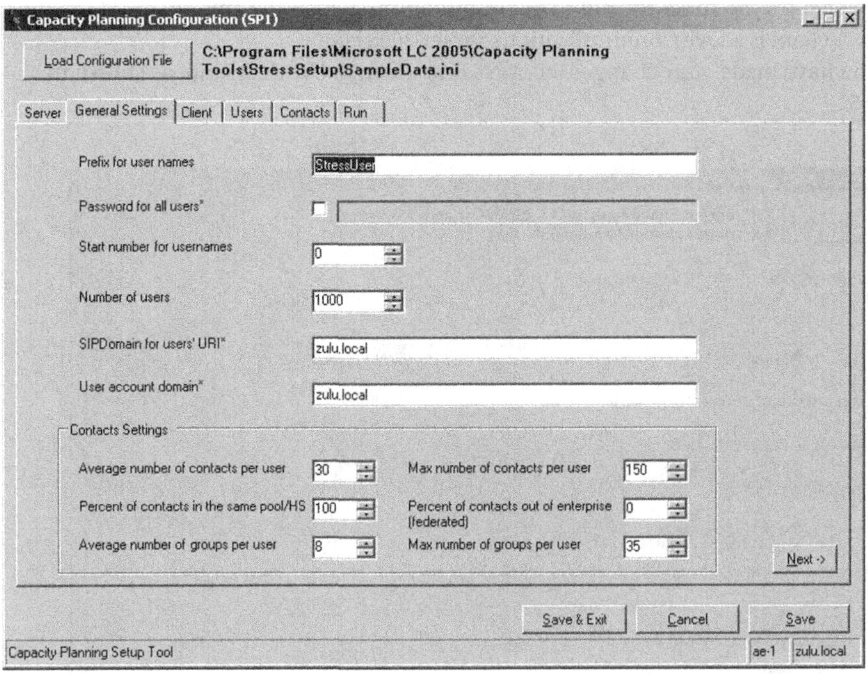

Figure 22-13. *General Settings tab*

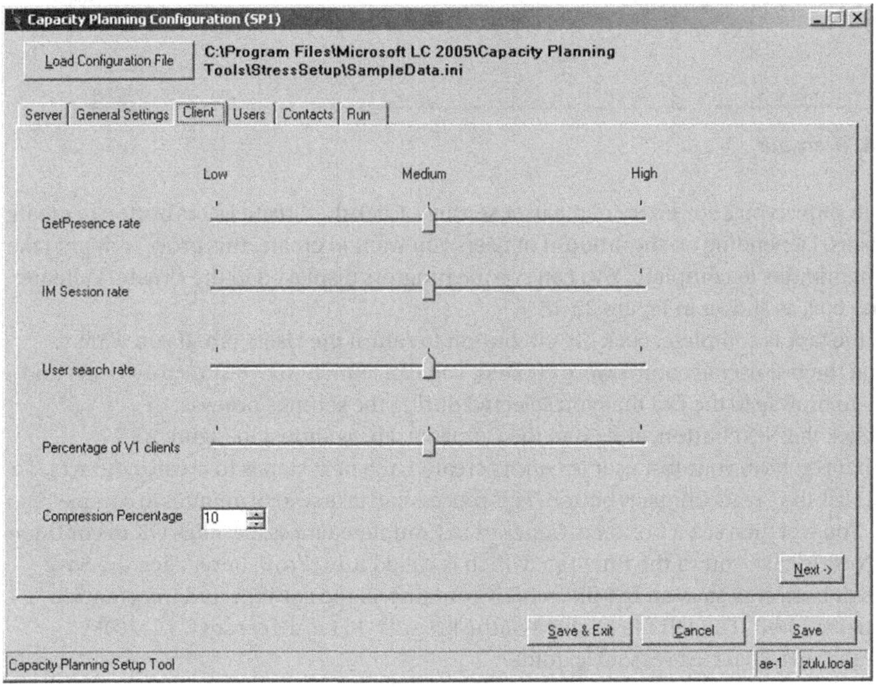

Figure 22-14. *Client tab*

This tab enables you to set specific client information, such as the amount of IM sessions per hour. A V1 client is a Live Communications Server 2003 client.

After you have made your changes, click Next to move to the Users tab, as shown in Figure 22-15.

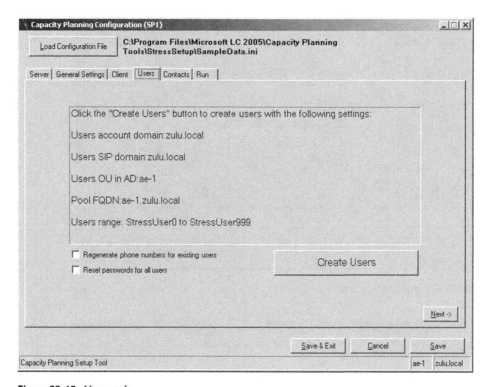

Figure 22-15. *Users tab*

This tab shows you a summary of the user settings. Click the Create Users button to create your test users. Depending on the amount of users you want to create, this process might take a number of minutes to complete. You can see the progress displayed in the Create/Validate Users dialog box, as shown in Figure 22-16.

When the task is complete, click the OK button to return the Users tab. If you want to confirm that the test user accounts were created, you can launch Active Directory Users and Computers to browse to the OU that you selected during the settings process.

Then click the Next button, and go to the Contacts tab, as shown in Figure 22-17.

Now that you have your test user accounts created, the next step is to create contacts. To do this, just click the Create Contacts button. This process can take several minutes to complete, so be patient. You will then see a Contacts Generation Completed message; click OK to continue.

Click Next to take you to the final tab, which is called Run. From here, click the Save or Save & Exit button to save an INI file, which contains all the settings and information you have just entered. The INI file is saved in the Program Files\Microsoft LC 2005\ Capacity Planning Tools\StressSetup folder.

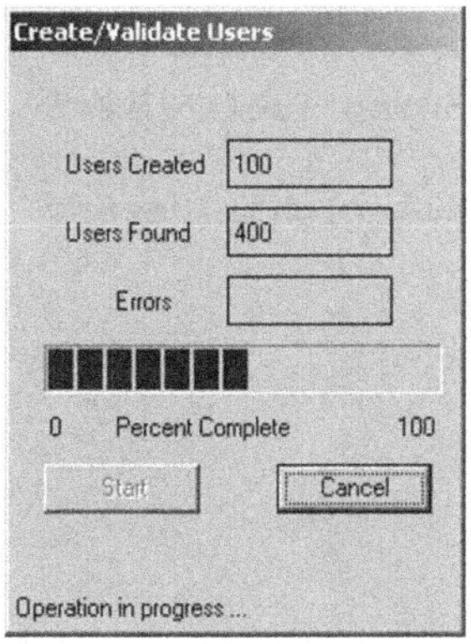

Figure 22-16. *Monitoring the progress of the test user creation*

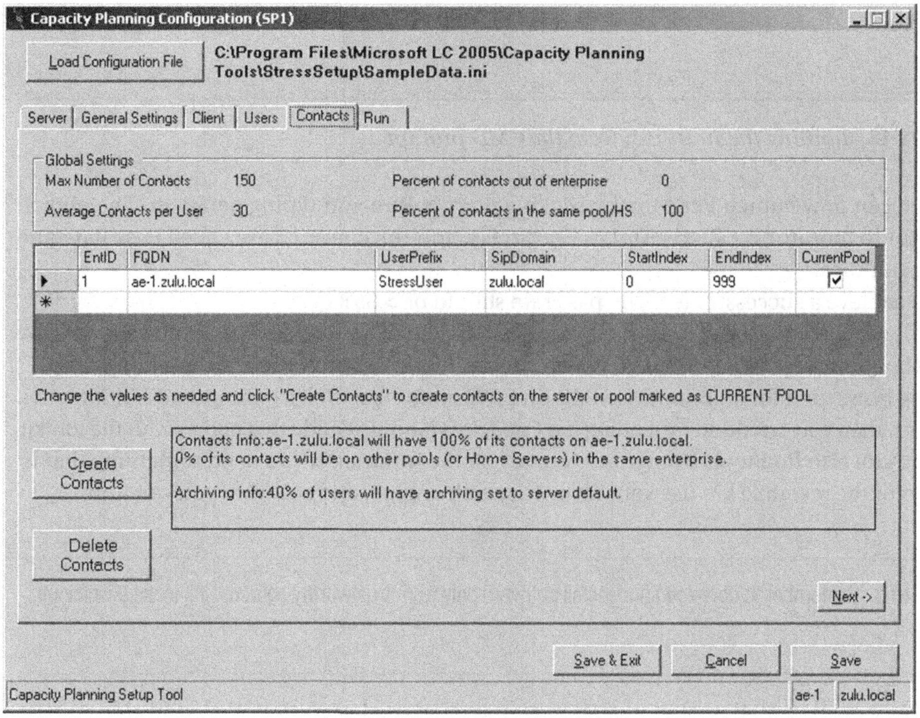

Figure 22-17. *Contacts tab*

Copy the INI file to the client machine you will be running the stress testing from, then open a command prompt, and finally go to the location where you put the INI file (which needs to be the UserStress directory on the client).

Type **LcsUserStress.exe -c [name of INI file.ini]** to start the stress testing.

You will then see the screen shown in Figure 22-18. If you want to stop the testing at any time, just press Ctrl+C.

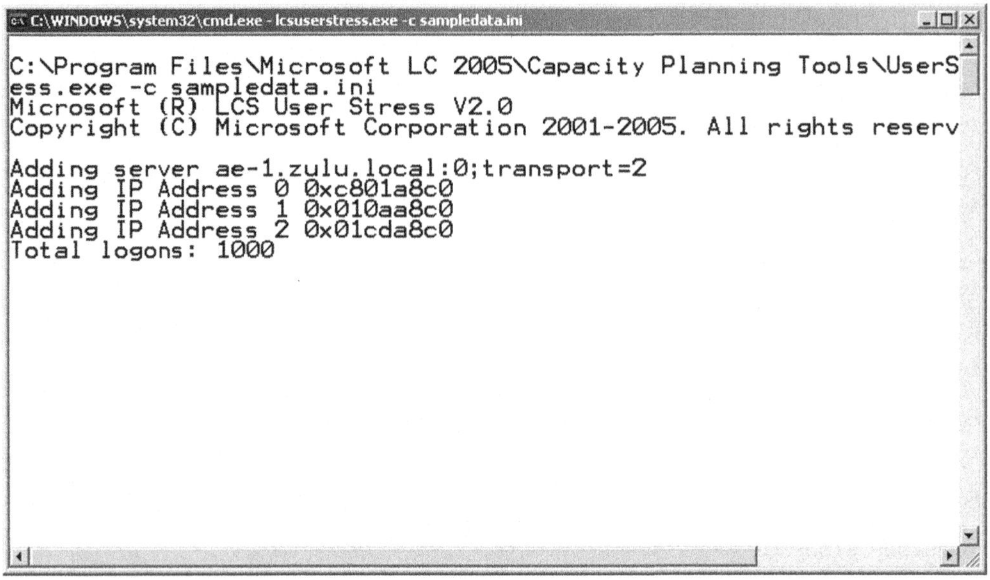

Figure 22-18. *Running the stress tool from the CMD prompt*

You can now launch PerfMon by clicking Start ➤ Run and typing **perfmon**. The object you want to monitor is called RTC LcsUserStress, and the counters are called Pass Rate and Online Buddies.

To achieve a successful test, the pass rate should be > 99%.

This section was a brief introduction to the Capacity Planning Toolkit. If you want to know more about the Capacity Planning Toolkit, such as learning about each of the settings and learning how run it for an Enterprise Edition Environment as well as a Standard Edition environment, then you can do so by reading the Capacity Planning Guide that comes with the toolkit.

You can also find tools from other sources on the Internet. If you need something that is not part of the resource kit, use your favorite search engine, and see what you can find.

■**Caution** Remember to download and install software only from trustworthy sources. If it looks suspicious, avoid it.

Microsoft Knowledge Base Articles

Another good place to find answers to your Live Communications Server problems is within the Microsoft Knowledge Base (KB).

You can access the Microsoft Knowledge Base for Live Communications Server directly from http://support.microsoft.com/ph/924, as shown in Figure 22-19.

If you happen to know the KB article number for something you are looking for, you can enter it in the box, and it will be displayed, assuming it is available. If you don't have a KB article number, enter your query, and search through any displayed results until you come to something that matches your requirements.

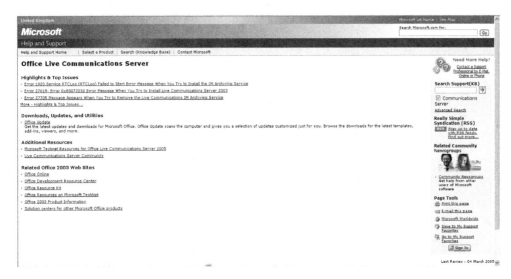

Figure 22-19. *The Microsoft Knowledge Base, Office Live Communications Server*

Partner Solutions

Finally, it is worth mentioning that there are many solutions from Microsoft Partners for Live Communications Server 2005, including antivirus products, mobility solutions, backup and restore products, and many, many more.

If you are looking for something specific that is not provided in the base product or you are just curious what else is available, you can access the full list at http://www.microsoft.com/ office/livecomm/prodinfo/partners.mspx.

Also, if your organization develops a solution for Live Communications Server, this is the place to advertise it. Contact Microsoft to discuss the various partner opportunities that are available.

Summary

This chapter gave you an overview of some of the additional resources that are available for Live Communications Server 2005 and Office Communicator. These resources ranged from online help, which should provide up-to-date information from Microsoft, to newsgroups, where you can post your own questions and read other people's posts that might provide help to your specific issue. You can also use several tools such as the Live Communications Server 2005 with SP1 Capacity Planning Toolkit, which helps you plan your Live Communications Server 2005 environment and reduce the amount of potential capacity problems later in your deployment. Also, Microsoft Partners, which are changing all the time, offer solutions, so you should keep your eyes open in case something is released that might be useful to you and your organization. Many more resources are available; you just have to look for them.

■ ■ ■

Advanced Tips

This appendix covers tips for how to deploy Live Communications Server 2005 SP1 in a resource forest. In addition, it includes two helpful flowcharts: one to help you determine which "prep steps" to run to meet your Active Directory infrastructure requirements and the other to help you keep track of the sequence of steps for deploying a Standard Edition Server or Enterprise pool.

Deploying in a Resource Forest

Many organizations deploy multiple Active Directory forests for various reasons. To allow autonomy, organizations may allow each of their business groups to host their own forest. Other organizations might choose to separate business functions into different forests to reduce dependencies and risk to business disruption from IT activity. Organizations have different and varying business reasons for deploying a resource forest. This document details how to deploy Live Communications Server in a resource forest Active Directory.

An Active Directory resource forest is a forest dedicated to deploying server infrastructure such as DHCP, DNS, Microsoft Exchange Server, and Microsoft Live Communications Server that relies on Active Directory. Although nothing restricts creating user accounts in the resource forest, user accounts are mostly created in separate Active Directory forests to maintain the clear separation of user infrastructure versus server infrastructure. Active Directory forests where only users are deployed will be referred to as *user forests* in this appendix.

The "Resource Forest Model" sidebar is an excerpt from the TechNet article at http:// www.microsoft.com/technet/solutionaccelerators/wssra/raguide/DirectoryServices/ igdrbp_2.mspx; it defines what an Active Directory resource forest is.

RESOURCE FOREST MODEL

A separate forest is used to manage resources in the resource forest model. Resource forests contain only the resources and any user accounts required for service administration or those accounts that are used to provide alternate access to the resources within the forest. User accounts are held in the organizational forest(s) associated with the organization. Forest trusts are established to provide resource access to the forests where the user accounts reside.

Resource forests are used to provide service isolations to protect areas of the network that need to maintain high availability. For example, an organization with a manufacturing facility can use this design to ensure the availability of the manufacturing resources even if the network connectivity between this forest and the organizational forest is unavailable.

Advantages

The advantages of the resource forest model include the following:

- **Autonomy from service owners in the other forests**: Because resources are managed in their own forest, it has complete autonomy of its data and services from other service owners in the organization.

- **Isolation from service owners in the other forests**: Because resources are managed in their own forest, its data and services are completely isolated from other service owners in the organization.

- **Explicit setup of trusts**: The members of each organizational forest do not automatically participate in trust relationships between forests. These relationships must be set up explicitly, either at the domain level or at the forest level, enabling increased control over which trusts should exist.

Disadvantages

The disadvantages of the resource forest model include the following:

- **Costly to implement**: This is an expensive model to implement from an administrative point of view. Additional personnel must be trained to maintain the forests, and additional hardware and software must be acquired to support the model.

- **No default Kerberos authentication between forests**: By default, two forests cannot use Kerberos v5 authentication between them. However, a forest-level trust can be implemented to provide this capability.

- **No single global catalog of objects**: Global catalogs do not replicate across forest boundaries. To get a unified view across multiple forests, directory synchronization software such as Microsoft Metadirectory Services must be implemented, which adds to the administrative burden.

Active Directory Requirements

Before you can deploy Live Communications Server in a resource forest topology, you must create a resource forest if one doesn't already exist. Creating a resource forest is no different from creating a new Active Directory forest. The only possible difference is you likely won't need to create multiple child domains. A resource forest with a single domain is often sufficient.

If the resource forest hosts its own DNS service integrated with Active Directory, then the user forest's DNS must be able to resolve DNS queries to the resource forest, as explained in the following TechNet article: `http://technet2.microsoft.com/WindowsServer/en/library/ 517b4fa4-5266-419c-9791-6fb56fabb85e1033.mspx?mfr=true`. Different options are possible, as documented in this TechNet article: `http://www.microsoft.com/technet/prodtechnol/ windowsserver2003/technologies/activedirectory/mtfstwp.mspx#EHAAC`. You can achieve this using delegation defined at the root DNS server, specifying DNS conditional forwarding, or adding an entry to the Root Hints list in the root DNS server.

To allow the user forest's DNS service to resolve DNS queries to the resource forest, launch the DNS MMC snap-in (`dnsmgmt.msc`) from the `Administrative Tools` folder. Select the NETBIOS name of the user forest in the scope pane. Double-click the Root Hints entry shown in the status pane. The property page will appear. In the Root Hints tab, click Add. The New Resource Record property page will appear. In the Server Fully Qualified Domain Name (FQDN) field, type the FQDN of the root domain of the resource forest. In the IP Address field, enter the IP of the resource forest's primary DNS server. This is usually the primary domain controller of the root domain. Click OK to finish your configuration.

For users to have single sign-on (SSO) experience when logging on to Live Communications Server using Microsoft Office Communicator, a minimum of a one-way trust relationship must be created. The direction of the trust is from the resource forest to the user forest, with the resource forest trusting the user forest. If the current domain functional level for both forests is Windows Server 2003, then the trust relationship can be forest level; otherwise, you must create domain-level trusts.

Note If the trust level between the forest is not a forest-level trust, then the Live Communications Servers must be configured for NTLM authentication only. Kerberos authentication will fail. Open the property pages of the home server/pool to configure this authentication protocol in the Live Communications Server's Admin Tools MMC snap-in, as illustrated in Figure A-1.

To determine the forest's domain functional level, launch the Active Directory Domains and Trusts MMC snap-in from the `Administrative Tools` folder. To raise the domain functional level, see the following TechNet article: `http://technet2.microsoft.com/WindowsServer/en/ library/5084a49d-20bd-43f0-815d-88052c9e2d461033.mspx?mfr=true`.

To create a one-way domain- or forest-level trust from the resource forest to the user forest, launch the Active Directory Domains and Trusts MMC snap-in from the `Administrative Tools` folder using a computer joined to the user forest. Use a user account member of the Domain Administrators group from the root domain of the user forest. Right-click the forest FQDN node in the scope pane, and select Properties. Click the Trusts tab. Click the New Trust button. This will launch the New Trust Wizard. Click Next to go past the welcome page. In the Name field, type the FQDN of the resource forest, and then click Next. On the Trust Type page, select the Trust with a Windows Domain radio button option, retype the name of the domain, and click Next and finally Finish to complete the wizard.

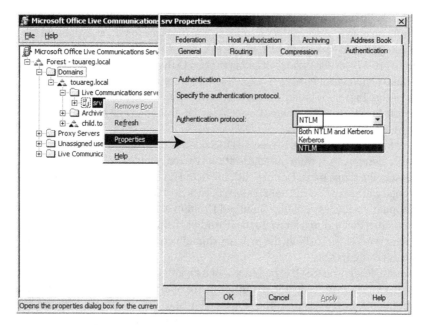

Figure A-1. *Configuring Live Communications Server for NTLM authentication*

To illustrate with an example, Figure A-2 shows two Active Directory forests: the user forest called `zulu.local` and the resource forest named `touareg.local`. Note the red arrow indicates a one-way forest-level trust between the two forests. A pool is deployed in the resource forest `touareg.local`. This pool's FQDN is `srv.touareg.local`.

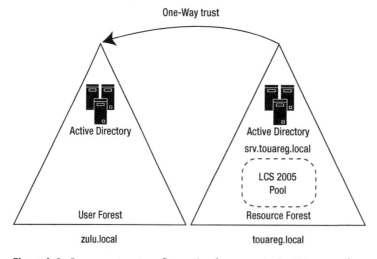

Figure A-2. *One-way trust configuration between Active Directory forests*

To verify the trust relationship is working properly, select the trust entry. When using the Active Directory Domains and Trusts MMC snap-in from the user forest, this trust entry will appear in the *incoming trusts* table. If viewing this trust from the resource forest, this trust entry will appear in the *outgoing trusts* table. Click the Properties button after selecting the trust entry. To confirm the trust relationship, click the Validate button from the property page. You can find more details about how to determine trust relationship configurations in the following Microsoft article: `http://support.microsoft.com/?kbid=228477`.

This completes the minimum Active Directory requirements for a resource forest topology. Next, we describe the requirements necessary to deploy Live Communications Server in this resource forest.

DNS Requirements

Most organizations that deploy Live Communications Server use the automatic configuration setting when deploying Communicator instead of the manual configuration, which is the default setting. Using the automatic configuration setting removes the need to configure each Communicator client with the user's home server/pool FQDN setting. When deploying Communicator to thousands or tens of thousands of users, the logistics of communicating each user's FQDN becomes difficult and costly because this effort may result in support calls.

To use the automatic configuration of Communicator, you must define a DNS SRV record for SIP in the authoritative DNS server(s) in the user forests. If the resource forest has its own DNS service, it is not necessary to create an SRV record for SIP in the resource forest since only users will need to query it.

To add a DNS SRV record for SIP, launch the DNS MMC snap-in for the root domain of the user forest. Expand the root node in the scope pane. Expand the Forward Lookup Zones node. Expand the user forest FQDN node (not the node that starts with _msdcs.<domain>) until the _tcp node is shown. Right-click the _tcp node, and select Other New Records. The Resource Record Type dialog box will appear. Search for the service location (SRV) in the Select a Resource Record Type field. Click Create Record. The New Resource Record property page will appear.

When making sure the entire resource forest deployment works, it's easier not to get confused with certificates just yet. Leave the Protocol field set to _tcp. Specify the FQDN of the Standard Edition Server or Enterprise pool if using a single pool in the resource forest or the FQDN of the Director if using multiple pools in the Host Offering This Service field.

Depending on whether you plan to use TLS or TCP for internal client-to-server connections, you'll create a different type of SRV record. The following SIP SRV records are supported:

1. _sipinternaltls._tcp.<domain>

2. _sipinternal._tcp.<domain>

3. _sip._tls.<domain>

4. _sip._tcp.<domain>

If you require clients to connect to Live Communications Server over TLS, then your SRV record should be of the format 1 or 3. If clients are connecting to Live Communications Server over TCP, then the SRV record should be of the format 2 or 4. Only Communicator will understand SRV records of the form 1 and 2. Specify one of the previous four options in the Service field.

If using TCP, specify 5060 in the Port Number field. If using TLS, specify 5061 in the Port Number field. Click OK to finish.

To verify that the SRV record is resolvable, start a Command Prompt window (cmd.exe), and enter **nslookup**. Type the command **set qq=srv** in the session. Then type the SRV record created. In the following example, the two queries to _sip._tcp.zulu.local and _sipinternal._tcp.zulu.local resolved to srv.touareg.local. Figure A-3 illustrates this verification.

```
Command Prompt - nslookup                                          _□×

C:\temp>nslookup
Default Server:  localhost
Address:  127.0.0.1                  ──── Set query type to SRV
> set qq=srv
> _sip._tcp.zulu.local  ◀──────────────────────── Resolve SRV query
Server:  localhost
Address:  127.0.0.1

_sip._tcp.zulu.local      SRV service location:
          priority       = 0
          weight         = 0
          port           = 5060
          svr hostname   = srv.touareg.local
srv.touareg.local      internet address = 192.168.3.1
> _sipinternal._tcp.zulu.local  ◀───────────────── Resolve SRV query
Server:  localhost
Address:  127.0.0.1

_sipinternal._tcp.zulu.local    SRV service location:
          priority       = 0
          weight         = 0
          port           = 5060
          svr hostname   = srv.touareg.local
srv.touareg.local      internet address = 192.168.3.1
>
```

Figure A-3. *Resolving DNS SRV records with NsLookup*

From the earlier example, these DNS SRV records are created in the zulu.local forest, as shown in Figure A-4.

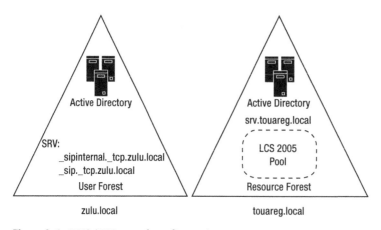

Figure A-4. *DNS SRV record configuration*

PKI Requirements

Before rolling out certificates for your Live Communications Servers, it's recommended that you ensure your deployment in a resource forest topology is functional. It's simpler to troubleshoot problems before compounding additional complexity.

Once you start rolling out more than one pool, server certificates will be required. Also, if you want to encrypt client-to-server traffic, then server certificates will be needed. Please refer to Chapter 8 for more information about configuring certificates for Live Communications Server.

Deploying Live Communications Server

Live Communications Server can be deployed at any stage as long as the resource forest is available. Documenting it at this stage made for a logical transition to focus on enabling user accounts in the user forest for LCS in the resource forest. Deploying LCS in a resource forest is no different from deploying it in a single-forest topology. All the same steps apply. Please refer to Chapters 7, 10, and 11.

Configuring Users for Live Communications Server

The process for enabling users for Live Communications in a resource forest topology requires some additional steps beyond the regular process for enabling users for Live Communications in a single forest. Since the user's account is located in the user forest, a corresponding account must be created in the resource forest. For security reasons, this account in the resource forest must be marked as disabled.

To avoid users maintaining passwords in two different user accounts (that is, the account in the user forest and the account in the resource forest), the user account in the resource forest is mapped to the user account in the user forest referred to as the *user principal account.* This mapping is done by copying the objectSID value from the NT principal account into the msRTCSIP-OriginatorSid attribute of the corresponding disabled user account in the resource forest. Figure A-5 demonstrates how to perform this mapping manually using AdsiEdit.msc.

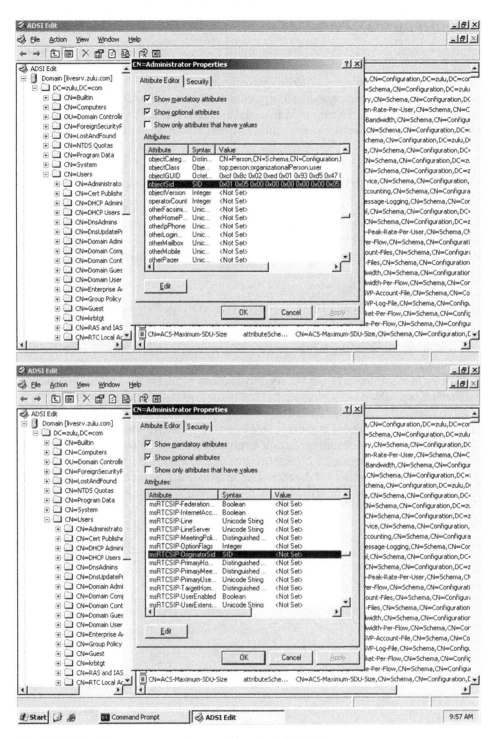

Figure A-5. *Mapping user accounts manually using AdsiEdit.msc*

Figure A-6 shows the logical representation of this user account mapping. You can now enable the account in the resource forest for Live Communications. When the user logs on to their desktop/laptop using their Active Directory credentials from the user forest, Communicator should be able to log on to Live Communications Server.

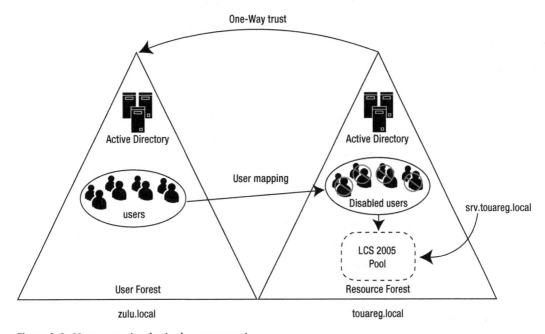

Figure A-6. *User mapping logical representation*

This process of creating a corresponding user account in the resource forest, marking the account as disabled, mapping the objectSID, and finally enabling the account for Live Communications can be tedious and error prone. Consider using Identity Integration Feature Pack (IIFP), a free version of MIIS for Active Directory only, or finding third-party tools that are available. For example, LcsSolutions provides a tool, LcsMap, to automate these steps.

Alternatively, the Live Communications Server 2005 SP1 Resource Kit offers a tool that can be handy when the resource forest already has Exchange deployed in this topology. In this case, disabled user accounts have already been created and mapped to the user principal accounts in the user forest for Exchange. The Live Communications Server 2005 SP1 Resource Kit tool, SidMap.wsf, copies the objectSID from the msExchMasterAccountSid attribute to the msRTCSIP-OriginatorSid attribute on the disabled user account. Once this step is completed, the administrator can use the Live Communications Server 2005 SP1 MMC to enable these disabled user accounts for Live Communications. For more information, please refer to the tool's accompanying documentation called sidmapreadme.htm, which is available in the resource kit.

In addition to mapping the SID from the NT principal account in the user forest to the disabled user account in the resource forest to enable single sign-on, you'll want to map other user information so those users can be searchable in the Address Book via any of the values listed in Table A-1. LcsMap automatically maps these additional settings, and you can configure IIFP to synchronize these settings as well.

Table A-1. *User Settings Mapping Table*

Attribute	User	Corresponding Disabled Account
Cn	Rui	Rui
ObjectSID	sid(Rui)	Sid(X)
msRTCSIP-OriginatorSID		sid(Rui)
telephoneNumber	555-1234	555-1234
displayName	Rui	Rui
givenName	Rui	Rui
surname	Maximo	Maximo
physicalDeliveryOfficeName	30/3250	30/3250
l (city)	Issaquah	Issaquah
st (state)	WA	WA
country	U.S.A.	U.S.A.
title	Lead program manager	Lead program manager
mail	ruim@touareg.com	ruim@touareg.com
company	Touareg	Touareg

Checklist

To help keep track of the tasks necessary to deploy a resource forest topology, the following is a convenient checklist when deploying:

1. Configure a root DNS server in the user forest to resolve servers in the resource forest.

2. Create a one-way trust.

3. Validate a trust relationship.

4. Create an SRV record in user forests.

5. Verify the record route using the Nslookup.exe tool.

6. Request the server certificate (this is optional).

7. Deploy Live Communications Server 2005 or newer.

8. Configure user accounts for Live Communications Server 2005 on the resource forest:

    a. Create a corresponding user account in the resource forest for each user.

    b. Disable the user account.

    c. Map the disabled account to the user's account from the user forest.

    d. Provision the disabled account for Live Communications.

Flowchart Guide to Active Directory Prep

Figure A-7 illustrates the logical flow to determine which "prep steps" to run to meet your Active Directory infrastructure. Use this flowchart as an aid to help you.

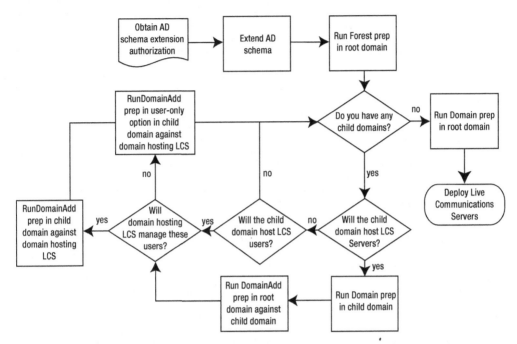

Figure A-7. *Active Directory prep flowchart guide*

Flowchart Guide to Deploying Live Communications Server

Refer to my website, http://www.ruimaximo.com, for a diagram of the logic flow you should observe to deploy a Standard Edition Server or Enterprise pool. Use this flowchart as an aid to ensure your server deployment is correctly completed.

Conclusion

Using the resource forest topology to deploy Live Communications Server offers the advantage of isolating the AD schema extensions required from your production forest into a separate forest. In an organization with multiple forests, the resource forest topology provides a way to centralize your Live Communications Server infrastructure. Since Exchange also supports the resource forest topology, you can leverage the same resource forest to centralize your Live Communications Server and Exchange deployment.

Index

Find it faster at http://superindex.apress.com

Find it faster at http://superindex.apress.com

Find it faster at http://superindex.apress.com